LAW MORALITY AND THE BIBLE

A symposium

EDITED BY BRUCE KAYE & GORDON WENHAM

Sir Norman Anderson

Oliver Barclay

David Bronnert

Bruce Kaye

Robin Nixon

James Packer

Gordon Wenham

Dennis Winter

InterVarsity Press
Downers Grove
Illinois 60515

InterVarsity Press is the book-publishing division of
Inter-Varsity Christian Fellowship, a student
movement active on campus at hundreds of universities,
colleges and schools of nursing.
For information about local and regional activities,
write IVCF, 233 Langdon St., Madison, WI 53703.

Distributed in Canada through InterVarsity Press,
1875 Leslie St., Unit 10, Don Mills,
Ontario M3B 2M5, Canada.

Quotations from the Bible are from the Revised Standard
Version (copyrighted 1946 and 1952, © 1971 and 1973, by the
Division of Christian Education, National
Council of the Churches of Christ in the United States
of America), unless otherwise stated.

ISBN 0-87784-795-9
Library of Congress Catalog Card Number: 78-18549

Printed in the United States of America

Preface

The essays in this book aim to throw light on some questions current in Christian circles about the nature and content of biblical moral teaching, and the way it applies in life today. The authors were members of a working party on Morality and Law which was convened in 1967 by the joint initiative of the Inter-Varsity Fellowship (now the Universities and Colleges Christian Fellowship) and Latimer House, Oxford, and which met regularly till 1972. The main theses of the present volume were formed in that group, though the material has been revised for publication. In the group were exegetes, theologians, philosophers, lawyers and parochial clergy; and the range of the essays reflects this fact. It is hoped that together they will help to re-establish landmarks in several disputed areas.

Earlier in this century evangelical Christians gave their attention to questions of dogmatics rather than ethics. (I leave aside the question of whether ethics should not be treated as a branch of dogmatics, as Barth urges; the conventional distinction between dogmatics as being about what you believe and ethics about what you do is sufficient for us here.) In those days it was evidently felt that the field of dogmatics was where the action was; such truths as biblical inspiration and the substitutionary sacrifice of Christ needed fresh exposition and defence, whereas Christian morals, which when the century opened were part of the English-speaking cultural heritage, could safely be left to look after themselves. Whether that was really so then may be doubted, but there is no doubt that it is not so now. Morals, as is often and truly said, are in the melting-pot. Since the Second World War ended, the good life for man has been under constant discussion in terms of 'permissive' Western secularism: in terms, that is, of the assumptions that self-exploration and self-discovery is our prime task, and any means to that end which does not violate others' freedom or destroy their well-being should be thought allowable, and that toleration of deviant behaviour should be practised up to the limit, as being both a civilized virtue and a universal duty. With this, the Christian view of man, the ethical subject, as God's image-bearer, a free and responsible moral agent aware of moral absolutes, has been widely replaced by behaviourist views of man's nature and relativist views of his moral intuitions. Traditional moral codes are sniffed at, and free-wheeling anarchies take their place. Finally (and it was this which provoked the convening of the working party) 'situation ethics' has invaded the churches, proclaiming that what Scripture presents as laws of God are no more than rules of thumb which are not always binding. It is into this complex ferment of 'post-Christian' ideas that the present book speaks.

The essays fall into two groups. Those in the first group explore basic biblical themes: grace, freedom, law, order. Those in the second group, building on the results of these biblical enquiries, seek to characterize Christian morality and to show how Christian moral reasoning must operate in particular fields. Thanks are due to Gordon Wenham and Bruce Kaye for editorial work on the first and second parts of the book respectively. Thanks are also due to members of the working party who helped its thinking forward, in several cases by writing papers that are not included here; to Professor Sir Norman Anderson and Dr O. R. Barclay, who between them hosted all the working party's meetings; to the IVF, for underwriting the costs involved; and finally to the publishers for the almost superhuman courtesy and patience with which they waited for overdue scripts.

J. I. PACKER
Trinity College,
Bristol.

Chief abbreviations

AV	The Authorized (King James') Version of the Bible, 1611.
ed.	editor.
ET	English Translation.
GNB	The Good News Bible (Today's English Version), (NT 1966, 4th edition 1976; OT 1976: The Bible Societies and Collins).
H	Hebrew verse numbering.
HL	Hittite Laws.
JB	The Jerusalem Bible (Darton, Longman and Todd, 1966).
LH	Laws of Hammurabi.
LXX	The Septuagint (pre-Christian Greek version of the Old Testament).
mg.	margin.
MT	Massoretic Text (of the Hebrew Bible).
MAL	Middle Assyrian Laws.
NEB	The New English Bible (NT 1961, 2nd edition 1970; OT 1970).
NT	New Testament.
OT	Old Testament.
RSV	The Revised Standard Version of the Bible (NT 1946, 2nd edition 1971; OT 1952, 2nd edition 1973).
Strack–Billerbeck	H. L. Strack and P. Billerbeck (eds.), *Kommentar zum Neuen Testament aus Talmud und Midrash*, 5 vols., 1922–56.
TSF Bulletin	Journal of the Theological Students' Fellowship.
ZNW	*Zeitschrift für die Neutestamentliche Wissenschaft*.

Part 1

Basic Biblical Themes

1

Grace and law in the Old Testament

Gordon Wenham

Introduction

St Paul insisted that 'a man is not justified by works of the law but through faith in Jesus Christ' (Gal. 2:16), that 'we are not under law but under grace' (Rom. 6:15). These are key phrases in the apostle's argument against Judaizers who wished to make Gentile converts to Christianity keep the Old Testament law. Paul trenchantly attacks these Judaizers and insists that men are saved only by the grace of God, his unmerited forgiveness in Christ; that as far as earning salvation is concerned, the Old Testament law is an irrelevance. It serves only to show up man's weakness and sinfulness. In that it can never be fully observed, it is unable to make a man acceptable to God. The gospel on the other hand frees man from the attempt to win God's favour by keeping the law.

Because Paul was dealing with opponents who held that keeping the law was the path to salvation, it is often assumed that this was the Old Testament teaching. In the Old Testament era, it is said, a man was saved by doing good works, *i.e.* by obeying the injunction of the law, not through the grace of God. It is the purpose of this chapter to examine this assumption. Was a man saved by the law in Old Testament times or by the grace of God? Where does the law fit into the Old Testament scheme of salvation?

Grace and covenant in the Old Testament

The first thing to say about the relationship of grace and law in the Old Testament is that this way of phrasing the question is foreign to the Old Testament. Saving history[1] in the Old Testament is built on a series of covenants. After the calamitous start to human history in Genesis 1–8 the future security of mankind is sealed in

3

a covenant with Noah (Gn. 9). With the call of Abraham a new phase in human history begins, the history of Israel. This history revolves around three covenants: the Abrahamic, the Sinaitic and the Davidic covenants.[2] The content of these covenants is not identical, but they all constitute turning-points in the history of Israel and are keys to the interpretation of that history. The covenant with Abraham with its triple promises of land, offspring and blessing holds together the whole narrative in Genesis.[3]

Most of the rest of the Pentateuch is taken up with expositions of the Sinai covenant. The book of Joshua shows how national fidelity to the Sinai covenant brought prosperity,[4] while Judges shows the reverse. The covenant with David introduces a new factor into the historical situation. The king of Jerusalem enjoys a special relationship with God and therefore has special responsibilities. The remaining historical books and the prophets are devoted to assessing the nation's and the kings' performance in the light of their covenant obligations.

Although the Old Testament does not describe them as such, all three covenants are aptly described as acts of divine grace; that is, they are arrangements initiated by God out of his spontaneous mercy, not because of the deserts of those with whom the covenants are made. This is especially clear in the case of the Abrahamic and Davidic covenants. These are essentially promissory covenants, that is, the covenant consists mainly of divine promises: the obligations placed on David and Abraham are mentioned very briefly. For example in Genesis 12:1–3 Abraham is promised that his descendants will form a large nation and that he will enjoy great blessing. The one command, to leave his own country, is really a further promise in disguise, that God will give him a new land to live in. Similarly David was promised an eternal dynasty, that he would always have a son ruling on his throne no matter how he behaved. Iniquity would indeed be punished, but not by the loss of his throne (2 Sa. 7:14f.).

It seems likely that both the Abrahamic and Davidic covenants are modelled on royal grants of land and dynasty. As a reward for faithful service great kings used to present vassals or leading officials with land, or in the case of vassal kings with land and dynasty. Much of the biblical terminology reflects the usage of these royal grants.[5] The biblical texts make it abundantly clear, however, that it was divine grace, not human merit, that prompted these covenants and their promises. Nothing is recorded of Abraham's achievements before his call. Genesis portrays his career as created by the call of God. The narrative in Samuel emphasizes the insignificance of David, before Samuel at God's bidding anointed him king (1 Sa. 16). David himself confesses that God's promises to him and his descendants are totally unmerited: 'Who am I, O Lord God, and what is my house, that thou hast brought me thus far?' (2 Sa. 7:18).

The Sinaitic covenant is not modelled on a royal grant but on a vassal treaty, a legal form in which the vassal's obligations are much more prominent. But even here the laws are set in a context of a gracious, divine initiative. Obedience to the law is not the source of blessing, but it augments a blessing already given.

Exodus presents the release from Egyptian slavery and the Sinai covenant as God fulfilling his promise to the patriarchs that he would give the land of Canaan to their descendants (Ex. 2:24 – 3:17). Half-way between Egypt and Canaan the Sinai covenant is concluded. It begins with a reminder of what God has done thus far: 'You have seen what I did to the Egyptians, and how I ... brought you to myself' (Ex. 19:4). Israel's obligations are then alluded to: 'Now therefore, if you will obey my voice and keep my covenant'. Then finally a promise is added: 'You shall be my own possession among all peoples' (Ex. 19:5).

This last promise closely resembles what God has already done in bringing them to himself (verse 4). Israel thus finds herself in a virtuous circle. Obedience to the law issues in further experience of the initial grace of God, who brought them to himself. It may be diagrammatically represented as follows:

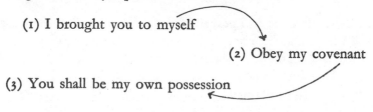

(1) I brought you to myself

(2) Obey my covenant

(3) You shall be my own possession

It is important to note the sequence—God's choice (1) precedes man's obedience (2), but man's obedience (2) is a prerequisite of knowing the full benefits of election (3).

A similar virtuous circle is to be found in the material dealing with the erection of the tabernacle. After the experience of God's presence on Mount Sinai, God offers to dwell among Israel permanently if they build him a suitable shrine. When the tabernacle is completed, God does indeed appear in it (Ex. 24–40). The book of Leviticus points out, however, that the divine presence in Israel is always at risk because of sin. Various regulations about holiness in life and worship are introduced to deal with this problem. They conclude with a series of promises, the last of which is: 'I will walk among you, and will be your God, and you shall be my people' (Lv. 26:12). The word 'walk' (*hithallēk*) is not used very often of God, and may be an echo of the Garden of Eden story (Gn. 3:8). Thus, according to Leviticus obedience to the law can bring man back to a near-paradise situation. But once again this is only possible through the prevenient grace of God, who made himself known to Israel in the first place. It should be noted that for Leviticus at least the greatest divine blessings are spiritual; the presence of God is more important even than peace and prosperity.

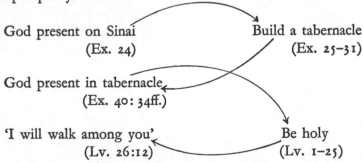

God present on Sinai (Ex. 24) Build a tabernacle (Ex. 25–31)

God present in tabernacle (Ex. 40: 34ff.)

'I will walk among you' (Lv. 26:12) Be holy (Lv. 1–25)

Deuteronomy is also pervaded by this notion of grace and law. God has already brought the nation into partial possession of the land. Israel is posed to take possession of the rest of their inheritance, but this depends on total obedience to the law and its demands. Only whole-hearted fidelity to God's directions will ensure them victory over their enemies and peace and prosperity within the land promised to their forefathers.

Within the Sinaitic and Deuteronomic covenants law and grace are not antithetic. Law is the gift of a gracious, saving God. Through keeping the law man can experience more of God's grace. These concepts have been brought into focus by modern studies of the covenants, especially the comparisons with oriental vassal treaties. To these studies we now turn.

Covenant terminology

Many investigations have sought to discover the etymology of the Hebrew word for covenant (*bᵉrît*) in the hope that it would shed light on its meaning. But none of the suggested etymologies[6] is totally convincing, and since it is clear that the writers of the Old Testament were unaware of its derivation its etymology is therefore quite irrelevant to its meaning.

All important for determining the meaning of *bᵉrît* is actual usage. In a secular context *bᵉrît* is often translated 'treaty' (*e.g.* Gn. 21:27, 32; 26:28; 31:44; 1 Ki. 5:12; 20:34; *cf.* Gn. 14:13, 'ally'), but when it refers to God's treaty with Israel it is translated 'covenant'. It is perhaps a pity that the translation is different in different contexts, because it obscures the parallel between God's relationship with Israel and the political relationships that existed in ancient empires. Recent studies have shown that the terminology, structure and ideology of the Sinaitic and Deuteronomic covenants have been adapted from that used in drawing up international vassal treaties.[7] These treaties shed light on the distinctive features of the biblical covenants and help to explain the order and content of the Old Testament passages dealing with the covenant.[8]

Secular vassal treaties and the Sinai covenant

In the biblical era various types of treaty were used, but the most common were the so-called vassal or suzerainty treaties. Great empires were held together by force of arms and vassal treaties. The kings of the great empires, *e.g.* Egypt, the Hittites and Assyria, called themselves 'great king' as opposed to lesser kings who ruled a city or two in Canaan (*e.g.* Jos. 12). When the 'great king' conquered a minor king, he might allow the latter to continue in control of his kingdom as long as he swore allegiance to the 'great king'. The oath of allegiance took the form of a vassal treaty, in which the vassal pledged his support of the 'great king'. Stereotyped forms and language were used in drafting these treaty documents. It seems to me that the Old Testament uses the analogy of God as 'great king' quite deliberately, just as it draws on images from other realms of human activity such as the family. Certainly the idea of the divine suzerain throws into high relief the sovereignty and grace of God in his dealings with Israel. In the Psalms God is frequently spoken of as king, and even as 'great King' (Ps. 95:3). In Old Testament contexts many other terms drawn from the treaties make an appearance: they include 'own possession', 'to go after' other gods (*i.e.* serve as vassal), 'to love', 'to fear', 'to sin', 'to hearken to his voice', 'to do as he commands'.

Just as the Old Testament is indebted to the treaty tradition for covenant terminology, so it is heavily dependent on this source for the basic structure of the covenant. As a rule Hittite vassal treaties begin with a brief section listing the suzerain's titles. This is followed by a longish historical section outlining the great king of Hatti's mercy and kindness towards his vassal. 'The description always amounts to saying that the vassal concerned is bound to be eternally grateful for all the benefits, honours and favours which he has already received from the great king.'[9] In Deuteronomy 1–3 we find a similar section outlining God's love and care and forbearance towards Israel during the years in the desert. The earlier Sinai covenant similarly opens with a brief statement of God's saving mercy in the words: 'I am the Lord your God, who brought you out of the land of Egypt' (Ex. 20:2).

The next main section of the treaty is the stipulations section in which are outlined the duties of the vassal towards his suzerain. Basically he must be faithful to him at all times, support him in battle, bring him tribute, hand over subversive rebels, *etc*. This section finds parallels in the Old Testament collections of law, especially in Exodus 20:3 – 23:19 and Deuteronomy 4–26.[10]

Polytheistic Hittites then invited the gods to witness the treaty, before invoking blessings on those who kept the treaty and curses on those who did not. The Old Testament naturally omits the god list, but it retains the blessings and the curses.

The covenant context of Old Testament law

The laws of the Sinai and Deuteronomic covenants are to be found in Exodus 20 – Leviticus 25 and Deuteronomy 4–26, which, following the treaty analogy, may be called the stipulations section. For a proper appreciation of the place of the law in the Old Testament it is essential to bear in mind that nearly all the laws in the Pentateuch appear within a covenant framework. Law is therefore integral to God's saving plan which is worked out through covenants.

A number of consequences follow from the covenant context of Israelite law:

First, these laws are more than an abstract system of morality. They are the *personal demands* of the sovereign, personal God on his subject people. This is stressed time and time again in different ways. 'The Lord came down upon Mount Sinai, to the top of the mountain; and the Lord called Moses to the top of the mountain, and Moses went up' (Ex. 19:20). The law was given orally and in writing. Often the very formulation of the laws, as direct speech, emphasizes that it comes from God himself. Commenting on the events at Sinai Deuteronomy 4:32f. says:

'For ask now of the days that are past, which were before you, since the day that God created man upon the earth, and ask from one end of heaven to the other, whether such a great thing as this has ever happened or was ever heard of. Did any people ever hear the voice of a god speaking out of the midst of the fire, as you have heard, and still live?'

The personal character of the relationship enshrined in the laws is emphasized by its exhortations. Israel must follow justice in her courts, and protect the weak because this is how God acts (Dt.

9

10:17ff.; 14:1; 16:18ff.,*etc.*).Israel is to 'be holy . . ., for I the Lord am holy' (Lv. 20:26). Motive clauses like these are scattered throughout the Pentateuch and are a distinctive feature of Old Testament law,[11] for they are not found in other ancient Near Eastern laws. They serve to reinforce a point that is often made explicitly in the Old Testament, that the covenant creates a personal relationship between God and Israel.[12]

This was part of the promise to Abraham: 'I will establish my covenant . . . to be God to you and to your descendants after you' (Gn. 17:7). That such a relationship is the goal of the covenant is reiterated before the law-giving at Sinai: 'Now therefore, if you will obey my voice and keep my covenant, . . . you shall be to me a kingdom of priests and a holy nation' (Ex. 19:5f.). As priests are set apart from ordinary men for the service of God, so a holy nation is to be set apart from other nations. Elsewhere the Israelites are called 'sons of God'. Through obedience to the covenant Israel confirms her calling to be God's chosen people. It is the law which transforms Israel from being simply the descendants of Abraham into a nation (*gôy*), a society organized for the service of God.[13]

Secondly, the covenant setting of the law emphasizes that *salvation is not based on works*. The covenant was made with those who had already been saved from Egypt: 'You have seen what I did to the Egyptians, and how I bore you on eagles' wings and brought you to myself' (Ex. 19:4). The Decalogue itself is preceded by a reminder about the exodus: 'I am the Lord your God, who brought you out of the land of Egypt, out of the house of bondage' (Ex. 20:2). The structure of the covenant form, with the historical prologue preceding the stipulations section, makes it clear that the laws are based on grace. In Deuteronomy the saving acts of God (Dt. 1–3) are related before the stipulations are imposed on Israel (Dt. 4ff.). Israel is expected to obey because God has brought the people out of Egypt and preserved them in the desert. The priority and absoluteness of God's grace are constantly reiterated: 'The Lord your God is not giving you this good land to possess because of your righteousness; for you are a stubborn people . . . . Even at Horeb you provoked the Lord to wrath' (Dt. 9:6, 8). God's grace in history is always the primary motive for obedience to the demands of the covenant. Deuteronomy 4–11 is a passionate plea to love God with all the heart, soul and mind. This demand is constantly being reinforced by appeals to the past history of Israel. These chapters freely mix historical reminiscence with exhortation, but even later in the more prosaic chapters 12–26 dealing with specific questions, historical allusions are often introduced in support of particular laws (*e.g.* Dt. 24:8f.; 25:17–19).

A *third* feature of the Old Testament collections of law distinguishes them from extrabiblical collections. The latter consist almost entirely of case law. If a man does X, his punishment shall be Y. They deal only with ordinary matters of legal dispute. The Old Testament of course contains many examples of this type of law, but it includes as well straight prohibitions and numerous religious regulations. The covenant basis of law explains why there is such a *mixture of subjects dealt with*. The primary command of the covenant is to 'love the Lord your God with all your heart', or to put it negatively to 'have no other gods before me'. And as in the New Testament, love is not conceived of as mere feeling but as faithfully obeying all that God commanded. 'You shall therefore love the Lord your God, and keep his charge, his statutes, his ordinances, and his commandments always' (Dt. 11:1). Among the specific requirements of the Sinai covenant, the Ten Commandments occupy a very special place, summarizing as they do the basic religious and moral principles that must control Israel's behaviour.[14] Other more specific demands of the covenant have close parallels with stipulations in ancient treaties. God as the great sovereign requires his vassal Israel to behave as a good subject ought. Israel must recognize her exclusive allegiance to her only Lord and King. In practice this means that Israel must wage war on God's behalf against his enemies, destroying heathen idols and their worshippers (Ex. 23:23f.; Dt. 7:1–5).[15] It also involves the regular offering of sacrifice and tithes to him in acknowledgment of his sovereignty (Ex. 23:14ff.; Dt.12:1ff.; 14:22ff.; 16:1ff.), just as earthly vassals had to bring their annual tribute to their suzerain. Vassals were supposed to read their treaty documents regularly, so too Israel is expected to read the law (Dt. 27 and 31).

Negatively, allegiance to the Lord means the avoidance of anything that has associations with pagan cults (Dt. 12–13).

The *fourth* aspect of the law highlighted by the covenant form is the section of *blessings and curses* (*e.g.* Lv. 26 and Dt. 28). Earlier it was noted that God's grace in choosing Israel should lead Israel to obey the Lord, and in consequence enjoy a further measure of divine grace. This virtuous circle receives formal expression in the very structure of the covenant documents themselves. They begin with a historical prologue recalling God's past mercies, their central section consists of stipulations (laws), and they conclude with blessings. To quote Deuteronomy 28:1: 'And if you obey the voice of the Lord your God . . . the Lord your God will set you high above all the nations of the earth.' But both Leviticus and Deuteronomy are at pains to point out that if Israel disobeys the law, she will quickly find herself in a vicious downward spiral with disaster following disaster: 'If you will not obey the voice of the Lord your God . . . then all these curses shall come upon you and overtake you' (Dt. 28:15).

Thus opens a horrendous list of curses containing some of the most spine-chilling passages in the whole Old Testament. The promise of continued peace and prosperity if Israel keeps the covenant, and woe and destruction if she does not, is not confined to Deuteronomy 28. Time and time again in the exhortations attached to the law Israel is reminded of the consequences of her action. Her persistent rebelliousness is recalled, and its results: 'Remember and do not forget how you provoked the Lord your God to wrath in the wilderness. . . . Even at Horeb you provoked the Lord to wrath, and the Lord was so angry with you that he was ready to destroy you' (Dt. 9:7f.). On the other hand the promise of blessing is constantly being held out if Israel is faithful: 'Honour your father and your mother, as the Lord your God commanded you; that your days may be prolonged, and that it may go well with you, in the land which the Lord your God gives you' (Dt. 5:16). As the new covenant was based on grace, so was the old. We may draw another parallel here. Both in the New Testament and in the Old Testament the promise of reward and the threat of punishment continue to play a role for those under the covenant. Thus I think that it is fair to say that because the law in the Old Testament has its basis in the covenant, it can never be a disinterested ethic. It is not merely the love of God which compels, but also the fear of God.

Finally we must draw attention to another aspect of covenant which has a bearing on the law, namely its *irrevocability*[16] (*cf.* Rom. 11:29). God cannot break his promises to the patriarchs. 'It was not because you were more in number than any other people that the Lord set his love upon you and chose you, for you were the fewest of all peoples; but it is because the Lord loves you, and is keeping the oath which he swore to your fathers' (Dt. 7:7f.). Similarly, Leviticus 26:40ff. and Deuteronomy 30 say that even after the covenant has been broken and Israel has experienced the worst consequences of the covenant curses, there may still be restoration if the people repent. There is therefore an unshakeable hope built into the covenant itself. It means that the history of Israel must always be significant. Nothing happens to her by chance. Even if she rebels, her destiny is always under her sovereign Lord.

The Davidic covenant

One other Old Testament covenant deserves a mention: the covenant with David. This has little to do with the law, but it does illustrate some of the aspects of covenant we have focused attention on in connection with the Sinaitic and Deuteronomic covenants. It is commonly stated that, originally, the Davidic covenant was unconditional, devoted wholly to promise and without any stipulations or threats attached to it.[17] This is not true, however, of the principal account of the Davidic covenant found in 2 Samuel 7. The prophet Nathan had rashly assured David that the Lord would like him to build a temple. At night Nathan was told that he was wrong. Instead he had to tell David that God was making an eternal covenant with the house of David, *i.e.* that the descendants of David would always be kings of Israel. Much the same features which characterize the Mosaic covenant are found in the Davidic covenant too. First, it is a relationship based entirely on divine grace demonstrated in history: 'Thus says the Lord of hosts, I took you from the pasture, from following the sheep, that you should be prince over my people Israel; and I have been with you wherever you went, and have cut off all your enemies from before you' (2 Sa. 7:8f.). Secondly, even more clearly than with the Sinai covenant, the drawing up of a covenant creates a state of grace and blessing: 'I will be his father, and he shall be my son' (verse 14). Thirdly, maintenance of this blessing depends on obedience to the divine commands: 'When he commits iniquity, I will chasten him with the rod of men' (verse 14). Here we find implicit what is explicit in Deuteronomy, namely that disobeying the covenant stipulations will bring the curse of economic disaster and military defeat. Fourthly, the covenant is eternal; though disobedience may bring trouble for a time, it will not last: 'I will not take my steadfast love from him, as I took it from Saul . . . your throne shall be established for ever' (verses 15f.).

Covenant ideas elsewhere in the Old Testament

For the whole of the rest of Old Testament religious history both the Sinaitic and Davidic covenants are of fundamental importance. The Psalms, many of which were sung in the Jerusalem temple, were most influential in moulding popular religious thinking. Some of them speak directly of the great covenants (44, 78, 89, 105, 132, *etc.*); in many others, covenant ideas are simply presupposed. The books of Kings in recounting the history of the monarchy make the decisive test of a king's character whether he was faithful to Mosaic law and Davidic practice (*e.g.* 2 Ki. 18:1–8; 14:3–6; 16:2–4).[18] Kings tries to show how the success of a particular king correlates with his adherence or otherwise to the covenant. The blessings and curses built into the covenant are demonstrated working out in history.

The covenant is also basic to the preaching of the prophets,[19] though they do not often use the word itself. Superficially they may appear to be straightforward preachers of righteousness fervently denouncing the moral and political ills of their time. But such a judgment misses the way in which the covenant structures the prophets' message. Appeals to Israel's history recur frequently, reminding the people that God's electing grace is not only a cause for thanksgiving but a ground for accountability: 'Hear this word that the Lord has spoken against you, O people of Israel, against the whole family which I brought up out of the land of Egypt: "You only have I known of all the families of the earth; therefore I will punish you for all your iniquities" ' (Am. 3:1f.).

According to the prophets the fault of Israel lay in her flouting of the covenant stipulations, thereby making all her outward allegiance in worship an empty show. Israel had broken the solemn treaty with her partner, and therefore God had declared war on his rebellious vassal. There is more than a formal similarity between some of the Old Testament 'controversies' (*rib*, Is. 1) and secular declarations of war.[20] Hosea cites the commandments that have been broken: 'The Lord has a controversy with the inhabitants of the land. There is no faithfulness or kindness, and no knowledge of God in the land; there is swearing, lying, killing, stealing, and committing adultery; they break all bounds and murder follows murder. Therefore the land mourns, and all who dwell in it languish' (Ho. 4:1ff.). As the 'therefore' makes plain, the mourning of the land is intrinsically related to the preceding sins (*cf.* Is. 24:5f.).[21] Every statement of the covenant concludes with a section of blessings and curses. The prophets proclaim that the guilt of Israel is such that the land is already suffering the effects of these curses and worse is to be expected in the near future. To mitigate their suffering Israel must repent forthwith. But the prophets' words go unheeded and they regretfully announce the imminent loss of the ancient institutions popularly supposed to have been guaranteed by the covenant. National sovereignty, the temple in Jerusalem and the Davidic dynasty will all be forfeit, at least in the immediate future. It was little wonder that the prophets faced such opposition from the ecclesiastical and political establishment; their message could plausibly be construed as an attack on the divine promises themselves.[22]

There are gleams of light in many prophetic passages, however, which show that they did believe the divine promises were eternal even though generations might pass without enjoying them. They look forward to a new age, when Israel will have received its fill of punishment and be reconstituted a purified people of God. In that day there will be a new Davidic king whose rule will extend over the whole earth (Is. 9 and 11). In this fashion Isaiah, who had earlier told Ahaz that his unbelief meant the end of the Davidic dynasty (Is. 7), yet holds out hope that the covenant with David will be renewed.[23] Similarly Jeremiah promises the renewal of the Mosaic covenant:

> 'Behold, the days are coming, says the Lord, when I will make a new covenant with the house of Israel and the house of Judah, not like the covenant which I made with their fathers when I took them by the hand to bring them out of the land of Egypt, my covenant which they broke, though I was their husband, says the Lord. But this is the covenant which I will make with the house of Israel after those days, says the Lord: I will put my law within them, and I will write it upon their hearts; and I will be their God, and they shall be my people. And no longer shall each man teach his neighbour and each his brother, saying, "Know the Lord," for they shall all know me, from the least of them to the greatest, says the Lord; for I will forgive their iniquity, and I will remember their sin no more' (Je. 31:31–34).

The law written on the heart is for Jeremiah the guarantee that the old external law will be kept. Ezekiel (chapters 34–37) takes up Jeremiah's idea of a new covenant enshrining the principles of the Mosaic covenant and combines it with the notion of a new Davidic covenant. Through the power of the Spirit of God Israel will be raised to new life and under a Davidic prince they will fulfil the law of God. For Ezekiel at least there is no dichotomy between the new life through the Spirit and adherence to the law. In fact it is only the Spirit that makes adherence possible. 'A new heart I will give you, and a new spirit I will put within you; and I will take out of your flesh the heart of stone and give you a heart of flesh. And I will put my spirit within you, and cause you to walk in my statutes and be careful to observe my ordinances' (Ezk. 36:26f.).

Written at least 150 years after Ezekiel, the books of Chronicles again emphasize the significance of the Davidic covenant in the history of Israel. The books of Ezra and Nehemiah both include records of solemn covenants. Ezra 10 deals with a pledge to divorce foreign wives. Nehemiah 10 covers a wider range of topics, endorsing various pentateuchal laws. In both cases the legal enactments are clearly set in a covenantal context. The laws themselves are preceded by a long historical prologue recalling the divine mercy and national apostasies which had resulted in their present unhappy plight. Re-endorsement of the covenant promises is put forward as the path to national blessing and prosperity. Thus, though there is no concluding section of blessings and curses in Ezra and Nehemiah, it is evident that basic covenant concepts have undergone little change in the 800 years from Moses to Ezra.

Throughout the Old Testament, then, law is consistently set in the context of covenant. This means that law both presupposes grace and is a means of grace. Law presupposes grace because law is only revealed to those God has called to himself. Law is a means of grace because through obedience to it the redeemed enter into a closer relationship to their divine king and enjoy more of the blessings inherent within the state of salvation.

Covenant in the New Testament

In view of the importance of the covenant in the Old Testament, it is mentioned remarkably rarely in the teaching of Jesus and Paul. The epistle to the Hebrews is the only book in the New Testament to develop the idea that Christ has inaugurated a new covenant. Does this mean then that most New Testament writers reject the relationship of grace and law enshrined in the Old Testament covenants?

We should be wary of too hastily assuming a continuity between Old and New Testament teaching on this point, since five centuries separate the covenants of Ezra and Nehemiah from the writing of the New Testament. As Christians we feel bound to assert that Christ fulfils the Old Testament law, but that must not be allowed to obscure the fact that at certain points he surpasses the teaching of the Old Testament.[24] On this particular issue, the relationship of law and grace, I believe the New Testament is in essential agreement with the Old. The nature of the saving event has changed, but the response expected of the believer to the call of God has not. Under the old covenant Israel was saved in the exodus from Egypt. She was expected to respond by accepting the kingship of Yahweh and obeying his covenant law. Under the new covenant the new Israel is saved by the coming of Christ. She is expected to respond by acknowledging that Christ is Lord and following his teaching.

To demonstrate this thesis is very much more complicated, and I can only indicate the lines along which the detailed argument might proceed. The first step is to examine the beliefs of Judaism at the turn of the era. Did they still accept the covenant basis of law, which permeates the Old Testament? The second stage is to examine the teaching of the New Testament itself. Did Jesus, Paul and the other writers see the relationship of grace and law in covenant terms?

It has often been asserted that the covenantal basis of law expressed so clearly in the Old Testament was lost in later Judaism, that in inter-testamental times a new understanding of the place of law in the scheme of salvation came to be generally accepted, namely that obeying the law earned a man salvation. A works-legalism tended to replace the view that salvation was through God's gracious covenant with Israel. This view is a total distortion of the true picture. In fact the Old Testament view of the relationship of grace and law was retained in inter-testamental and early rabbinic Judaism.[25] Most of the apocryphal and pseudepigraphical works of immediately pre-Christian times, the Essene writings from Qumran, and the tannaitic literature of the first centuries AD, agree on the basic essentials of the way of salvation, which Sanders terms 'covenantal nomism'.

'The "pattern" or "structure" of covenantal nomism is this: (1) God has chosen Israel and (2) given the law. The law implies both (3) God's promise to maintain the election and (4) the requirement to obey. (5) God rewards obedience and punishes transgression. (6) The law provides for means of atonement, and atonement results in (7) maintenance or re-establishment of the covenantal relationship. (8) All those who are maintained in the covenant by obedience, atonement and God's mercy belong to the group which will be saved. An important interpretation of the first and last points is that election and ultimately salvation are considered to be by God's mercy rather than human achievement.'[26]

It should also be noted that just as in the prophets, the term 'covenant' appears relatively rarely in the rabbinic literature. Sanders argues, convincingly in my opinion, that the reason for the scarcity of discussion of the word is that it was so fundamental to their thought. 'The covenant was presupposed, and the rabbinic discussions were largely directed toward the question of *how* to fulfil the covenantal obligations.'[27] In the Dead Sea Scrolls on the other hand, covenant is mentioned quite frequently, probably because the Essenes regarded themselves as members of the new covenant foretold by Jeremiah and were anxious to assert their identity over against mainline Judaism. But the Essenes shared the same general view of the relationship of covenant and law that characterized the rest of Judaism in the New Testament era, that salvation was through God's election of Israel and that keeping the law kept one within God's mercy but did not secure that grace. They held that the rest of Jewry was lax in its adherence to the law and therefore in grave danger of forfeiting the salvation that was all Israel's inheritance. But the same pattern of covenantal nomism is present in their works as well as in rabbinic literature.

An understanding of first-century Jewish thinking about the covenant and the law puts the teaching of Jesus and Paul in a clearer perspective. That they rarely mention the covenant does not prove they regarded it as unimportant. It could be that just like the rabbis they assumed it was fundamental, and therefore required no discussion. This latter possibility is confirmed, I believe, by an examination of the teaching of Jesus and Paul.

Jesus' only reference to the covenant occurs in the solemn context of the last supper. On that occasion Jesus said, 'This is my blood of the covenant' (Mk. 14:24). For our present purpose it is unnecessary to establish exactly what Jesus meant when he said this; what is significant is that he assumed that his disciples would understand and also that the evangelists supposed their readers would understand the remark without further explanation. They simply anticipate familiarity with the notion of covenant.

More important still, many aspects of Jesus' teaching[28] directly recall various details of Old Testament covenant thinking. First and foremost his parables are about the kingdom (kingship might be a more appropriate translation) of God. It will be recalled that all the Old Testament covenants presuppose that God is the king of Israel. Within the parables and his other sayings Jesus sets out a view of the relationship of God and man that finds many parallels in the Old Testament covenant. He declares that the kingdom of God has drawn near (Mk. 1:15; *cf.* Ex. 19:9). His parables and his treatment of publicans and sinners declare that men are forgiven through the unmerited grace of God (*e.g.* Lk. 14–18). He presents his teaching as a new law which at once fulfils and surpasses the law of Moses (Mt. 5). Those who obey his teaching and follow his example will be called blessed on the day of judgment; those who do not will be called accursed (Mt. 7:21ff.; 25:31ff.). It is therefore quite appropriate to describe the message of Jesus so far as the relationship of grace and law is concerned as a type of covenantal nomism rooted in the Old Testament.

In certain very important respects, however, Jesus' teaching gives a radical, fresh interpretation to the covenantal nomism common both to the Old Testament and to first-century Judaism. The central difference concerns his person and role. The kingdom of God comes not on another Sinai but with him. He is the king of Israel. His teaching, not Moses', is the final authority for men. His death, not that of the lambs prescribed in Leviticus, is the ransom for the sins of mankind. He is the judge who will pronounce the blessing and the curse on the last day. Another point of difference between his teaching and that of the Old Testament concerns the scope of election. Many of his remarks challenge the usual equation of Israel with those who are being saved. On the one hand he warns many of those who regard themselves as righteous that God does not and will not accept them. On the other, penitent sinners are repeatedly assured of God's mercy, and there are several hints that this mercy extends to those outside of Israel. Implicit in our Lord's teaching is a universalizing of the Old Testament view, opening up the covenant to all who acknowledge the kingship of Christ.

Similarly in Paul the basic covenantal scheme is clearly present.[29] Indeed his formulation of the relationship of law and grace was the starting-point of our essay. But like his fellow rabbis Paul was no antinomian. Unlike them, however, he was under the law of Christ; that is, he was guided by Christ's precept and example. He warns the Corinthians that they can expect God's judgment, as ancient Israel did, if they persist in immorality. He looks forward to receiving a reward for faithful service, just as Israel knew blessing when they were loyal to the Lord.

When Paul's writings are compared with the Gospels the centrality of Jesus in the new covenant is more evident. In the Gospels the kingdom of God is presented somewhat mysteriously in parables; Paul categorically affirms that Jesus is Lord. In the Gospels Jesus occasionally welcomes non-Jews as his followers. Paul declares, 'There is neither Jew nor Greek . . . you are all one in Christ Jesus' (Gal. 3:28). The universalization of the old covenant is complete; the kingdom of heaven is open to all believers.

In stressing the essential continuity of the Old and New Testaments as regards the relationship of law and grace, it is easy to give the impression that the Gospels and Paul are little more than a revamping of the old covenant in a universalistic and Christocentric framework. There is very much more to the ethical teaching of Jesus and Paul than this and it is the purpose of some of the later essays[30] to expound these aspects in greater detail. The purpose of the next essay is to lay the groundwork for the discussion of a particular problem that arises out of Jesus' affirmation that his teaching, not the Old Testament law, is the final authority. He also emphatically affirms, however, that the law was Godgiven, that his teaching does not contradict it but fulfils it, and indeed Jesus claims that his teaching sometimes recovers the true intention of the law which his contemporaries had forgotten. Jesus' attitude to the law is thus highly paradoxical: on the one hand he and his teaching replace it, on the other he is witnessed to by the law and he agrees with the law and its divine authority. To help resolve this paradox, the next essay examines the content of the Old Testament law in its original setting. This aims to make clear the essential continuity of old and new covenant ethics, without obscuring the occasional points of real difference between them.

NOTES

1. By this I mean the theological interpretation of Israel's history presented in the canonical books of the Old Testament as opposed to a modern critical understanding of that history. See G. von Rad, *Old Testament Theology,* I (Oliver and Boyd, 1962), pp. 105ff. Furthermore, our present concern is the theology of the books in their final form rather than that of the underlying sources. For a justification of this approach see H. J. Kraus, *Die biblische Theologie: ihre Geschichte und Problematik* (Neukirchen, 1970), pp. 367ff.; B. S. Childs, 'The Sensus Literalis of Scripture', in H. Donner (ed.), *Beiträge zur alttestamentlichen Theologie: FS für W. Zimmerli* (Vandenhoeck und Ruprecht, Göttingen, 1977), pp. 80–93.

2. D. R. Hillers, *Covenant: The History of a Biblical Idea* (Johns Hopkins, Baltimore, 1969); J. Bright, *Covenant and Promise* (SCM Press, 1977).

3. On the Abrahamic covenant see R. E. Clements, *Abraham and David* (SCM Press, 1967) and N. Lohfink, *Die Landverheissung als Eid* (Katholisches Bibelwerk, Stuttgart, 1967).

4. See G. J. Wenham, 'The Deuteronomic Theology of the Book of Joshua', *Journal of Biblical Literature* 90, 1971, pp. 140–148.

5. See M. Weinfeld, 'The Covenant of Grant in the Old Testament and in the Ancient Near East', *Journal of the American Oriental Society* 90, 1970, pp. 184–203; *idem,* 'Covenant, Davidic', *The Interpreter's Dictionary of the Bible,* Supplementary Volume, (Abingdon, New York, 1977), pp. 188–192.

6. There are four main possibilities: $b^e r \hat{\imath}\underline{t}$ could come from (1) *brh* 'to eat' (2) *brh* 'to see' (3) *birīt* 'between' (4) *birītu* 'fetter, band'. For further discussions see E. Kutsch, *Verheissung und Gesetz* (de Gruyter, Berlin, 1973), pp. 28ff.; J. Barr, 'Some Semantic Notes on the Covenant', *Beiträge zur alttestamentlichen Theologie* (Vandenhoeck, Göttingen, 1977), pp. 23–38; M. Weinfeld, 'Berit', *Theological Dictionary of the Old Testament,* II (Eerdmans, Grand Rapids, 1977), pp. 253–278.

7. Of the many modern discussions D. J. McCarthy, *Treaty and Covenant* (Pontifical Biblical Institute, Rome, 1963) and *Old Testament Covenant: A Survey of Current Opinions* (Blackwell, 1972) and M. Weinfeld, *Deuteronomy and the Deuteronomic School* (Clarendon Press, 1972) are among the most useful.

8. Some studies suggest that the arrangement of Near Eastern collections of law may also have influenced Old Testament covenant texts, and that the Old Testament covenant form could be described as a cross between the treaty and 'law-code' form. See my article in *The Churchman* 84, 1970, p. 219; S. M. Paul, *Studies in the Book of the Covenant in the Light of Cuneiform and Biblical Law* (Brill, Leiden, 1970), pp. 27ff.; M. Weinfeld, *Deuteronomy and the Deuteronomic School,* pp. 146ff.

9. V. Korošec, *Hethitische Staatsverträge* (Weicher, Leipzig, 1931), p. 13.

10. M. Weinfeld, *Deuteronomy and the Deuteronomic School,* pp. 59ff.

11. B. Gemser, 'The Importance of the Motive Clause in Old Testament Law', *Supplement to Vetus Testamentum* 1, 1953, pp. 50–66.

12. Ex. 4:22; Dt. 1:31; 14:1; *cf.* 32:6. Secular treaties were also thought to create a family relationship. The vassals are called 'sons' of the suzerain, and 'brothers' of each other (*cf.* Am. 1:9) and address the suzerain as 'father' (McCarthy, *Old Testament Covenant,* p. 66).

13. S. M. Paul, *op. cit.,* pp. 30ff.

14. For further discussion see next chapter.

15. The command to exterminate the Canaanites (*e.g.* Dt. 7:1ff.) raises acute problems. It is often seen as the expression of bellicose nationalism dressed up as a divine command. In context the ban on the Canaanites appears in a different light. It is because the Canaanites serve other gods and will deflect Israel from total loyalty to the Lord that Israel must eliminate them. Deuteronomy chapter 13 is equally severe on Israelite towns, families or individuals who forsake the Lord. They must be ruthlessly sought out and executed. Similarly Deuteronomy 28:15-68 warns that wholesale ruin will face Israel if they are not careful to do all the words of this law. Judgment on sin is just as much part of the fabric of New Testament theology as it is in the Old Testament. For a fuller discussion of the ethical issues see J. W. Wenham, *The Goodness of God* (Inter-Varsity Press, 1974), pp. 119ff.

16. Here I part company with the usual view (*cf.* J. Bright, *Covenant and Promise,* pp. 26ff.) that the Abrahamic and Davidic covenants were basically eternal and unconditional, whereas the Sinaitic/Deuteronomic covenant was conditional and not necessarily eternal. Rather, as J. Barr (*Beiträge zur alttestamentlichen Theologie,* p. 33) points out, all biblical covenants are eternal. It is also clear that all the covenants had conditions attached to them, at least in the texts as we now have them.

17. *Cf.* M. Weinfeld, 'Covenant, Davidic', *The Interpreter's Dictionary of the Bible,* Supplementary Volume, pp. 188-192.

18. G. von Rad, *Old Testament Theology,* I, pp. 334ff.

19. J. Bright, *Covenant and Promise;* R. E. Clements, *Prophecy and Covenant* (SCM Press, 1965), pp. 18ff.; W. Zimmerli, *The Law and the Prophets* (Harper and Row, New York, 1967).

20. J. Harvey, *Biblica* 43, 1962, pp. 172ff.

21. D. R. Hillers, *Treaty Curses and the Old Testament Prophets* (Pontifical Biblical Institute, Rome, 1964).

22. See J. Bright, *Covenant and Promise,* pp. 140ff.

23. So R. Kilian, *Die Verheissung Immanuels* (Katholisches Bibelwerk, Stuttgart, 1968) and J. A. Motyer, 'Context and Content in the Interpretation of Isaiah 7:14', *Tyndale Bulletin* 21, 1970, pp. 118ff.

24. See next essay for some examples in the realm of food laws and sexual ethics.

25. E. P. Sanders, *Paul and Palestinian Judaism* (SCM Press, 1977) discusses the issues with great thoroughness.

26. *Ibid.,* p. 422.

27. *Ibid.,* p. 421.

28. Among the vast literature on this subject the following are especially useful. R. J. Banks, *Jesus and the Law in the Synoptic Tradition* (Cambridge University Press, 1975); W. D. Davies, *The Sermon on the Mount* (Cambridge University Press, 1966); J. Jeremias, *The Parables of Jesus*[2] (SCM Press, 1963); J. Jeremias, *New Testament Theology, I: The Proclamation of Jesus* (SCM Press, 1971) and J. W. Wenham, *Christ and the Bible* (Inter-Varsity Press, 1972).

29. See E. P. Sanders, *Paul and Palestinian Judaism,* pp. 431ff.

30. By R. E. Nixon and B. N. Kaye.

2
Law and the legal system in the Old Testament

Gordon Wenham

Introduction

In the first chapter we looked at the relationship of law and grace within the Old Testament, a relationship that can be summed up in the word covenant. We saw that God's love for Abraham, Israel and David was the basis of the three most important covenants. In each case the human partner had to respond, by loving God in return. They were assured that such loving obedience would lead to a yet fuller experience of divine mercy and blessing.

But how can a man or a nation love God? Without some revelation of God's will human efforts to please God may well be misdirected. It is for this reason that law occupies such a central position in the Old Testament. It shows what love for God means in daily life: how man is to worship God in a way that is acceptable to his Creator and how he should treat his neighbour. To this end it offers a short but comprehensive statement of religious and moral principles in the Ten Commandments.

Were man unfallen, the Decalogue would no doubt be a sufficient guide to living. But that is not the case. Even members of the covenant nation failed to observe the commandments from time to time. For social and theological reasons it was therefore necessary to have a penal system to punish transgressors. Any society which fails to censure wrongdoers is liable to disintegrate, and in Israel's case to lose the blessings of the covenants as well. To maintain, or restore when broken, the relationship between God and man is the purpose of the many regulations about worship in the Old Testament; to restore relations between man and man and to bear witness to the moral principles of the Decalogue is the purpose of the penal law. Where worship or morality is neglected, Israel will start to experience the covenant curses, both at a national and at an individual level. This covenant context of Israel's law gives a special urgency to its penal law and makes its scale of values rather different from that of its neighbours. By surveying the types of punishment enshrined in the Pentateuch light is shed on its scale of values.

Finally, the organization of society has a material influence on the way people behave. Law must be known if it is to be obeyed, and there needs to be a means of enforcing obedience on the recalcitrant. Every society has its own set of devices for this purpose; in ancient Israel judges, law-teachers, prophets, kings and other rulers all played their part in undergirding the covenant law, and they will form the final subject of our enquiry.

The nature of the material

Before studying the laws themselves it is wise to ask some preliminary questions about the nature of the collections of law found in the Old Testament. Are they all-embracing codes of law intended to cover every aspect of Israelite life? How far do they conform to the patterns of other ancient legal collections? Can we discern any general principles running through biblical law which mark it off from other systems?

Various collections of law are to be found in the books of Exodus, Leviticus and Deuteronomy, and records of legal cases are to be found in many parts of the Bible. Comparison of these laws with other collections of Near Eastern law shows that Hebrew law was heavily indebted to the tradition of cuneiform law originating in Mesopotamia.[1] It is now generally agreed that these extrabiblical documents are not comprehensive codes of statute law, but collections of traditional case law occasionally introducing certain innovations and reforms. It seems likely that the biblical collections of law are to be interpreted similarly. In many cases the Old Testament introduces changes into the traditional law of the Near East, but in other cases it simply assumes it (*e.g.* laws about oxen Ex. 21:28ff., divorce Dt. 24:1ff.).

Theory of law

In Mesopotamia the king was the author of law. He was held to have been divinely endowed with gifts of justice and wisdom which enabled him to devise good law. Law was therefore a basically secular institution. In Israel, however, God himself was the author and giver of law, and this divine authorship of law had several consequences. First it meant that all offences were sins. They did not merely affect relationships between men but also the relationship between God and man. As we have seen, law was a central part of the covenant. Therefore, if the nation rejected the law or connived at its non-observance, curses came into play bringing divine judgment on the whole people.

Secondly, because all life is related to God, and the law came from God, moral and religious obligations are all to be found in a single law book. This is true of the Pentateuch as a whole and of the smaller collections of law within it (*e.g.* Ex. 21–23). Mesopotamia maintained a sharp distinction between these spheres: their collections of law consist almost entirely of civil legislation.

The third implication of the Old Testament views of law is that not just the king but every Israelite was responsible for its observance. He had to keep it himself and ensure that the community of which he was a member did so too. There was thus both an individual and a national responsibility to keep the law (*cf.* Dt. 29:18ff.).

Finally, since the law came from God, it was not to be a secret understood only by lawyers, but by everyone. There was therefore an obligation on the national leaders to teach and explain it to the people. The public character of the biblical legislation is reflected in the large number of motive clauses which give reasons why certain laws should be obeyed (*e.g.* 'that your days may be long in the land'). Such reminders are more in character in a sermon addressed to the nation than in a piece of literature designed only for the edification of those administering the law. Hammurabi invited all who were oppressed to come and read his laws.[2] In this limited sense he was looking for a popular knowledge of the law. The Bible stresses to a much greater degree the importance of everyone knowing the law. It is addressed to 'all Israel'. Moses was appointed to explain the laws given at Sinai, and the law had to be read out every seven years at a national assembly (Dt. 5:1; Ex. 20:18ff.; Dt. 31:10f.). Thus law in the Old Testament is not simply intended to guide the judges but to create a climate of opinion that knows and respects it.

This fits in with the express purpose of the law: to create 'a kingdom of priests and a holy nation' (Ex. 19:6). The prologue and epilogue of the Laws of Hammurabi dwell on the political and economic benefits that law brings—justice, peace, prosperity and good government. But 'the prime purpose of biblical compilations is sanctification'.[3] As has been stressed before, law-giving is integral to the covenant. The law itself is the divine means of creating a holy people. Obedience to it renews the divine image in man and enables him to fulfil the imperative to 'Be holy, for I am holy' (Lv. 11:44f.; 19:2; 20:7, 26, *etc.*).

The Ten Commandments

The distinctive features of Old Testament law find expression in the opening words of the Decalogue: 'And God spoke all these words saying . . . '. Here the divine authorship of the following laws is simply stated. After a brief historical prologue reminding Israel of what God had done on their behalf, there follows a series of injunctions covering both religious and social matters. God, the author of these laws, unlike earthly kings, is concerned with the whole of life.

Case law or moral principle? The Ten Commandments are rightly regarded as the quintessence of Old Testament law. It has been suggested in the previous chapter that they are to be understood as part of the stipulations of the Sinai covenant. But is it possible to be any more precise? How, for instance, are they related to the other laws in the Pentateuch? Should they be regarded as laws in their own right, or are they rather a set of moral principles, which could be enshrined in case and statute law? These questions have been debated intensively in recent years, and it is not possible to review the problem in depth here. The answers given depend on the view taken of the development of Israel's law, since the interpretation of the commandments depends to some extent on the historical situation in which they were formulated. In spite of many attempts to disengage the commandments from their present context and recover earlier phraseology and meanings, no consensus of opinion has emerged.[4] We can, however, be more certain how the author of Exodus understood the commandments, since he must have known them in the present form and have been responsible for the literary context in which they are found. It is the context and content of the commandments as they now stand that form the basis of the following exposition, not hypothetical reconstructions of the original form of the Decalogue.[5]

On this basis it becomes clear that we should not regard the commandments as case or statute law. No human penalties are specified for their transgression; rather divine curses are pronounced on those who break certain of the laws, and blessings are promised to those who keep them. These characteristics are more appropriate in a treaty text than in a collection of laws.[6] The Decalogue itself does not state what punishment the community will impose on those who break the commandments. It is misleading to describe the Decalogue as Israel's criminal law, for it is not a list of offences that the state would itself prosecute, let alone for which it would always exact the death penalty.[7] Ancient law does not sharply distinguish between criminal and civil offences. Dishonouring parents, murder, adultery and theft were all cases in which the prime responsibility for bringing the offender before the courts was left to the injured party or his family. Since, however, the death penalty could be imposed for some of these offences, they might be called crimes.[8] Religious offences could more aptly be described as crimes, since the whole community had to take action to punish the sinner. That the Decalogue cannot be classed as criminal or civil law is most clearly demonstrated by the tenth commandment, for a human court could hardly convict someone of covetousness. The Ten Commandments should therefore be looked on as a statement of basic religious and ethical principles rather than as a code of law.

Commandment and law. The principles of the Decalogue are illustrated and, in the laws which follow, put into a form that human judges can handle (Ex. 20:23ff.; Dt. 6–26). To revert to the treaty analogy, the commandments constitute the basic stipulations which precede the detailed stipulations in a covenant document. In the exposition that follows I shall therefore try to illustrate the meaning of the commandments by reference to the laws in the Pentateuch, though it should always be remembered that the commandment is more fundamental and wide ranging than the corresponding laws.

It should be noted that the special status of the Decalogue in both Jewish and Christian tradition is not a mere fancy of later exegetes; the Old Testament itself regards the Ten Commandments as different and more important than the other laws. They alone were written by the 'finger of God'. The narrative in Exodus clearly emphasizes the unique significance of the Decalogue in the way it prepares for it and sets it apart from the case law which comes after.[9] Similarly Deuteronomy, when harking back to the law-giving at Sinai, focuses exclusive attention on the commandments, though the other laws in Exodus are clearly presupposed in Deuteronomy. The Ten Commandments are thus acknowledged to be the heart of the covenant law, a special revelation of God in the fullest sense of the phrase.

But though every commandment expresses the will of God, and breach of any one of them is a sin calling down on the offender the wrath of God, their order is not haphazard: the most vital demands are placed first. This is confirmed by the penal law. Flagrant disregard of the first six commandments carried a mandatory death penalty. For the seventh death was probably optional, not compulsory. Only in exceptional cases would breach of the eighth and ninth commandments involve capital punishment. And it is most unlikely that the tenth commandment was ever the subject of judicial process. The order of the commandments thus gives some insight into Israel's hierarchy of values and this should be borne in mind in their exegesis.

First commandment. The principal concern of every vassal treaty was to secure the sole allegiance of the vassal to his suzerain. This is the thrust of the first commandment: 'You shall have no other gods before me.' It is not certain whether this commandment implied absolute monotheism, *i.e.* the existence of only one God, but it undoubtedly was a demand for practical monotheism, worship of the Lord alone. This terse command is expanded in great detail in the book of Leviticus in particular, which gives instructions about the correct rituals in worship. But perhaps the laws for the instruction of the laity found in Exodus 20–23 and Deuteronomy give a better impression of the primacy of worship. Both collections begin their detailed stipulations section with laws about the place of worship.[10] They also require the offering of tithes and the attendance of all Israelite men at the three national festivals, as well as the extermination of all pagan cults and their adherents (Ex. 23:14ff.; Dt. 12; 14:22ff.; 16). Apostasy involving the worship of foreign deities was punishable by death (Nu. 25; Dt. 13).

It has also been suggested[11] that the need for whole-hearted allegiance to the Lord explains the ban on eating certain foodstuffs (Lv. 11; Dt. 14; *cf.* 1 Cor. 8). The unclean animals were either worshipped or sacrificed by the Canaanites or Egyptians and therefore Israel must shun them. But this explains too few of the regulations to be convincing. More probably, the reason for the prohibitions was that the unclean animals symbolized the unclean nations, the Gentiles, with whom Israel was forbidden to mix, whereas the clean species represented the chosen people of Israel.[12] Thus, every time an Israelite ate meat he was reminded of God's grace in choosing Israel to be his people, and that as one of God's elect he had a duty to pursue holiness.

Second commandment. The second commandment bans all visual representation of God for use in worship. Images of gods in human and animal form are well known in Egyptian and Canaanite religion. Deuteronomy 4:15ff. justifies this prohibition by appeal to Israel's experience at Sinai, where they heard God but did not see him (*cf.* Rom. 1:18ff.).

The wording of this commandment shows that it is not a ban on art as such. Characteristically of biblical legislation the decisive condition or prohibition comes towards the end of the sentence, in this case: 'You shall not bow down to them or worship them' (verse 5). Had the commandment meant to ban all artwork and sculpture it should have ended with verse 4. This interpretation of the law is confirmed by the following chapters (25ff.). The tabernacle itself was richly decorated with the likeness of many things in heaven and earth, and the ark, the earthly throne of God, was surmounted by two winged cherubim. But by making the golden calf and inviting the people to worship it, Aaron broke this commandment and threatened the whole nation with extinction (Ex. 32).

The commandment is followed by a motive clause explaining why it should be observed: 'For I the Lord your God am a jealous God, visiting the iniquity of the fathers upon the children to the third and the fourth generation of those who hate me, but showing steadfast love to thousands of those who love me and keep my commandments' (Ex. 20:5f.). Motive clauses like this are a characteristic feature of Israelite legislation, showing that the commandment was supposed to be public law which had to be taught to the people. In this clause there are several reflections of basic covenant ideology, in particular the exclusive nature of the relationship, 'I the Lord . . . am a jealous God', and the blessing on those who keep the law and the curse on those who do not. In secular treaties 'bowing down', 'serving' and 'loving' are the appropriate actions of a vassal towards his lord. It is also worth noting that loving God is equated with keeping his commandments (*cf.* Jn. 14:15). Finally, the long-range effect of obedience and disobedience should be observed. Actions do not just affect the individual but also his descendants, up to the great-grandchildren in the case of transgression and as far as the thousandth generation in the case of obedience (Dt. 7:9). This disproportion is one of many illustrations in the law of how God's mercy far exceeds his anger.

Third commandment. The third commandment forbids any misuse of the name of God, whether in frivolous speech or in such dark deeds as witchcraft and magic (Lv. 24:11ff.; Mt. 5:33ff.; Acts 19: 13ff.). In biblical thinking the name of God expresses the character of God himself. Again this commandment adds a motive clause reminding any transgressor that he will not escape the covenant curses, even if he escapes human judgment.

Fourth commandment. The fourth commandment forbids all work on the sabbath day.[13] There are few indications of exactly how this was interpreted in early days. Ordinary, everyday work such as trading was forbidden. More lowly tasks such as collecting manna or sticks were also prohibited, on pain of death (Ex. 16:22ff.; Nu. 15:32ff.). Positively, it was a day set aside for worship (Is. 1:13). Like the tithe, the setting apart of one day in the week is a token of the consecration of the whole. The reason given in Exodus for the observance of the sabbath is imitation of God, who rested from the work of creation on the seventh day. In Deuteronomy it is remembrance for God's deliverance from Egypt; under the new covenant Sunday commemorates the resurrection. It is probable that the rules about the sabbath were not so strict in early days as in post-exilic times. For instance, the commandment does not forbid the wife to work, journeys were permitted (2 Ki. 4:23), and the temple guard was changed on the sabbath (2 Ki. 11:5-8). Therefore Jesus' more flexible attitude to the sabbath over against the strictness of his Pharisaic opponents may really reflect the original practice in early Israel (Mk. 2:23ff.). Looking to the future, Hebrews 4 views the sabbath as a type of the rest of the saints in heaven.

Fifth commandment. 'Honour your father and mother.' To honour (*kibbēd*) is most often used in the Old Testament with respect to God or his representatives such as prophets and kings.[14] It may be that parents are envisaged as representing God to their children, and this would explain the very severe penalties prescribed for those who dishonour their parents (Ex. 21:15, 17; Dt. 21:18–21). But the motive clause, 'that your days may be long in the land which the Lord your God gives you', draws attention to the blessings of obedience. 'The "promise" attached to this first manward command shows the family as the miniature of the nation. If the one is sound, it implies, so will be the other. To put it more accurately, unless

God's order is respected at the first level, his gifts will be forfeited at all others.'[15]

Sixth commandment. The sixth commandment forbids murder and other actions that may result in loss of life (Dt. 22:8). It does not rule out the judicial execution of murderers and other heinous criminals, or killing in war. The death penalty is insisted on for murder. Genesis 9:5f. sets out the theological principle involved: 'For your lifeblood I will surely require a reckoning; of every beast I will require it and of man; of every man's brother I will require the life of man. Whoever sheds the blood of man, by man shall his blood be shed; for God made man in his own image.' The laws in the Pentateuch show how the principle was applied in practice. A man or an animal which causes the death of another man must be put to death (Ex. 21:12, 28ff.). Where a man is responsible for someone's death, deliberate and accidental homicide are carefully distinguished (Ex. 21:13f.; Nu. 35:9ff.). It was common in other legal systems to allow composition in the case of homicide; instead of being executed the homicide could pay appropriate damages to the dead man's family. Numbers 35 expressly excludes this arrangement in Israel. In the case of murder the murderer must be executed; if the killing was not premeditated the homicide must live in the city of refuge until the death of the high priest.[16] The Pentateuch is not only concerned with the punishment of homicides, but with the prevention of accidental death. Owners of dangerous animals are warned to keep them in (Ex. 21:29, 36), and house-builders are told to put a parapet around the roof to stop people falling off (Dt. 22:8).

One law (Ex. 21:22-25) specifically deals with the death of a foetus as the result of a brawl. Close parallels to this rule are known in cuneiform law (LH 209-14; HL 17: MAL A 21, 50-2) but the interpretation of the biblical law is highly complex.[17] Three things are clear, however, in the present law. First, the miscarriage and the injury to the woman were caused accidentally, a by-product of a quarrel between two men. Secondly, this suggests that the talion formula 'life for life . . . stripe for stripe' which refers to the woman's injury should be regarded as a formula insisting on a punishment proportionate to the injury, not necessarily literal retribution (*cf.* verses 26–27). 'Life for life' only applies in cases of premeditated killing. Thirdly, the loss of the foetus is compensated for by the payment of damages. Biblical law therefore does not deal with the case of deliberately induced abortion. On the basis of certain passages in Job and the Psalms[18] it seems likely that the child in the womb was regarded as a human being, under the protection of its Creator (Jb. 10:8–12; Pss. 51:5f.; 139:13–16; *cf.* Lk. 1:15, 44), and that Old Testament writers would have shared the abhorrence of the Assyrians at artificially induced abortion.[19]

The Old Testament discourages wanton destruction and slaughter in war as well as in peace (Dt. 20:10ff.). It regards death in war, however, as one of God's judgments (Dt. 28:25ff.), and therefore inevitable as long as men go on sinning. In the same way that 'all Israel' is summoned to execute judgment on criminals, so nations may be called to punish other nations (*cf.* Ex. 23:23ff.; Is. 10:5ff.), though when they undertake this task, they are warned not to exceed their brief.

Seventh commandment. Immediately following the prohibition of murder comes the prohibition of adultery (*nā'ap̄*), *i.e.* sexual relations between a married woman and a man who is not her husband.[20] A comparison of this commandment with various laws in the rest of the Pentateuch which deal with sexual offences is very revealing, in showing how the commandment expresses a bare moral principle, whereas the detailed laws apply the principle in various situations.

If the sixth commandment seeks to uphold the sanctity of human life, the seventh seeks to preserve the purity of marriage. Genesis 2:24 states the positive theological principle undergirding matrimony: 'A man leaves his father and his mother and cleaves to his wife, and they become one flesh.' This poetic couplet expresses rather cryptically one of the fundamentals of Old Testament marriage law, that in marriage a woman becomes, as it were, her husband's closest relative. A man could therefore call his wife, rather misleadingly in some circumstances, his sister (Gn. 12:13, 19; 20:2; Ct. 4:9; 5:2). Other implications of this verse are not developed in the Old Testament. One group of first-century Jews held that it entailed monogamy. Our Lord added that it meant that marriage should be indissoluble, even though in practice human sinfulness ('the hardness of men's hearts') often led to its breakdown (Mt. 19:5f.).

Similarly the commandment forbids adultery, a sin whose very nature involves breaking the marriage bond. What happens when marriages break up is the concern of the other laws in the Pentateuch. They are concerned with the situations that arise and not with theological utopia. This Old Testament legislation can, I believe, be seen to have a similar goal to the New Testament teaching on marriage, namely the creation and preservation of stable marriages.

As usual the Decalogue prescribes no human penalty for breach of this commandment. Other passages make it clear that the standard penalty for adultery was death. If caught, both parties, the man and the woman, were put to death (Lv. 20:10; Dt. 22:22). The severity of the sentence is undoubtedly very shocking to modern readers. Certain observations may perhaps mitigate our sense of shock. First, the death penalty for adultery is not unique to the Old Testament; it is common to most of the legal systems of the ancient Near East. Secondly, the death penalty was not mandatory; if a husband wished to spare his wife, he had to spare the other man as well.[21] Thirdly, where the circumstances suggest that the woman was coerced, she would be pardoned and only the man would be put to death (Dt. 22:25–27). Nevertheless, in spite of these considerations, the penalties for adultery are still striking, and reflect a much harsher condemnation of those who deliberately break up marriage, home and family than is made in modern Western society.

In contrast the penalties imposed for other sexual misconduct are lighter. After betrothal, effected by the payment of a large present to the bride's father (often equal to several years' wages), a girl was legally as good as married and intercourse with her by a third party was regarded as adultery and therefore liable to the death penalty (Dt. 22:23–27). But when an unbetrothed girl was caught lying with a man, both escaped more lightly. The man was made to marry the girl and give the appropriate betrothal gift to the girl's father, which by his action he had, as it were, by-passed. In addition his right to divorce was forfeit. If the girl's father did not want her to marry the man concerned, he could still demand the betrothal gift from the man, but that was all (Ex. 22:16f.; Dt. 22:28f.). It can be seen that running through all these laws is a concern to promote stable marriages. The financial payments associated with marriage and divorce were also very effective in stabilizing marriages.[22]

Marriages did break up in Old Testament times, however, and remarriage was permitted. Nowhere does the Old Testament give any instructions about divorce itself. Contemporary custom is simply presupposed. What it does do, in fact, is regulate remarriage after divorce or widowhood. This is clearest in Deuteronomy 24:1–4 which allows a divorced woman to contract a second marriage, but if her second husband dies or divorces her, she may not return to her first husband. The thinking behind this law has puzzled commentators. A common view is that the law regards the second marriage as adulterous[23] and is concerned to discourage such unions. There is no hint of this motive in the law, however, and as there were other powerful legal and financial deterrents to divorce and adultery in the Old Testament, this view seems inadequate. More plausible is Yaron's suggestion[24] that the law is designed to protect the second marriage from interference by the first husband. Perhaps jealous of her second husband, her first partner might try to woo her back without the safeguard of this law. But this idea founders on the fact that the rule also applies after the second husband's death (verse 3).

A more probable explanation[25] of this law emerges from a comparison with the incest rules in Leviticus 18. These forbid sexual intercourse between brother and sister, grandfather and granddaughter and so on. They also prohibit intercourse between brother-in-law and sister-in-law, or father-in-law and daughter-in-law. The logic of these prohibitions is as follows: in marriage a woman becomes her husband's closest relative, his sister as it were, and therefore a sister to his brothers, a daughter to his father and so on. Therefore if it is wrong for a man to marry his sister or daughter, it is equally wrong for him to marry his sister-in-law or daughter-in-law. Now these prohibitions on intermarriage with one's daughter-in-law only become relevant after the end of her first marriage in divorce or the death of her first husband. Up to that point such a union would be adulterous. The same logic applies in Deuteronomy 24 to remarrying one's former wife. If one cannot marry one's sister, one cannot marry one who has become a sister through a previous marriage, *i.e.* one's former wife. Thus while the Old Testament does not affirm the practical indissolubility of marriage, it does maintain its theoretical indissolubility, in the sense that the kinships created between the spouses and their families are not terminated by death or divorce.

In certain respects, then, Old Testament marriage law is less strict than that of the New Testament. Infidelity by the husband does not count as adultery in the Old Testament. It does in the New Testament. 'Every one who divorces his wife and marries another commits adultery' (Lk. 16:18 parallels Mt. 19:3-12; Mk. 10:2-12).

These Gospel sayings also explicitly rule out remarriage after divorce and, by implication, polygamy as well, equating them with adultery. Thus at three points—polygamy, remarriage,[26] and a husband's adultery—the Old Testament laws plainly conflict with the New Testament ideal of life-long monogamous marriage. But in practice the differences were quite slight. The great expense of marriage and divorce meant that few could afford a second marriage, while the legal restrictions placed on the choice of marriage partners for divorcees and widows bore witness, even in Old Testament times, to the permanency of the relationship established by marriage.

Eighth commandment. Theft is prohibited by the eighth commandment. Theft in this context covers all attempts to deprive a man of his property and livelihood whether by brute force or stealth and cunning. In the Old Testament, land and property are seen as the gift of God and essential for a man's livelihood (Dt. 11:9ff.; 1 Ki. 21:3). But again the commandment only represents the negative side of the law. At various other points a positive concern to support the poor and weak members of society comes to expression (*e.g.*

37

Dt. 24:10–22). For instance, every third year tithes are to be given to the Levite, the immigrant, the orphan and the widow (Dt. 14: 28f.). Every harvest-time corn is to be left ungathered round the edges of the fields for the poor to glean (Lv. 19:9f.). Most far-reaching of all are the laws of the sabbatical and jubilee years, under which a man who had become so poor that he had been forced to sell his land to someone else or himself into slavery, recovered his property and his freedom. In this way the tendency for wealth to accumulate in fewer and fewer hands would have been checked (Ex. 21:1ff.; Lv. 25; Dt. 15:1ff.).[27]

Ninth commandment. After dealing with duties toward God and actions against neighbours the last two commandments deal with sins of speech and thought. The ninth commandment forbids false witness, primarily in a court of law, but it covers all other unfounded statements as well (Ex. 23:1f., 7; Dt. 17:6; 19:15ff.; 22:13ff.). It should be noted that the command is in the negative; the Old Testament does not demand that the full truth has to be disclosed on every occasion (1 Sa. 16:2).

Tenth commandment. The tenth commandment forbids all desiring of another's property.[28] Though covetousness cannot have been punished by the courts, feelings are not outside the realm of biblical law in the broader sense. On the one hand the Israelite was commanded to love God; on the other not to hate his neighbour in his heart or covet his goods (*e.g.* Dt. 6:5; Lv. 19:17). This inward aspect of biblical morality is even more prominent in the book of Proverbs, which has much to say about motives, feelings and speech. The whole of a man's life must be lived out in the presence of God, who weighs the heart. It may therefore be concluded that the Old Testament contains as comprehensive and demanding an ethic as is to be found anywhere in the ancient world.

Principles of punishment in the Pentateuch

An outstanding feature of biblical law is the pre-eminence it accords to human values, as opposed to the economic considerations of much cuneiform law. This emerges particularly clearly in its penal law.[29] In Israel, religious offences and offences against life and the structure of the family tended to be punished more severely than elsewhere; whereas cuneiform law tended to rate financial loss as more serious than loss of life, or at least see loss of life in economic terms. For instance, Babylonian law punished by death, breaking and entering, looting at a fire and theft.[30] But in Israel no offences against ordinary property attracted the death penalty.[31] By contrast, in Israel the death penalty was mandatory for murder, because man is made in the image of God (Gn. 9:5f.), whereas other legal systems permitted monetary compensation.[32]

The humanitarian outlook of the biblical law is also illustrated by its abolition of substitutionary punishment. Substitution was often allowed in cuneiform law, *e.g.* if through faulty construction a house collapses killing the householder's *son*, the *son* of the builder who built the house must be put to death (LH 230). But Deuteronomy explicitly forbids this kind of substitutionary punishment: 'The fathers shall not be put to death for the children, nor shall the children be put to death for the fathers; every man shall be put to death for his own sin' (24:16). It is only in specifically religious matters that the principle of corporate guilt comes into play. Though Deuteronomy insists that sons shall not be put to death for the fathers, it also insists that a village should be wiped out, if some of its inhabitants commit idolatry (Dt. 13:12ff.), while the Decalogue mentions that God will visit the sins of the fathers upon the children (Ex. 20:5; Dt. 5:9).

The purpose of punishment

The principles underlying the biblical laws on punishment are summarized in Deuteronomy 19:19f., a passage dealing with the punishment of a false witness: 'You shall do to him as he had meant to do to his brother; so you shall purge the evil from the midst of you. And the rest shall hear, and fear, and never again commit any such evil among you.' Five principles are alluded to in this passage and may be illustrated from other parts of the Pentateuch.[33]

(1) The offender must receive his legal desert, which is not simply to be equated with revenge. The penalty must correspond with the crime. This is perhaps most clearly seen in Genesis 9:6: 'Whoever sheds the blood of man, by man shall his blood be shed', and in the general principle of talion enunciated in various places: 'Life for life, eye for eye, tooth for tooth' (Dt. 19:21; Ex. 21:23f.; Lv. 24:18ff.). This talion formula is just a formula however; it is not to be taken literally except in the case of premeditated murder (Nu. 35:31). Where the formula occurs, it is usually evident that the lawgiver is not demanding its literal fulfilment, but some payment to compensate for the offence (see Ex. 21:22ff.).[34]

(2) Punishment is designed to 'purge the evil from the midst of you'. What does this mean? 'The evil' cannot refer to the offence itself, for it cannot be undone. Nor can it refer to the possible repetition of the offence. Rather it refers to the guilt that rests upon the land and its inhabitants. This concept, though foreign to our secular way of thinking, occupies an important place in the Bible. In Genesis 4:10f. the blood of Abel cries out to God from the ground, and the ground is accursed for his sake. In Leviticus 18:24–28 it is said that the offences of the heathen cause them to be expelled from Canaan. Still clearer is Deuteronomy 21:1–9 where a rite is prescribed to atone for the crime of an unknown murderer. The attempt to discover the murderer has proved futile, and therefore a calf is killed by a stream and various rites are performed. This series of actions does not undo the murder, nor does it ensure that no murders are committed in future, but it does atone for the blood guilt which rests upon those whose responsibility it is to execute punishment, and the whole people. The elders say: 'Forgive, O Lord, thy people Israel, whom thou hast redeemed, and set not the guilt of innocent bood in the midst of thy people Israel' (verse 8).

(3) Punishment should deter others from committing the offence: 'The rest shall hear, and fear, and shall never again commit any such evil among you' (Dt. 19:20; *cf.* 13:11; 17:13; 21:21).

(4) Punishment allows the offender to make atonement and be reconciled with society. After he has paid the penalty the offender suffers no loss of his civil rights. Degradation of the offender as a motive for punishment is specifically excluded by Deuteronomy

25:3, where the number of strokes is limited to forty, 'lest, if one should go on to beat him with more stripes than these, your brother be degraded in your sight.' The degrading brutality of many punishments under Assyrian law is in marked contrast to the Hebrew outlook. Mutilation is only demanded once in the Pentateuch, in an extreme case (Dt. 25:11f.), and there the penalty is mild compared with some of those in the Assyrian laws (*e.g.* MAL A4–5, 8–9, 40).

(5) Punishment allows the offender to recompense the injured party. Hebrew, like Mesopotamian law, had no system of fines. Instead it imposes damages so that the one who suffered, and not the state, benefits from the punishment (*e.g.* Ex. 22; Lv. 6:1ff.; *cf.* H 5:20ff.).

Civil and criminal law

The use of damages rather than fines highlights an aspect of the biblical legal system of which the layman is not usually conscious; it is basically a system of civil law on to which various criminal law features have been grafted. This means that many offences are regarded as torts, wrongs against individual private citizens for which the injured party has to seek redress on his own initiative through the courts.

The number of offences which can properly be called crimes, actions which the state itself forbids and seeks to stamp out, is very limited in Near Eastern law, though it is considerably augmented in the Old Testament by the large number of religious crimes. It is somewhat artificial to attempt to distinguish civil and criminal law in the Old Testament, since the whole of life is viewed as being lived under God and therefore all wrongdoing is sin. No sin can be viewed with equanimity by the community, since it is likely to provoke God's wrath. Nevertheless if one wishes to distinguish the criminal and civil law elements, the type of penalty imposed may provide a criterion. Monetary compensation suggests that the offence should be regarded as falling within the realm of civil law, while the death penalty or corporal punishment suggests that the offence should be viewed as a crime. The prosecution of murderers, however, shows how foreign the civil/criminal law distinction is in biblical thinking. Though murder is viewed as a crime, in that the payment of damages to the victim's family is prohibited, the state does not take a hand in prosecuting the criminal. It is left to a relative, the avenger of blood, to kill the murderer if he can, or if he cannot, to chase him to the city of refuge and there convince the city authorities that the homicide is a murderer. The avenger of blood must then execute him (Ex. 21:12–14; Nu. 35:10ff.; Dt. 19).

Types of punishment

The Pentateuch lays down three main types of punishment: the death penalty for the gravest public sins against life, religion and the family, 'cutting-off' for grave private sins, and restitution for property offences.

(a) *The death penalty*. The death penalty is prescribed for a wide range of crimes: premeditated murder (Ex. 21:12ff.; Nu. 35; Dt. 19); man-stealing (Ex. 21:16; Dt. 24:7); persistent disobedience to authorities and parents (Dt. 17:12; 21:18ff.); adultery (Lv. 20:10; Dt. 22:22); homosexuality (Lv. 20:13); the worst forms of incest (Lv. 20:11f.); false prophecy (Dt. 13:1ff.); profanation of the sabbath (Nu. 15:32ff.); blasphemy (Lv. 24:13ff.); idolatry (Lv. 20:2ff.); magic and divination (Ex. 22:18; *cf.* H17). Some of these crimes were also punishable by death under Babylonian law.[35]

It is not clear in how many cases the death penalty was actually exacted and how often composition was permitted. Composition is explicitly prohibited in the case of murder (Nu. 35:31), and this seems to be the force of the phrase, 'your eye shall not pity' in Deuteronomy 19:13, and by analogy in 13:8 (idolatry), 19:21 (false witness) and 25:12. It would seem to me unlikely that composition was permissible in those cases where the mode of execution is prescribed (Dt. 21:21; 22:21). In the case of blasphemy and profanation of the sabbath, it evidently depended on the gravity of the particular offence whether the ultimate penalty was exacted

(Ex. 31:13–17; Nu. 15:32–36; Lv. 24:11f.). It was only profaning the sabbath by actual work, or blaspheming the name of Yahweh as opposed to God, that merited death. This shows that *the penalties prescribed in the law were the maximum penalties.* Where there were mitigating circumstances, lesser penalties would have been enforced. These were cases in which the evidence was clear. The demand for at least two witnesses (Dt. 19:15) would have in practice limited the application of these penalties to flagrant violations of the law. Many secret offences would inevitably have escaped punishment.

(b) *'Cutting-off'.* The law refers a number of times to God cutting off an offender, or the guilty person being cut off from among his people (*e.g.* Ex. 12:15, 19; Lv. 7:20f., 25, 27; 17:4, 9, 14; 18:29; 19:8; 20:3, 5f., 17f.; Nu. 15:30f.). It is a punishment generally reserved for religious and sexual offences. Since some of these offences may also attract the death penalty, 'cutting-off' might be an alternative way of describing capital punishment (*e.g.* Lv. 20:6 and 27). However, since cutting-off is contrasted with judicial execution in Leviticus 20:2ff. (the man who escapes stoning must still face the possibility of being cut off), something different must be meant. For one case of incest Babylonian law demands expulsion from the community, whereas biblical law speaks of the guilty man being 'cut-off' (LH 154, *cf.* Lv. 20:17f.). It could be argued that 'cutting-off' means excommunication from the covenant community. But this treatment is reserved for the unclean rather than criminals (Lv. 13:45f.; Nu. 5:1–4). It therefore seems best to retain the traditional interpretation of 'cutting-off': it is a threat of direct punishment by God usually in the form of premature death. In so far as many of the offences punishable by 'cutting-off' would easily escape human detection, a threat of divine judgment would have been the main deterrent to committing them.[36]

(c) *Restitution.* In cases of theft or misappropriation of property, restitution of the stolen property was demanded. Additional penalties vary with the degree of penitence shown by the thief. If he is penitent, he restores what he has stolen plus a fifth (Lv. 6:5, *cf.* H5:24).[37] If he is caught with the goods on him, he restores double. If he has already disposed of the goods by sale or other means, he must restore four or fivefold. The penalty may have been increased in the latter case because of the greater difficulty of proving his guilt, and because the thief had made a deliberate attempt to cover his traces (Ex. 22).[38] If a thief cannot pay, he may be taken as a slave by the injured party until he has worked off the debt (22:3; *cf.* H2). His slavery would usually be for a maximum of six years (Ex. 21:1ff.; Dt. 15:12ff.) or until the year of jubilee (Lv. 25:39ff.). Slavery in the ancient Orient was not nearly as ghastly as it was in more modern times. There was little difference between a slave and a hired labourer (Lv. 25:39–55). Indeed it could be argued that Hebrew slavery was more humane than its modern equivalent—imprisonment. Neither in the laws of Hammurabi nor in the Pentateuch is imprisonment laid down as a punishment, though it was known in Egypt and under the later monarchy. To quote Driver and Miles: 'This last punishment, which is expensive to the community, generally corrupting to the prisoner and often bringing unmerited hardship to his dependants, is the invention of a later age.'[39] Twice it is mentioned in the Pentateuch that someone was kept in custody while awaiting trial (Lv. 24:12; Nu. 15:34). The nearest thing to primitive imprisonment was the restriction imposed on a manslaughterer, who is bound to live in a city of refuge until the death of the high priest (Nu. 35:26ff.).

Law enforcement in Israel

If ancient Israel had a most searching ethical code in the Ten Commandments and an elaborate penal system, did it also have means of enforcing the law? Did it just depend on public goodwill, or was there a recognized organization to maintain law and order? These are not easy questions to answer, for it is in those periods when law was not being enforced that the problem emerges in the Old Testament. It was when the country lacked strong central government that injustice was most evident, and most is said about the lack of good government. 'In those days there was no king in Israel; every man did what was right in his own eyes' (Jdg. 17:6;

cf. 18:1; 19:1). Hence we are better informed about the failures of government than about its successes.

However, a good deal can be pieced together from the Old Testament and neighbouring cultures about how government worked.[40] But certain things must be borne in mind. First, the village culture of ancient Israel was very different from Western urban society, and the problems of law enforcement were trivial compared with ours. They lived in small, closely-knit communities in which everyone knew everyone else, and it would therefore have been extremely difficult for any local person to commit an offence without its becoming common knowledge. In the mass anonymity of modern society it is very much easier for criminals to remain undetected. Secondly, it was a conservative and authoritarian society, and therefore less likely to lead to social deviancy. Finally, because society was so much more compact, there was inevitably less specialization. One man could easily play the role of city councillor, judge and policeman in his spare time, and be a farmer the rest of the week. So we should not necessarily expect to find a professional police force. This was only introduced into imperial Rome by Augustus.

But though this means that the problem of law enforcement was much smaller than in our society, it does not mean it was non-existent. We can distinguish various devices for encouraging observance of the law. First, knowledge of the law was promoted by a seven-yearly festival at which the law was read (Dt. 31:9ff.) and by the Levites who were sent out to instruct people in the law (2 Ch. 17:8f.). By these means a public opinion was created that at least knew what the law demanded. In other words the Levites played a role equivalent to the mass media in modern society. Secondly, in the early period there was a system of tribal democracy. It seems likely that each tribe or village elected elders to govern its affairs and act as judges in legal disputes. In the monarchy period there was added to this older system a central court of appeal in Jerusalem to decide disputed cases (2 Ch. 19:8ff.).

Within this system specific remedies were available against law-breakers. When an offence was committed, it was up to the injured party or his family to bring the culprit before the court and prove

45

his guilt. A man who suspected his wife of infidelity had to bring her before the court and prove it (Dt. 22:13ff.). Parents who had a stubborn and rebellious son had to report the case to the elders (Dt. 21:18ff.). In the case of murder it was up to a relative, the avenger of blood, to execute the murderer (Nu. 35). Essentially, then, the system was one of self-help regulated by the courts. Witnesses were publicly summoned to report crimes (Lv. 5:1; Jdg. 17:2). Thus for most offences the initiative for the prosecution rested in private hands.

In the majority of cases it seems as if the plaintiff was also responsible for enforcing the court's decision. But there is evidence that the plaintiff was sometimes aided by 'officials' (*šōṭᵉrîm*). The word literally means 'scribe', so one of their functions may have been to record court decisions. They also had the job of mustering the army and are mentioned alongside the judges in one or two cases (Dt. 16:18; 20:5; 1 Ch. 23:4), so they may have had the job of bailiffs or constables deputed to ensure that the judgment was carried out, but this is not too clear. As has already been explained, it is likely that an individual had several functions in society.

For the most part, then, law enforcement was a private matter for which the injured person was responsible. Religious offences, however, were more serious and public prosecutions could be instituted (*e.g.* Dt. 13:12ff.). Furthermore when the injured party was too weak to secure his legal rights by himself he could appeal to the king (*e.g.* 1 Ki. 3:16ff.). One of the fundamental duties of the king was to promote justice in the land, to 'defend the cause of the poor of the people, give deliverance to the needy, and crush the oppressor' (Ps. 72:4). David's failure to fulfil his duties in this regard gave Absalom an excuse for fomenting rebellion (2 Sa. 15).

Political authority in the Old Testament

The monarchy was one of several systems of government that Israel experienced. It may well be wondered whether in the bewildering array of political systems and attitudes to those systems there can be discerned any unifying principles. Abraham appears as a father of a wandering clan. Moses is chief, lawgiver, priest and prophet of a group of tribes. The judges exert an *ad hoc* authority in times of national emergency. Saul is the first king, but he looks more like a glorified judge than the later dynastic monarchs descended from David. For a time national leadership seems to have been eclipsed after the fall of Jerusalem. The last episode in the Old Testament shows Nehemiah, a patriotic Jew, governing Judah as a province of the Persian empire. There is thus great diversity in the systems under which the men of the old covenant were ruled, let alone how their contemporaries were governed. Nevertheless in spite of the differences in the form that political authority took and in the way it was exercised, there are a number of features common to all the systems under which Israel lived at various times.

First, political leaders and other authorities to enforce law were always found to be necessary in Israel. Moses, overwhelmed with the task of judging the people alone, had to appoint rulers over thousands, hundreds, fifties and tens to take over the work, so that he was left only with the hard cases (Ex. 18:13ff.). The leaders of Israel recognized that they needed someone to take over from Samuel and they asked him to find a king (1 Sa. 8:4f.). The book of Judges several times points out that the chaos it describes was caused by the lack of a national leader.

Secondly, these authorities were not only necessary but seen as God-given. Just as prophets and priests were anointed with oil as a mark of their divine calling, so were the kings of Israel and Judah. Sometimes other signs of their call are mentioned. The Spirit of God makes Saul prophesy on one occasion (1 Sa. 10:10ff.). The part played by the prophets in making God's choice of a leader known to the man himself is constantly emphasized in the Old Testament. On one occasion God's choice of a whole dynasty was announced through the prophet Nathan. Speaking to David he said: 'the Lord declares . . . I will raise up your offspring after you . . . and I will establish the throne of his kingdom for ever' (2 Sa. 7:11ff.). Rulers of other nations too are recognized as being appointed by God for their job. Cyrus, king of Persia, is called 'his messiah' (anointed one) (Is. 45:1). Even Pharaoh is said to have been raised up expressly by God to demonstrate his power (Ex. 9:16; Rom. 9:17). Because political leaders were called by

God, they were regarded as sacrosanct: 'You shall not revile God, nor curse a ruler of your people' (Ex. 22:28). Similarly David refused to lay hands on Saul, because he was the Lord's anointed. Prophets with their special access to God's hidden purposes could initiate revolution, but ordinary mortals whose knowledge was limited were expected to submit to God's chosen king and wait and pray for God's deliverance.[41]

But although political authorities, and in particular kings, were necessary and divinely ordained, this did not mean that they were above criticism. The prophets often told kings when they were going wrong or failing in their duties. These duties were clearly spelt out in the law and it was the leader's responsibility to teach and enforce that law. In Israel leadership, law and covenant were closely connected. When Moses was first called to lead his people out of slavery, he was told that the sign that God had sent him was that Israel would serve God upon this mountain, *i.e.* Mount Sinai (Ex. 3:12). Joshua, on taking over the leadership from Moses, was told to meditate on the law day and night (Jos. 1:8). Under the monarchy it was customary to mark the accession of a new king with a service in the temple to renew the covenant. In this service the law was read out.

Upholding the principles of the covenant law was a large assignment. On the one hand the king was supposed to encourage the true worship of God throughout his kingdom. The books of Kings lay the blame for the calamities that befell the Northern and Southern kingdoms largely on the kings who permitted and even encouraged Canaanite worship at the high places and in the temple. Furthermore the king had to maintain justice and peace throughout the land. This meant more than giving fair and equitable decisions in court, it meant actively helping the poor and weak and not leaving them to the mercies of the rich and strong.

> 'He delivers the needy when he calls,
> the poor and him who has no helper.
> He has pity on the weak and the needy,
> and saves the lives of the needy'
> (Ps. 72:12f.).

Nehemiah's tough measures against the nobles and officials who were enslaving their poverty-stricken neighbours are a fine example of the sort of behaviour looked for in political leaders (Ne. 5).

In spite of the necessity and value of human authorities, the Old Testament also recognizes their danger. Though one of the promises to the patriarchs was that their descendants should be kings, though Saul was chosen at God's instruction to be king, there is a persistent strain in the Old Testament disapproving of kingship, alliances and other political devices. It is not that kingship is bad in itself. Rather it is what people may do with divinely established authority. On the one hand the king may not live up to the expected standards and may abuse his powers (1 Sa. 8:7). The elders' demand that Samuel should make them a king was not wrong in itself, but the reason that inspired it was. They wished to eliminate the risk involved in waiting for God to raise up a leader or judge to save them in a crisis, and to have instead a strong human authority ever to hand, on which they could rely. They had more faith in the institution than in the power of God. Similarly misplaced trust in a God-given institution prompts occasional prophetic polemic against sacrifice, prayer and the temple. But this does not mean the prophets regarded these things as bad in themselves, only that men were misusing them.

So far we have concentrated on kings and other national leaders to the neglect of lesser officials. The latter certainly existed, both in Mosaic times and in the monarchy period. But we know very little of how they were appointed or how they functioned. Deuteronomy 1:13 and 15 no doubt correctly underline the two most important qualifications looked for in such officials: wisdom and experience. It is interesting that in this passage the people are asked to *choose* men with these characteristics. Whether this means that there was some sort of popular election is conjectural.

In conclusion, the Old Testament presupposes a well-developed system of political authorities within the state, but with the exception of the top man it tells us little about their powers and duties. Throughout the biblical period there generally appears to be one leader at the head of the nation, except in times of chaos or defeat. His title varies: Moses and Joshua are not given one; Nehemiah was a Persian provincial governor; others were kings. But though his title changed, his authority and duties remained much the same. He was regarded as a necessity and endowed with divine authority. For his part, he was responsible for the spiritual and moral health of the nation. He had to enforce the covenant law and protect the interests of the weak.

Summary

Law and authority occupy a very prominent place in the Old Testament. This brief summary cannot hope to have done justice to the very wide variety of material the Old Testament contains. Brevity requires selection, and selection involves subjectivity. Even so, a rough sketch is better than a blank page. Nevertheless I believe certain abiding principles of ethics, of punishment and political authority can be seen to run through very large sections of the Old Testament. In the Old Testament we see these principles applied in a particular situation and culture. The particular laws and institutions we find there are the result of applying these general principles in one particular society. In the New Testament, however, we meet different situations. First-century Palestinian society had changed somewhat from that prevailing a millennium earlier. The wider Graeco-Roman world was even less like ancient Israel. Therefore even if the New Testament endorsed all the theological and ethical principles of the Old, we would not necessarily expect an identical set of laws and institutions to be the result. The changed situation would demand, at some points at least, different applications of the old principles. Just how far the basic principles of Old Testament law are accepted by New Testament writers, and how far new circumstances demand new applications, is the subject of the following chapters.

NOTES

1. S. M. Paul, *Studies in the Book of the Covenant in the Light of Cuneiform and Biblical Law* (Brill, Leiden, 1970). For a list of parallels between biblical law and other oriental sources see S. Greengus, 'Law in the Old Testament', *The Interpreter's Dictionary of the Bible,* Supplementary Volume (Abingdon, New York, 1977), pp. 532–537.
2. LH xxvb:3–14.
3. Paul, *op. cit.,* p. 41.
4. The version found in Deuteronomy varies slightly from that in Exodus. The

variant phrases are typical of the book of Deuteronomy, and it would therefore seem likely that the Exodus version is closer to the original. However, attempts to go further and, for example, to reduce each commandment to one short sentence, have not led to a scholarly consensus. See J. J. Stamm and M. E. Andrew, *The Ten Commandments in Recent Research* (SCM Press, 1967); E. Nielsen, *The Ten Commandments in New Perspective* (SCM Press, 1968); A. C. J. Phillips, *Ancient Israel's Criminal Law* (Blackwell, 1971).

It has been customary to assign the first four commandments to the first table of the law and the last six to the second. A better suggestion (M. G. Kline, *Westminster Theological Journal* 22, 1960, pp. 133–146) is that one tablet was a duplicate of the other, so that there were ten commandments on both.

5. My approach is thus similar to B. S. Childs. See for example his commentary on Exodus.

6. Curses may be appropriate at the end of a collection of laws, but not within it.

7. B. S. Jackson, *Essays in Jewish and Comparative Legal History* (Brill, Leiden, 1975), pp. 202ff.; *cf.* A. C. J. Phillips, *op. cit.*

8. The definition of crime in ancient law is difficult, see Jackson, *op. cit.*, pp. 55ff.

9. *Cf.* B. S. Childs, *Exodus*, pp. 364ff.

10. Ex. 20:23ff.; Dt. 12.

11. *E.g.* by M. Noth, *The Laws in the Pentateuch and Other Essays* (Oliver and Boyd, 1966), pp. 56ff.

12. See M. Douglas, *Purity and Danger* (Routledge and Kegan Paul, 1966), pp. 51ff., and *Implicit Meanings* (Routledge and Kegan Paul, 1975), pp. 249ff. This explanation has the merit of explaining why the early church saw fit to abolish the food laws. In the church there was to be no distinction between Jew and Gentile (*cf.* Acts 10). For further discussion see G. J. Wenham, *The Book of Leviticus* (Eerdmans, Grand Rapids, forthcoming), chapter 11, and G. J. Wenham, 'The Theology of Unclean Food', *Evangelical Quarterly*, forthcoming.

13. For a modern discussion see R. T. Beckwith and W. Stott, *This is the Day* (Marshall, Morgan and Scott, 1978).

14. *E.g.* Jdg. 9:9; 1 Sa. 2:30; 15:30; Pr. 3:9; Is. 29:13.

15. F. D. Kidner, *Hard Sayings: The Challenge of Old Testament Morals* (Inter-Varsity Press, 1972), p. 12.

16. Only where murder was premeditated was the death penalty mandatory. B. S. Jackson, *op. cit.*, pp. 91f. A. Phillips, 'Another Look at Murder', *Journal of Jewish Studies* 28, 1977, pp. 105–126, thinks intention as opposed to premeditation distinguished murder from manslaughter in biblical law.

17. See the discussions of S. M. Paul, *op. cit.*, pp. 70ff.; B. S. Jackson, *op. cit.*, pp. 75–107; S. E. Loewenstamm, 'Exodus 21:22–25', *Vetus Testamentum* 27, 1977, pp. 352–360.

18. See B. K. Waltke, 'Reflections from the Old Testament on Abortion', *Journal of the Evangelical Theological Society* 19, 1976, pp. 3–13.

19. MAL A 53 sentences a woman who procures an abortion to death followed by impaling on a stake without burial. Without proper burial a person could not enjoy rest in the underworld.

20. Relations between a married man and an unmarried woman did not count as adultery. If the laws in Ex. 22:16 and Dt. 22:28f. applied to married as well as unmarried men, the man would have been forced to take the woman as a second wife. This would fit in with the practice of polygamy, allowed in Old Testament times. However, the expense of marriage made a second wife a luxury only kings and patriarchs could afford.

21. This is explicit in non-biblical law, and implied in Pr. 6:32ff. (which warns a would-be adulterer against counting on the offended husband being satisfied with

Law, morality and the Bible

damages) and also in Dt. 22:13ff. (see my article in *Vetus Testamentum* 22, 1972, pp. 330ff.).

22. Not only did the bridegroom give a large present to his father-in-law on betrothal, but his father-in-law gave an even larger gift of land or other property to the couple on their marriage. This dowry belonged to the bride, but while the marriage lasted the husband could dispose of it as he wished. Should he divorce her though, he had to return the dowry and maybe make other payments as well. This dowry system kept divorce rates down to 5% among Palestinian Arabs earlier this century.

23. *E.g.* A. Toeg, 'Does Deuteronomy 24:1–4 Incorporate a General Law on Divorce?', *Dine Israel* 2, 1970, pp. 5–24; P. C. Craigie, *The Book of Deuteronomy* (Eerdmans, Grand Rapids, 1976), p. 305.

24. R. Yaron, 'The Restoration of Marriage', *Journal of Jewish Studies* 17, 1966, pp. 1–11.

25. See my articles, 'The Biblical View of Marriage and Divorce', *Third Way* 1.20, 21, 22, 1977, pp. 3–5, 7–9, 7–9; 'The Restoration of Marriage Reconsidered', *Journal of Jewish Studies* (forthcoming). On Leviticus 18 see my commentary, *The Book of Leviticus*.

26. Whether the New Testament permits remarriage after divorce for unchastity is disputed. Those against remarriage include J. Dupont, *Mariage et divorce dans l'évangile* (Desclée de Brouwer, Bruges, 1959); Q. Quesnell, 'Made Themselves Eunuchs', *Catholic Biblical Quarterly* 30, 1968, pp. 335–358; and G. J. Wenham, *Third Way* 1.22, 1977, pp. 7–9. This was also the standard patristic view; see H. Crouzel, *L'Eglise primitive face au divorce* (Beauchesne, Paris, 1971). Those allowing remarriage in cases of unchastity include J. Murray, *Divorce* (Presbyterian and Reformed, Philadelphia, 1961) and J. R. W. Stott, *Divorce: the Biblical Teaching* (Falcon, 1972).

27. The implementation of these laws must have been difficult. See R. Westbrook, 'Jubilee Laws', *Israel Law Review* 6, 1971, pp. 209–226.

28. Attempts to reinterpret 'covet' as a species of taking are unconvincing. See B. S. Jackson, *op. cit.*, pp. 202ff.

29. M. Greenberg, 'Some Postulates of Biblical Criminal Law', in M. Haran (ed.), *Yehezkel Kaufmann Jubilee Volume* (Magnes Press, Jerusalem, 1960), pp. 5–28; E. M. Good, 'Capital Punishment and its Alternatives in Ancient Near Eastern Law', *Stanford Law Review* 19, 1967, pp. 947–977; S. M. Paul, *Studies in the Book of the Covenant in the Light of Cuneiform and Biblical Law* (Brill, Leiden, 1970); J. J. Finkelstein, 'The Goring Ox', *Temple Law Quarterly* 46, 1973, pp. 169–290 and B. S. Jackson, *op. cit.*, pp. 25–63.

30. LH 6–11, 21–22, 25.

31. Theft of booty dedicated to God in holy war was punishable by death (Jos. 7).

32. *Cf.* HL 1–6.

33. See J. L. Saalschütz, *Das Mosaische Recht* (Heymann, Berlin, 1853 reprinted 1974), pp. 439ff. for fuller exposition.

34. For a modern discussion see B. S. Jackson, *op. cit.*, pp. 75–107.

35. *E.g.* Murder LH1, sorcery LH2, adultery LH129, incest LH157.

36. See further discussion in my commentary on Lv. 17.

37. This is the traditional view, and is to be preferred to B. S. Jackson's suggestion in *Theft in Early Jewish Law* (Clarendon Press, 1972), pp. 172ff., that what Leviticus intends for secular offences is restitution of two and a fifth times the amount stolen.

38. For other explanations see Jackson, *Theft in Early Jewish Law*, pp. 154ff.

39. G. R. Driver and J. C. Miles, *The Babylonian Laws*, I (Clarendon Press, 1952), p. 501.

40. R. de Vaux, *Ancient Israel: Its Life and Institutions* (Darton, Longman and Todd, 1973), pp. 150ff.; D. J. Wiseman, 'Law and Order in Old Testament Times', *Vox Evangelica* 8, 1973, pp. 5–21.

41. 1 Sa. 24, 26.

3

Fulfilling the law: The Gospels and Acts

Robin Nixon

Introduction

The overall evidence that we have suggests that neither Jesus himself nor the earliest Christians were on the one hand flagrant breakers of the current Jewish law, nor on the other hand slaves to it.[1] 'Law-breaking' in the normal sense of the word does not seem to have been the reason why Jesus was put to death. Some of the things which he did undoubtedly caused fierce opposition, but the real trouble was the claims, explicit or implicit, which he made for himself. These were seen by some to pose a threat to a variety of Jewish institutions if they were taken seriously. The apostles seem to have been brought up before the Jewish authorities in Acts not so much for 'law-breaking' as for preaching Jesus as the Messiah and for their attitude to the inclusion of the Gentiles.

There emerges from the New Testament the pattern of a religion which has sufficiently liberated itself from legalism to make it into a universal faith in which one of the main emphases is the freedom of the Spirit. How far is this conclusion justified from the actions and teaching of Jesus himself? How far is there in New Testament Christianity continuity with and discontinuity from all that had gone before?

The priority of the grace of God and the need for a human response to that grace are writ large over the face of the New Testament (Mk. 1:15, *etc.*). There is in this a basic continuity with the old covenant, as has been indicated in the previous chapter. No-one reading the New Testament in its proper context could fail to see that it is God's initiative which reaches out to sinners who are thereby transformed and enabled to live the sort of life which he wishes them to live (Rom. 12:1f.). Repentance, forgiveness and a new relationship to God come first but those who experience them have as an inevitable consequence a new desire and ability to do God's will. The incarnation, however, makes a watershed in the dealings of God with men. Previously things had been done to a large extent by what could now be seen as shadow and symbol; in Christ they were achieved in reality. The prophets often spoke in general terms of 'the day of the Lord' and people looked forward to something beyond their present experience. The elaborate sacrificial system was a model which demonstrated God's forgiveness without itself achieving it (Heb. 10:1). The historical life, death and resurrection of Jesus showed God in action in a new way and gave fuller meaning to all that had gone before. Much of the apparatus of the Mosaic legal system ceased, therefore, to have any function because that to which they pointed had come. Jesus came not just to call men to repentance, nor to save them from their sins by his atoning death, but to provide for them a pattern of humanity as it was meant to be and to fall short of which was sin (Rom. 3:23). This was a pattern of humility and service, overthrowing conventional ideas of greatness (Jn. 13:12–17; Phil. 2:5–11). He therefore became the central point of reference, not only for salvation but also for ethics, and his life as well as his death has always provided inspiration for Christian living.

1. THE SYNOPTIC GOSPELS

a. The kingdom

One of the central themes of the teaching of Jesus as it is recorded in the Gospels is 'the kingdom of God' (or of heaven). This expression meant primarily the 'reign' rather than the 'realm' of God. In the Old Testament it is often stated that God is King (*e.g.* Pss. 93–99). This means that he has supreme authority not only over his people Israel but over all the affairs of the world. While the kingdom or reign of God was therefore a permanent reality it could be said to have come near in a new way in the person of Jesus whose ministry began with the assertion, 'The time is fulfilled, and the kingdom of God is at hand', which led to the command, 'repent, and believe in the gospel' (Mk. 1:15). Jesus not only proclaimed the kingdom of God, in a sense he also realized it (Mt. 12:28). Yet it waited for its consummation in a future age. When his followers were taught to pray 'Thy kingdom come' (Mt. 6:10), the request probably had both immediate and future, eschatological reference. The kingdom of God has its moral demands upon those who would enter it, demands which mean a new approach to the law of the Old Testament (Mt. 5:17-20). Keeping the law was not a means of entry into the kingdom of God. This could be attained only by means of repentance and faith. Yet the fact and the coming of the reign of God calls for an ethical response such as is set out, for example, in the Beatitudes (Mt. 5:1-12). Likewise the new revelation of the Fatherhood of God, given in Christ, has ethical consequences (Mt. 5:43-48). While only those who have responded to the gospel can make such responses appropriately, it would be wrong to infer that God had no moral claims upon others or that 'kingdom ethics' could be set in opposition to 'creation ethics' (see Part 1, chapter 6).

b. Fulfilment of the law

The concept of 'fulfilment' is the key to the understanding of the teaching and actions of Jesus in relation to the Old Testament law. Yet this word needs defining, as it has been interpreted in a number of different ways which have ranged from the abolition of every element of law in Christian living to strengthening the demands of the law upon the life of the disciple.

There is a saying which indicates that the law and the prophets have a limited period of validity, or perhaps, one should say, of dominance. They were 'until John' (Mt. 11:13; Lk. 16:16f.). 'Since then the good news of the kingdom of God is preached . . .' The preaching of the kingdom and the incarnation of the kingdom in Jesus in some way supersede the law and the prophets just as they supersede the temple. The saying as a whole is a difficult one and from it we must turn to another difficult passage, but one which is the key to the understanding of the concept, Matthew 5:17-20.[2]

In this saying Jesus first defends himself by implication against charges that he had come to abolish the law and the prophets. There must have been some who thought his untraditional ways involved that intention. His intention, however, which he also achieved in practice, was to fulfil the law and the prophets. We can learn from the use of the word 'fulfil' elsewhere in Matthew's Gospel, in connection with prophecy, that it means 'give the full meaning to'. The prophecies made in the Old Testament dealt with situations which were in some sense paralleled by the life of Jesus. Only the immediate meaning could be seen in the original Old Testament context. The fuller meaning, in the whole context of Scripture, was seen in the action of God in the life of Christ. So it would appear here that Jesus had come to give the full meaning to the law, as he did to righteousness (Mt. 3:15).

The law is said to be something from which the smallest piece cannot pass until all is accomplished. Some have taken this as being the teaching of a strict Jewish-Christian party in the church which has been inserted into a saying of Jesus. Others have taken it as being rather sarcastic: 'If you are going to rely on the law you will find that there will never be any change in that!' It is probably correct to see 'all is accomplished' (Mt. 5:18) as referring to all the things which Jesus is to do. Nothing will pass until he has done what he came to achieve. If that is so there will be no need to understand the teaching of the next verse as inculcating literal obedience to the smallest commandment in the law in order to achieve greatness in the kingdom of heaven. It would be more natural to take it with the passage which follows (Mt. 5:21–48), in which instances are given of the way in which the new approaches of Jesus would operate. When Jesus says that the righteousness of his disciples must exceed that of the scribes and Pharisees it is evident that he intends this in the sense of quality rather than quantity.

If this is so, the rest of chapter 5 is very instructive. Jesus goes behind a number of the commandments and draws out their real meaning. He applies to each instance the principle of love. Law is essentially something which is imposed upon people from outside themselves and with which they may or may not agree. Every society has to have its system of law because of the wickedness and blindness of human nature, and it also needs sanctions to enforce it. In Israel the Torah was conceived of as divine revelation and its regulations were therefore properly thought of as being for the good of God's people (Dt. 6:24). Yet the highest form of ethical conduct comes not so much from obeying what comes from outside as from responding in a spirit of love, inspired by gratitude to God and a sense of relationship to him, to the inward impulses which he implants in us (Je. 31:31–34; Ho. 6:6). This is the fruit of the new covenant.

So we see in the Sermon on the Mount, which is the nearest to a collection of the ethical teaching of Jesus which we have in the Gospels, how the commandment prohibiting killing needs to be seen in a wider context of banishing hatred. The law itself is upheld and in fact strengthened by this radical thrust at the heart. Casuistic regulations, which had set a limit on the irresponsible swearing of oaths or taking of revenge, are swallowed up by the more challenging principle of complete prohibition. The illustrations given are instances of the possible demands of love rather than a comprehensive guide to the legislation of the church or state on the matter. The implied interpretation of the command to love one's neighbour, that it meant one could hate one's enemy, is rejected. The family likeness to the heavenly Father who loves without discrimination should be shown in the love of his children even towards their enemies (Mt. 5:21–48).

This exposition of the true intention of the law was given by one who was prepared to 'fulfil all righteousness' in his own life (Mt. 3:15). The Gospels are full of evidence of the way in which all that he was and all that he did was determined by the scriptures of the Old Testament. The temptations were met from the book of Deuteronomy (Mt. 4:1–11; Lk. 4:1–13). Jesus understood his own mission as in some way recapitulating the history of Israel and it was appropriate therefore, at this test of his person and mission, that he should turn to the principles set out in a book which assesses the reasons for the success and failure of Israel. In obedience to the scriptures he went to his death (Mk. 9:12, *etc.*). It was written 'that the Christ should suffer and on the third day rise from the dead' (Lk. 24:46), and because of this, amongst other things, he was able to speak in authoritative tones, 'I say to you'. This was the reason why instead of directing people to obedience to the Torah he could say, 'Take *my* yoke upon you . . .' (Mt. 11: 28–30). Allegiance was to be given to him, but he was not at odds with the Torah. In his person and in his attitude he fulfilled the law, and to his disciples he gave the power to live with a new approach to it.

The teaching of the Synoptic Gospels on this is remarkably consistent. If Matthew treats the subject as being of the most importance, he is usually only making explicit what is implicit in Mark. For Matthew, almost certainly writing from and to a Jewish Christian milieu, it is important that Jesus' teaching on this subject should be recorded and understood. The nature of Matthew's Gospel as a kind of handbook of instruction in the basic principles of the Christian life, means that there are places where a movement towards a sort of Christian casuistry may be discerned. This might be compared with the sort of rulings which Paul gives in his letters. It is not intended to minimize the basic fact that the teaching of Jesus goes out primarily as a direct personal claim on the heart of man.

c. The temple and ritual

As Paul points out, Jesus was born 'under the law' (Gal. 4:4) and it is interesting to see how the Gospel of Luke, almost certainly written for Gentiles and probably by a Gentile, devotes its first two chapters to a description of the way in which Jesus was associated in his birth, babyhood and boyhood with a circle of piety which revolved around the temple in Jerusalem. If some had opted out of 'main line Judaism' because of its compromises and corruptions, it was clear that there was also a faithful remnant of pious people who waited for the coming of the Messiah within the context of the traditional religious institutions.

When we turn to the ministry of Jesus we find further contacts with the cultus.[3] After healing a leper Jesus sends him to show himself to the priest 'for a proof to the people' (Mk. 1:44; Mt. 8:4;

Lk. 5:14). The interpretation of the last phrase has been disputed, but even if it means testifying to the messianic claims of Jesus, it is interesting to note that this is done within the framework of the ritual law. The disciples who are addressed in the Sermon on the Mount are expected to take gifts to the altar (Mt. 5:23f.) though the offering is less important than the moral challenge to be reconciled with one's brother. Jesus follows in the prophetic tradition of seeing that attitudes and relationships are far more important than ritual. God's preference for mercy ('covenant love') over sacrifice is shown in the quotation from Hosea 6:6 used in Matthew 9:13 and 12:7. A similar point is made in the words of the young man to Jesus in Mark 12:33.

The coming of Jesus puts the temple, like the other religious institutions of Judaism, in a new perspective. 'I tell you, something greater than the temple is here' (Mt. 12:6). This something was the kingdom of God, present in the midst of men with the coming of the Son of God in human flesh. It was because the reign of God had greater claims upon his people than any of the outward symbols provided for them, that Jesus had to cleanse the temple. His action was not simply concerned with getting rid of the commercialization of religion. It was the court of the Gentiles which had been made 'a den of robbers'. Forgetting that her mission was to attract the Gentiles to the worship of her Lord, Israel was allowing people to feather their own nests. God had intended that the temple should be his house (Mk. 11:17; Mt. 21:13; Lk. 19:46). Only Mark records the full saying taken from Isaiah 56:7: 'My house shall be called the house of prayer *for all the nations.*' When Matthew and Luke wrote, such a quotation might have been misleading. In Matthew the same expression occurs at the very end of the Gospel. The apostles are to go out and make disciples of *all nations* in the power of the risen Lord (Mt. 28:18–20). The actions of the Jews had in fact made it 'their house' and it would be forsaken and desolate (Mt. 23:38; Lk. 13:35). The discourse on the last things (Mk. 13; Mt. 24; Lk. 21) indicates that the destruction of the temple in Jerusalem will be part of the judgment that God will bring upon his people who have lost their sense of calling and mission.

d. The synagogue

Jesus is recorded as visiting the synagogue on a number of occasions (*e.g.* Mk. 1:21; 1:39; 6:2). Every recorded visit was an occasion for him to exercise some ministry. The expression 'as his custom was' in Luke 4:16 could refer to his habit of ministering when he did attend rather than to his frequency of attendance. None the less it seems very likely that frequent ministry in the synagogue arose out of a regular attendance there, to join with the people of God in the worship of God in a place which had been hallowed by custom. Here he would be in a position to hear the scriptures upon which he was brought up and which so clearly moulded the course of his life.

e. The sabbath

There are a number of incidents recorded in the Gospels in which Jesus is shown to have come into conflict with the Jewish leaders because of his attitude to the sabbath.[4] All the Synoptics record the story of the disciples plucking the ears of corn on the sabbath (Mk. 2:23–28; Mt. 12:1–8; Lk. 6:1–5) and the healing of the man with the withered hand (Mk. 3:1–5; Mt. 12:9–13; Lk. 6:6–10). Luke includes two other stories: the healing of the bent woman (Lk. 13:10–17) and the healing of the man with dropsy (Lk. 14:1–6).

What emerges from these incidents is the fact that Jesus taught that there were claims of human need more important than a rigid observance of the sabbath law. This is summed up in the famous pronouncement, 'The sabbath was made for man, not man for the sabbath' (Mk. 2:27). The impression given is that Jesus obeyed the law of the sabbath as set out in its essence in the Decalogue but that he did not feel himself bound by the casuistic interpretations of it which had grown up in the oral tradition of the scribes. He saw the sabbath as a means of grace, and not as the burden which legalism had made it into. What he did was in accordance with the principle that people were meant to benefit from this gracious provision of God for them. Mark's Gospel includes the words, 'so the Son of man is lord even of the sabbath' (Mk. 2:28). This may be intended as the comment of the evangelist rather than as the words of Jesus, but, whichever way it is taken, it is of some importance. Even if the expression 'Son of man' here were to refer to mankind as a whole, it is still in Jesus as the most perfect expression of humanity that lordship over the sabbath is most clearly demonstrated. It is his coming which enables people to look at the whole principle underlying the sabbath law in a new way. The exhortation to the disciples to pray that their flight should not be on the sabbath (Mt. 24:20) is more likely to be given in the context of people who were unlikely to shed their old traditions than as an ordinance of the new Israel.

f. Fasting

There is evidence from the Gospels that Jesus fasted (Mt. 4:2; Lk. 4:2) and he seemed to approve the practice in general (Mt. 6:16–18). Yet questions were raised about the way in which the disciples failed to fast as did the Pharisees and John's disciples (Mk. 2:18–22; Lk. 5:33–38). Jesus justified his disciples' behaviour by explaining that this was a particular time when the bridegroom was with the wedding guests, at which fasting was inappropriate. A higher claim has come upon them, the claim of rejoicing in his presence. The idea of fasting as a mark of discipleship is by no means abrogated but it is seen as something which needs to have a specific purpose in the service of God and not to be an empty piece of ritual.

g. Divorce

There have always been notorious difficulties associated with this subject. It is the case today in the framing of suitable laws, and it is also the case in our understanding of the teaching of Jesus as recorded in the New Testament.[5] It was a matter of dispute between the schools of Hillel and Shammai, and the Pharisees came to Jesus to ask his views on the matter (Mk. 10:2–12; Mt. 19:3–9; *cf.* Mt. 5:31–32; Lk. 16:18). Jesus sends his questioners back to the law of Moses and they tell him what is written in Deuteronomy 24:1. There is a regulation here that a man may give his wife a certificate of divorce. Jesus explains this as a provision which was 'for the hardness of your heart'. As far as the principle is concerned he goes back beyond Deuteronomy to Genesis. There, in the creation story, one finds the reason for sexuality (Gn. 1:27) and therefore for marriage (Gn. 2:24). The teaching of Genesis is quite plain: what God has joined together man must not put asunder.

This is an approach to a problem typical of Jesus. He is a man cast in the prophetic mould whose role is to declare principles. He is not there to settle individual problems. When approached by someone wanting him to get his brother to divide the inheritance with him, his reply was 'Man, who made me a judge or divider over you?' (Lk. 12:13f.). He refused to take the bait when asked the question about the payment of tribute to Caesar which was supposed to hook him (Mk. 12:13–17; Mt. 22:15–22; Lk. 20:20–26). In fact his approach might be called apodictic rather than casuistic. He stated principles which were the will of God and he did not make rules of the sort which evolve when the principles have to be applied to individual cases.

The divorce law as it is set out in Deuteronomy 24 is intended to show what is to happen in a particular case. This must be secondary to the underlying principle stated in Genesis. Similarly, Jesus was apparently asked to give something rather more like a casuistic ruling by the disciples in the house (Mk. 10:10–12). The phrase 'except for unchastity' (Mt. 19:9) shows how Jesus' general prohibition of divorce was to be applied in a specific instance, just as the principle set out in Genesis was shown in application in Deuteronomy. Similarly we find Paul being asked by the Corinthians how to apply this principle in their lives. His answer is given in 1 Corinthians 7. It is to Matthew's Gospel, with its practical instruction and topical arrangement, that other Christians would naturally turn for this sort of guidance on a specific issue.[6]

h. The state

Old Testament law assumes that the government of the nation is in the hands of representatives of Yahweh. By New Testament times this was not so and the Romans were the latest of a number of foreign overlords. While attempts have been made to suggest that Jesus was a zealot seeking to overthrow the government by force, these attempts involve a certain selectivity in the use of the evidence. His answer to the loaded question about the payment of the tribute money (Mk. 12:13–17) seems to indicate his position better, because it is consistent with his leaving answers to questions of this kind somewhat open-ended in order that they should be thought through in each new situation. His asking for a coin and enquiring about the image on it may be significant, for a number of reasons, in the light of his final pronouncement, 'Render to Caesar the things that are Caesar's, and to God the things that are God's'. Not only must Caesar not be made an idol, but man bears the image of God and the secondary allegiance to the state cannot have precedence over God's claim on the whole man.

i. Traditions

When we come to the attitude of Jesus towards the religious traditions of his day we see more clearly, perhaps, the difference of approach which he brought. He gives a discourse about them arising from an incident in which the Pharisees criticized some of his disciples for eating without washing their hands in the approved manner (Mk. 7:1–23; Mt. 15:1–20). In this he makes the point that ritual must be supported by morality, for corruption and defilement are essentially internal and not external. The scribes and the Pharisees had lost their true sense of values and they could even be said to make void the Word of God through their tradition. The reason for this was that the written law was put through a strait-jacket of oral interpretation which made it almost impossible for people to face up to its challenge directly.

It ought to be remembered that many corruptions of truth have their origins in a good intention of some kind which has managed to get seriously out of proportion. The original good intention of the Pharisees in the oral tradition was to make the law relevant to all the various situations of daily life under different social conditions from those which applied when the law was given. It may be that we have something of this process going on in the Old Testament itself, by which the law is 'up-dated' to cover new situations which have arisen. The way in which the Pharisees did this soon became 'institutionalized'. The casuistic rules became more important than the underlying principles. This is particularly brought out in the strong condemnation of the scribes and Pharisees contained in Matthew 23: they neglected the 'weightier matters of the law, justice and mercy and faith' (Mt. 23:23).

It is interesting to note the twofold effect of this attitude. On the one hand Jesus could say that the Pharisees 'bind heavy burdens, hard to bear, and lay them on men's shoulders' (Mt. 23:4). On the other hand the men of Qumran could criticize the Pharisees as 'speakers of smooth things' who made the law practicable by their casuistry and so blunted its radical challenge (see K. Stendahl on Mt. 5:17–20 in *Peake's Commentary*). Jesus did not dispute the need to make the law relevant, but the ability to distinguish between application and principle was a leading characteristic of his ministry. This was one of the reasons why he always went back to scripture and found that the traditions of the elders so hedged scripture around that many people could not be touched by its claim.

j. The commandments as a whole

When the rich young ruler came to Jesus asking what he must do to inherit eternal life, he was given the answer, 'You know the commandments' (Mk. 10:17–22; Mt. 19:16–22; Lk. 18:18–23). There is then given to him a selection from the Decalogue, with the addition of a commandment not to defraud. Here it appears that Jesus is selecting those which are most applicable to the particular situation of the man in question. The context of the story suggests that while they are offered as the way of life, it is not possible for anyone to attain life simply by keeping them. In this case the man's love of his possessions is greater than his love of Christ.

On another occasion a scribe asked Jesus which commandment was the first of all (Mk. 12:28–31; Mt. 22:35–40; Lk. 10:25–28). It is interesting that Jesus does not reply from the Decalogue but quotes the command to love God and love one's neighbour (Dt. 6:4; Lv. 19:18). If the Decalogue is largely concerned with actions, the real heart of the Torah is concern for attitudes. Love is basic to all, and of the love which inspires obedience to the commandments, the love of God is primary. On another occasion the 'golden rule' is stated in terms of doing to others what you would wish them to do to you (Mt. 7:12; Lk. 6:31). In Matthew's version he adds, 'this is the law and the prophets'.

We are thus shown that Jesus apparently did not treat all the laws of the Old Testament in the same way. He was particularly concerned to stress those which dealt with attitudes and relationships to God and man. He is not recorded as saying that other commandments were unimportant, but the general drift of his ministry as recorded in the Gospels shows that his teaching emphasized underlying principles rather than the details of practice. In fact his approach was prophetic rather than legalistic.

2. ST JOHN'S GOSPEL

The differences between the Synoptic Gospels and the Fourth Gospel make it right for us to treat John separately. Yet, whatever the divergence between them in other areas, there is little to be discerned here. In the prologue Moses the law-giver is set over against Jesus as the one who brought grace and truth, principles more precious than the law. The trust that people have in Moses is brought out in John's Gospel, and its hollowness exposed. They do not really believe the Mosaic scriptures (5:45–47) and their claim to discipleship of Moses is used to try to negate the challenge of Christ (9:28f.).

The narrative part of John's Gospel is largely constructed round the visits of Jesus to Jerusalem at the time of the great festivals. The fact that he preached in the temple does not necessarily mean that he did not also go there as a worshipper. The incident of the cleansing of the temple as recorded in this Gospel is of special interest. Scholars differ as to whether this is the same event as that recorded in the Synoptics at the end of Jesus' ministry (Mk. 11:15–18; Mt. 21:12–16; Lk. 19:45–48; Jn. 2:13–22). Whatever the case may be, it is important to note the way in which a more explicit interpretation is given. Jesus says, 'Destroy this temple, and in three days I will raise it up.' The garbled version of this comes out in the evidence of the false witnesses at his trial which is recorded in the Synoptic Gospels (Mk. 14:58; Mt. 26:61). The explanation given by the evangelist is that Jesus was speaking of the temple of his body. Here is the indication that what the temple stood for in symbol is to be superseded by what Jesus is in reality.

John's Gospel also contains some controversies about the sabbath. After the healing of the crippled man at the pool Jesus is criticized for performing a miracle on the sabbath. The dispute on this point soon gets swallowed up in the more basic question of the origin and authority of Jesus (5:10–18; 7:14–24). On the latter occasion Jesus is shown to recognize that there may be at times a conflict of laws. The Jewish leaders were prepared to circumcise on the sabbath when it was the eighth day after a child's birth. How much greater was the case for healing a man's whole body on the sabbath.

The farewell discourse of Jesus contains some interesting teaching about his commandments. First there is the new commandment which he gives his disciples, that they should love one another (13:34f.). This is not entirely new in the sense that the Old Testament had inculcated love of one's neighbours. In its context, however, a new dimension is given to it by the love which Jesus had shown them. He then goes on to speak frequently of the importance of keeping 'my commandments' as a condition of receiving the Holy Spirit and living a life of love and fellowship with him. The commandments are not made explicit in detail. It is the general principle of love that pervades everything.

It can be seen that the teaching of John's Gospel does not differ much from the teaching of the Synoptics about the attitude of Jesus to the law. Here too he is shown as living a life fully within the framework of traditional Judaism and yet with his own person and teaching bringing into the situation an element which transcends petty legalism and institutionalism. He gives commandments which are to be obeyed, but they are commandments of principle, relating to attitudes and relationships. Here too he is shown as not having come to destroy but to fulfil.

3. THE ACTS OF THE APOSTLES

It is well to remember that the book of the Acts of the Apostles has a specific and limited purpose connected with the missionary expansion of the church. It would be unwise, therefore, to expect to find in it a record of all the controversies which may have gone on in the earliest days of the church. None the less there is much valuable information about some of the issues which arose concerning the law of Israel and the church.

The book opens with the disciples as a sect within Judaism who have accepted Jesus as the Messiah and are waiting for the gift of the Holy Spirit which he has promised. The descent of the Spirit on the day of Pentecost gives birth to the Christian church, though it did not recognize itself as such in the earliest times. Those who responded to the message which Peter proclaimed adopted a new life-style, one of the ingredients of which was regular attendance at the temple (2:46). The early chapters of the book show how frequently their worship and evangelism must have been centred round the temple.

One theme of Acts is that the mission of God's people was to become centrifugal rather than centripetal (1:8). It is important therefore to see how the attitude towards the temple changed. This is particularly brought out in the episode of Stephen (chs. 6 and 7).[7] Stephen was accused of speaking against the temple and the law. 'We have heard him say that this Jesus of Nazareth will destroy this place, and will change the customs which Moses delivered to us' (6:14). Luke stresses that they were false witnesses who said this. This seems to mean that they had got hold of something that Stephen was saying, had put it into this rather stark form and represented it as an all out attack on their most precious national institutions. The defence of Stephen which is recorded at some length in chapter 7 does not deal directly with this charge. He states that the 'Most High does not dwell in houses made with hands' (7:48). This reminder that the temple was purely symbolic was clearly unacceptable to them and was a step on the way to the 'spiritualization' by the apostolic church of the Jewish religious institutions. He says that they 'received the law as delivered by angels and did not keep it' (verse 53). He is therefore upholding the law but the whole tenor of his speech is that the law must be interpreted from a dynamic, prophetic standpoint.

The significance of Stephen in Acts is considerable. He is something of a pioneer thinker who is preparing the way for Paul. For it is Paul and the Gentile mission which now becomes the main concern of the book. Meanwhile the first Gentile converts are seen through the coming of the Spirit upon Cornelius and his companions as a result of the ministry of Peter (chs. 10 and 11). Peter has to be assured by a vision that it is right to accept the Gentiles, for 'what God has cleansed you must not call common' (10:15). When this great barrier has been overcome the way is soon open for definite missionary activity among the Gentiles.

The Gentile mission was bound to cause concern, not only among unbelieving Jews, but also among the more conservative Jewish Christians. Some therefore started teaching that 'unless you are circumcised according to the custom of Moses, you cannot be saved' (15:1). As a result of this a council was called at Jerusalem to consider the terms of Gentile admission to the church. The more extreme view was expressed that 'it is necessary to circumcise them, and to charge them to keep the law of Moses' (15:5). The case for acceptance was urged on the grounds of the work of the Holy Spirit and the grace of the Lord Jesus which made no distinction between Jewish and Gentile Christians. The judgment of James who presided was that they should 'abstain from the pollutions of idols and from unchastity and from what is strangled and from blood' (15:20) These regulations were drawn from Leviticus 17 and 18, where they were given as conditions of fellowship for foreigners in Israel. They are in the nature of a compromise to preserve the unity of the church. It is evident from the rest of the New Testament that these regulations were not regarded as binding upon all Gentile Christians at all times. Moreover it was not long before scribes who copied the New Testament manuscripts were interpreting them as moral commandments (idolatry, fornication and murder) rather than ritual ones.

The ability of Paul to compromise when he thought no principle to be at stake can frequently be seen in his letters. It is also shown in Acts 21:17–36 how he was prepared to submit himself to a ritual purification in order to avoid giving offence to Jewish Christians. It was his missionary activity among the Gentiles and the rumour that he had brought them into the temple which led to his being lynched.

Acts, then, shows that there was no quick, clean break with the law and institutions of Israel. The new position of the Christian church had to develop and there were occasions when compromises had to be made because there was no uniformity of practice. There were some Christians who felt themselves to be emancipated from the Mosaic law, or who had never had to obey it, while others continued in some measure to observe it. Yet the sense of fulfilment which came through the work of the Holy Spirit and the success of the Gentile mission was bound in due course to lead the church on to a new basis for its allegiance to God. It is to the Epistles that we must turn for a fuller working out of this theme.

Conclusion

We find, then, in the Gospels and the Acts a great deal of evidence about the way in which Judaism changed into Christianity. The Messiah and the gospel are born from the matrix of Judaism, and even the most Gentile-orientated of the evangelists does not discount the Old Testament heritage. There is continuity in the use of the scriptures of the old covenant and it is they which are taken as pointing towards the new. The action of God in Christ brings discontinuity too, as one dispensation yields to another. This is seen by all writers as the time of fulfilment, a new era, the 'last days'. Everything is changed in one sense because of the advent of the Messiah and the gift of the Spirit. Yet if the Torah was first and foremost the revelation of a personal God rather than a code of law, it is this new revelation of a personal God which alone can enable men to understand it truly and to obey it properly.

Law, morality and the Bible

Because of the personal nature of the incarnation it becomes clear that Jesus is more concerned with persons than with things, he is more concerned with attitudes and relationships than with actions. He uses the law as a challenge to the self-righteous. He draws out from the law the commandment to love. If the Pharisees thought that by making the fruit good the tree would become good, Jesus made it plain that it was only a good tree that could bear good fruit (Mt. 12:33–35; *cf.* Lk. 6:43–45; Mt. 7:16–20). The fruit of good deeds was the inevitable and essential evidence of the new man transformed by Christ.

How was the good fruit produced? Through responding to his love, through the work of the Spirit which reproduced the family likeness of the sons of God. The elements of love and freedom are to the fore in the new life-style of the disciples. Is that, then, something which has outgrown law? If law is taken in the sense of legalism the answer must be 'Yes'. Jesus does not give rulings in particular cases and he does not allow his disciples to be bound by the rulings of others. It is to the principles of the Torah that he goes and he expounds these in what he calls 'my commandments'. If the apostles have on occasions to make rulings, this is inevitable, but it is seen as having a validity very much secondary to the basic principles.

Jesus came to fulfil the law. He fulfilled it in what he was and what he did. By his perfect dedication of himself to its principles and by his redeeming death to take undeservedly its sanctions he gave it a new significance. Its full meaning was shown in a new awareness of personality and concern for the well-being of others which is set forth in his own teaching. But it is the same God who gave the Torah for the welfare of his people under the old covenant who expects obedience to his will as expounded in the teaching of Jesus under the new covenant. It may be right to think not so much of there being a change in the law as of there being a change in the relationship of God's people to it. This is because of the overriding significance of the action of God in Jesus Christ. As Robert Banks has put it: 'Even in those passages which define his attitude to it, it is not so much a question of "what is his relation to it?" that is at issue as "what is its relation to him?" '[8]

We should not think of Jesus as producing an ethical system, either for all people or just for his own disciples. Rather what he was, what he did and what he said created a new situation out of which principles of Christian ethics could arise. Law in the sense of legalism is rejected, but the whole concept of law does not disappear. For the love which is dominant in the life and teaching of Jesus is not mere sentiment, but attitude, principle, obedience springing from a new relationship with the one who is Lord of all.

NOTES

1. *Cf.* James Denney, 'Law (in the New Testament)' in *Hastings Dictionary of the Bible,* III (T. & T. Clark, 1900), pp. 72–76; B. H. Branscomb, *Jesus and the Law of Moses* (Hodder and Stoughton, 1930).

2. *Cf.* H. Ljungmann, *Das Gesetz Erfüllen* (Lund, 1954); T. W. Manson, *Ethics and the Gospel* (SCM Press, 1960), p. 65; C. H. Dodd, *Gospel and Law* (Cambridge University Press, 1951), pp. 64f.

3. *Cf.* E. Lohmeyer, *Lord of the Temple* (ET, Oliver and Boyd, 1961); R. J. McKelvey, *The New Temple: The Church in the New Testament* (Oxford University Press, 1969), pp. 58–74; B. Gärtner, *Temple and Community in Qumran and the New Testament* (Cambridge University Press, 1965), pp. 99–122.

4. *Cf.* W. Rordorf, *Sunday* (ET, SCM Press, 1968), pp. 54–79.

5. *Cf.* W. Lillie, *Studies in New Testament Ethics* (Oliver and Boyd, 1961), pp. 118–128.

6. But see Mark Geldard in *Churchman* 92.2, 1978; Gordon Wenham, 'The Biblical View of Marriage and Divorce', *Third Way* 1.21,22, 1977.

7. *Cf.* M. Simon, *St Stephen and the Hellenists in the Primitive Church* (Longmans, 1958).

8. R. Banks, *Jesus and the Law in the Synoptic Tradition* (Cambridge University Press, 1975), p. 245.

4
Law and morality in the Epistles of the New Testament

Bruce Kaye

THE EPISTLES OF PAUL

Introduction

Within the material covered by the Epistles of the New Testament, Paul is obviously the most important writer from the point of view of Christian morality. Not only have more of his writings come down to us, but what has come down is more significant than what we have from other writers. Paul therefore will be taken as the main concern of this section, though the other letters of the New Testament will also be considered.

Morality, or ethics, is a central concern of the New Testament writers generally. As far as Paul was concerned Christian behaviour was the mark of an individual's standing as a Christian. This can be seen in the priorities which appear in the prayers for his readers contained in many of his letters. This is true not only of the inter-cessory prayers, but also of the thanksgivings and benedictions. The prayer in Colossians 1:3–12 is a very good example of this. In verses 3–8 Paul gives thanks for what he has heard about the Colossians, their faith, love and hope; and then in verses 9–12 he records his intercession for the Colossians. He asks that they might know God's will in all wisdom and spiritual understanding, in order that they might walk worthy of the Lord in every good work. These general points are then elaborated a little in the last part of the prayer, which blends into a long Christological section.[1] Not only does Paul pray for his converts, he visits them, sends his assistants to them, and writes letters to them. The care of all the churches which daily presses upon Paul, and which is manifest in all his letters, is a care for the Christian life of his readers.

Law is an issue in this section because it occupies a place in Paul's letters, being an important question for Paul because of his Jewish heritage in which the law played a significant part in the definition of morality. This is law in the sense of Torah, the law of Judaism and the Old Testament. In this sense law, or the law, is part of the history of the revelation of the will of God to man. The incarnation is the culmination of this revealing. Jesus Christ is not just the paradigm 'man for others', he is Jesus the Messiah. Thus he comes in a certain historical tradition, he has a heritage, and thus an interpretative framework. The question 'Who is this?' may be answered at one level, 'the son of Joseph', but the more significant theological answer must derive from the consideration of Hebrews 1:1f.: 'In many and various ways God spoke of old to our fathers by the prophets; but in these last days he has spoken to us by a Son.' If the revelation of God to man is fulfilled in Christ, then the law is also, in some sense, fulfilled in him.

Law in the sense of legislation which defines the order of society, however, is not really discussed by the New Testament writers as such, although they are in touch with the social order and the law of society. In certain strands of the Old Testament, the law in the sense of the revelation of the will of God, includes legislation, since the Torah is addressed to the people of God who, as a society, are thought of as being ruled by God. As such, Israel may be described as a theocracy. Even within the Old Testament there are signs of a division between the moral law and social legislation.[2] This division becomes more manifest in later Judaism, but its roots can be traced to the establishment of the kingdom, and the seemingly inevitable consequence of that, the building of the temple. In the New Testament the division is complete, and a consideration of Christian morality does not begin with a definition of 'Christian' society, or how society should be ordered, but with the position of the Christian within a society which may be alien or even hostile.[3] The question of how far the New Testament helps us to deal with the question of social and political involvement is not dealt with here, but in chapter 5. Thus in this section we shall concern ourselves with the nature of Christian morality, as determined by the position of the Christian. We must also consider the relationship of law as Torah to fulfilment in Christ and also the moral life of the Christian. First of all, however, the gospel, as that to which a man responds in becoming a Christian, must be outlined, for this gospel not only provides the basis of the Christian's moral position but it also defines that position.

The gospel of God

The term 'gospel' seems to have been particularly adopted by the early Christians to describe their proselytizing activity, and the message which they preached. It is not common before the New Testament, but is widely used in it.[4] Whatever its background the noun (*euangelion*) and the verb (*euangelizomai*) are certainly used by Paul to describe his apostolic activity, and the subject-matter of his message (Rom. 1:9, 16; 15:16, 19; 1 Cor. 1:17; 15:1). This is very clear in Galatians 1 and 2 where he defends his gospel at length (see especially Gal. 1:6–11; 2:1–14). When Paul writes to the Romans he says (Rom. 1:15) that he is eager to 'gospelize' them although it is manifest that the people who would be the recipients of this ministry are already Christians. This is despite the fact that Paul later in that letter says that he has made it his aim to 'gospelize' where Christ is not named (Rom. 15:20). It is not absolutely clear what relationship Paul sees between his evangelizing where Christ has not been named, and his actions where he is working with Christians who have been converted as the result of someone else's ministry. What is clear is that Paul uses the verb 'evangelize' to indicate that activity for which he was called and which he pursued in the east generally, and specifically at Corinth and Galatia, and which he proposed to pursue at Rome.

The significance of this can be illustrated by reference to 1 Corinthians 4:15 where Paul says that he begot the Corinthians in Christ through the gospel. Thus the gospel is the instrument whereby those who are recipients of Paul's ministry become Christians. Yet the way in which people become Christians in the Pauline letters is described in a variety of ways, and the message preached is not described only as the gospel; it is also the word, Christ, or, more significantly for our purposes here, tradition. In 1 Corinthians

15:1 the terminology of tradition is used (the Corinthians 'receive' what Paul 'delivers' or hands on) and the substance of the tradition is the gospel which he preached. However in Romans 6:17 the content of the tradition is the 'standard of teaching', and it is a standard of teaching which clearly implies a certain ethical pattern of behaviour for those who are committed to it.

There are various ways in which Paul describes the step or process whereby a person becomes a Christian. At least eleven different motifs are employed by him to describe this change; they are justification, reconciliation, redemption, sanctification, adoption, inheritance, calling, salvation, deliverance, to create anew, to make peace.[5] These motifs are sometimes brought into relationship with each other, but not always in the same way, so that it is not really possible to establish a pattern of becoming a Christian and continuing in the faith (such as in Rom. 8:25f.) which can be said always to apply in Paul's letters. What can be said, however, is that the change which is described under these motifs places the Christian in a position which has distinct ethical consequences. Some motifs are more susceptible to this use than others, but the fundamental point is that the Christian, whether he is primarily thought of as justified, sanctified, redeemed, or whatever, is introduced into, or involved in the purpose of God. Thus, to be a Christian is to be committed, 'by definition', to the will of God in all its ethical aspects.

There is a further point about the gospel that should be noted here. The position of the Christian as involved in the will of God provides not only the basis but also the character of his ethical life. Thus the gospel message must be understood as revelation and tradition. It is not the case that there is a message called the gospel which is to be accepted and believed in order to be a Christian, and then some further message, which might be called 'teaching', which provides the pattern of Christian life for the person who has accepted the gospel message. This view is reflected in two popular ideas which are open to considerable doubt. First, a distinction is sometimes made between preaching (*kerygma*) and teaching (*didachē*).[6] The former is addressed to the non-Christian, and the latter to the Christian. But in the Pauline letters such a terminological distinction cannot be sustained. What Paul does with outsiders and with his converts is variously described in both these terms. The second mistake is similar to the first, and is the suggestion that the letters of the New Testament can be seen to fall into two sections: theology (usually the first half of a letter) and then ethics. It is thus thought that the ethical teaching of the New Testament is rightly understood only when it is viewed as based on theological truth (despite the great difficulties to which such a distinction leads, and which are similar to the problems associated with the so-called naturalistic fallacy).[7] Such a distinction is very difficult to sustain even on simple literary grounds. If Romans is taken as a typical example, it is suggested that chapters 1–11 contain the theological material and 12–15 the ethical material, introduced by a 'paraenetical therefore'.[8] But this is really inadequate. Chapters 6–8 are, as Schweitzer rightly remarks, among the most impressive passages ever written on ethics, a point which Chrysostom had noted some time before.[9] It is true that in chapter 12 Paul turns to *particular* ethical matters, whereas the ethical material in the first half of the letter is *general*, but that is very different from claiming a change from theology to ethics. We are thus left with the position that in Paul's letters the gospel is at once ethical and theological. To believe is to commit oneself to a certain ethical life, and to commit oneself to that (Christian) ethical life is to believe.[10] Having reached this point we must now turn to the question of fulfilment and the law, since Christ is seen as the fulfilment of the law, and the gospel is a message of salvation that has its roots in the historical purposes of God begun in Abraham and continued in Moses and Israel.

Fulfilment and the law

Paul's attitude to the law is to be understood in the context of his position in Judaism and his commitment to the law as a Pharisee, on the one hand, and his work as apostle to the Gentiles upon whom he did not place the yoke of the law, on the other. The difficulty is that Paul says things about the law which seem to indicate wholehearted support and endorsement of it, while at the same time saying things which suggest the opposite. These two aspects of Paul's writing are not easy to resolve.

Paul regards the doctrine of justification by faith as establishing and not annulling the law. Paul uses this last word in Romans 7:2 and 6 in the illustration of the man and wife, to say that the woman is free from the law of her husband when he dies. The same construction (*katargesthai apo* with the genitive) is used in Galatians 5:4 when Paul says that anyone who wishes or tries to be justified by the law is cut off from Christ. The verb and the noun forms of fulfil are used by Paul in relation to the law, but they do not have any special point in the Greek, beyond what the English indicates. This is also the case with *telos*, translated 'end', since it means not only the end in the sense of termination, last part or conclusion, but also in the sense of goal, the end in view. This point is of some importance in Romans 10:4 where Paul says that Christ is the end of the law.

Paul asserts that the law is to be the basis for action, which actions will be tested by the judgment of God (Rom. 1:32; 2:1–11. Compare Rom. 8:7 and 1 Cor. 7:19.) The law is not sin (Rom. 7:7), rather it is good (Rom. 7:13, 16). It does not bring death (Rom. 7:13), it is not against the promises of God (Gal. 3:21), and is what Paul the Christian delights in (Rom. 7:12).[11] The Jew has the advantage of having been entrusted with the oracles of God (Rom. 3:1–8), and one of the benefits of Israel is the giving of the law (Rom. 9:4). We may also note that in Romans 3:19–20 the law contributes to the whole world's being held accountable to God.

This last point might be thought to indicate a negative attitude to the law, since Paul goes on to expound a righteousness apart from the law (Rom. 3:21) by which a man is justified by faith apart from works of the law (Rom. 3:28, and see also the rhetorical question in Rom. 9:30–31). Thus in Romans 8:3 God has achieved in Christ what the law could not do, and the ethic of the Spirit and the mind of Christ are in contrast to the way of the law (Rom. 8:4–17). Similarly the Galatians did not receive the Spirit through works of the law, but through faith (Gal. 3:1–5), and in any case, if justification were through the law, then Christ died to no purpose (Gal. 2:21).

In Romans 10:4 Paul says that Christ is the end of the law with reference to righteousness for all who believe (see NEB mg., 'Christ is the end of the law as a way to righteousness for everyone who has faith'). In the preceding verses Paul has been describing the position of the Jews who have not come to salvation. They have a zeal for God, but it is ignorant zeal because they are ignorant of the righteousness from God, and seek to establish their own righteousness and do not submit to the righteousness from God. In other words they seek to establish their relationship with God themselves, rather than accepting the gift of God which established that relationship. Thus Christ is the end of the law in the matter of this righteousness, in the sense that he has demonstrated the impossibility of a legalistic attempt to establish a position over God, which the law had not done.[12]

Turning to a passage which deals with law as a guide to conduct rather than its potential misuse to establish relations with God, Romans 13:8 says that he who loves his neighbour has fulfilled the law. In explanation of this Paul quotes Leviticus 19:18b as a summary of the various injunctions of the law, and he is not the only person in the New Testament to do so (see Mt. 5:42; 19:18–19; 22:34–40; Lk. 10:25–37; Jas. 2:8; and Gal. 5:14). In Leviticus 19 the verse is not a summary of the law, but it was so understood by some of the rabbis.[13] In support of this summarizing of the law Paul argues that love does no wrong to the neighbour, and therefore it is the fulfilling of the law.[14] In other words the fundamental consideration here is the good of the neighbour.

In Leviticus the obligation to love is applied to the stranger who dwells with the Israelite. Thus it is not strictly correct to say that the neighbour in the Old Testament is the fellow Israelite, though there is a distinction between Israelite and non-Israelite. That distinction can be seen, for example, in the laws relating to slavery. An Israelite slave must be set free under certain circumstances, and the obligations to a fellow Israelite are far greater than they are to a non-Israelite in this situation. So great in fact that at least one rabbi speaks of an Israelite slave as a 'lord' of his master. In the New Testament the distinction between Jew and Gentile has been eliminated in Christ. The true sons of Abraham are those by faith, be they Jew or Gentile. This universalizing has a considerable effect on the law conceived of as the law given to Israel to guide and regulate the life of the nation. The social institutions and structures of Israel have dissolved in the New Testament. Christianity is no longer national, but universal in its scope and conception. The law is therefore not so significant as the fundamental principles which it embodies.[15]

The way in which Paul summarizes the commandments into one injunction, and the rationale in terms of good and evil, shows that Paul does not have a legalistic approach to the law when used as a guide to moral conduct. He is more concerned with the fundamental issues than with formal obedience (compare Dt. 10:16 in its context). This does not mean, however, that the law is of no value at all. Quite the contrary, it shows that the definition of those fundamental issues is made possible by the law. 'The will of God is not regarded as a mere vessel or form which is given its content by *agapē*; this idea would be commensurate with neither the Jewish understanding of the law nor with Paul's view of the *nomos*.'[16]

It is not possible to raise all the issues related to Paul's attitude to the law, and it is only possible to touch on the question of fulfilment in the briefest way.[17] In the matter of righteousness Paul sees the gospel of God as the one way, the way of faith, grace. This is in sharpest contrast to the attempt to achieve righteousness by the works of the law,[18] which in any case was a misuse of law. The law, however, reveals sin for what it is and thus, like the gospel itself, declares God's judgment. In so far as Jesus is understood by Paul as the Christ, then Paul sees the law providing part of the interpretative framework for an understanding of Jesus as the Messiah. Paul's ethics are not nomistic, however, but are better described as exemplarist.[19] It is the mind of Christ which guides those who walk according to the Spirit,[20] and growth in character is itself the work of the Spirit. This is because Christ is truly the end of the law, and the giving of the Spirit has put the law in its place.

Fulfilment and freedom

It is sometimes thought that because Paul found himself in conflict with people who insisted on legalistic observance of the law, and because he had such a firm sense of the fulfilment that is in Christ, he must have been in favour of freedom in something like the popular sense of 'free from all constraint'. It is true that Paul understands freedom chiefly in terms of the relationship of the Christian to Christ and that he deploys his arguments about freedom against a Jewish form of legalism. However, his discussion of freedom is not always set in this polemical context and this context does not provide the best way into an understanding of his statements. The Greek background, and particularly the Stoic development of the Greek tradition, afford the most illuminating way into Paul's understanding.

In the Greek tradition freedom was basically a political idea, understood within the context of the *polis*. Free men are understood in contrast to slaves or others. The free man is the citizen who exercises all his political rights. In this sense, however, the free man has his freedom in the context of the laws of the *polis*,[21] since the laws provide the secure framework within which the free man may live and where he may rule as well as be ruled.[22]

In later Greek philosophical writings this political idea is developed in a more personal way, particularly by the Stoic writers. Epictetus is a good example of this development. Freedom is a personal matter and is the result of knowing how to live.[23] 'Once prepared and trained in this fashion to distinguish what is not your own from what is your own possession, and the things which are subject to hindrance from those which are free from it, to regard these latter as your concern, and the former as no concern of yours, diligently to keep your desire fixed on the latter and your aversion directed towards the former, then have you any longer anyone to fear?—No one.'[24] Thus, liberation is from the world and is achieved by liberation from that which represents the world to and in me. This liberation is a matter of personal attitude and training. Diogenes is described by Epictetus as free, 'not because he was born of free parents, for he was not, but because he himself was free because he had cast off all handles of slavery, and there was no way in which a person could get close and lay hold of him to enslave him'.[25] Such freedom gives peace.

When we turn to Paul there are a number of significant passages which demand consideration. First, Galatians 5:1, 'For freedom Christ has set us free', is one of the strongest statements in the Pauline letters, in that not only is a change of status effected by Christ called 'deliverance' (*ēleutherōsen*) but also the new status is designated 'freedom' (*eleutheria*). This assertion comes in the context of an argument with those who are insisting on circumcision as a necessity. This point was touched in Galatians 2:4 with reference to Titus, and is dealt with in various arguments in chapters 3 and 4. In these chapters circumcision is argued against in terms of its being part of a righteousness achieved or sought by works of the law. The contrary argument is that faith (not the works of the law) is the way of deliverance. This argument is first given in 4:1–7. The Galatians and Paul are slaves to the elements of the universe (4:3) and are under law (4:4), but their position of slavery is changed by manumission effected by God in Christ. This manumission leads not to freedom but to sonship, and thus to being an heir. The argument is repeated in verses 8–11 in a slightly different way. This basic argument is followed by an argument based on the story of the two sons of Abraham (4:21–31), the conclusion of which is that Paul and his readers are the sons of the free woman. Galatians 5:1 is thus a summary assertion reverting to the basic argument of 4:1–11. The freedom to which the Galatians have been delivered is a state which is in contrast to their position before they became Christians. Thus the sons of God have a freedom from the law and the elements which they did not have before.

The contrast between the pre-Christian position of the Galatians and their Christian position is continued in chapter 5. In verses 2–4 Paul reiterates in the strongest possible terms that the attempt to justify oneself before God by the works of the law is fatally in conflict with the grace of God in Christ. The Christian position (verse 5) is that through the Spirit and by faith we wait for the hope of righteousness. The contrast is again present in verse 6; circumcision is contrasted with faith working through love. This phrase is one of the best summaries of Paul's basic understanding of the Christian's life as involving at once belief and action.

In the last part of chapter 5 the contrast is portrayed in more particular and concrete terms of 'life-style'. On the one hand the works of the flesh are: 'immorality, impurity, licentiousness, idolatry, sorcery, enmity, strife, jealousy, anger, selfishness, dissension, party spirit, envy, drunkenness, carousing, and the like' (verses 19–21). 'Paul doth not recite all the works of the flesh, but with a certain number for a number uncertain.'[26]

The list of the fruit of the Spirit is in the sharpest contrast: 'love, joy, peace, patience, kindness, goodness, faithfulness, gentleness, self-control' (verses 22–23). Perhaps Lightfoot is right to comment: 'Would you ascertain whether you are walking by the Spirit? Then apply the plain practical test.'[27] What is certain, however, is that Paul not only reinforces his exhortation of verse 16 by these two lists, but he also gives concrete expression to the character of the Christian's life-style. In this sense both lists contribute, for they complement one another to provide a picture of the character of God and his will when seen in terms of human behaviour. It is not surprising that the life-style described here reminds us of Jesus, to whom Paul and the Christians belong.

Romans 6 deals with the theme of freedom in terms of belonging to Christ more explicitly than does Galatians. The second half of Romans 6 deals with the question posed in verse 15: 'Are we to sin because we are not under law but under grace?' Verse 16 states the basic principle of the argument: slavery is a consequence of commitment. In political terms slavery was not something to which one committed or presented oneself, and it was terminated by manumission. Thus the slavery which is the result of putting oneself at the disposal of another is not political slavery. Nor is the imagery in this section that of political slavery, but of slavery to that which hinders or compels, and thus limits the inner freedom of the individual be he politically slave or free.[28] Thus the slavery that Paul here speaks of is a consequence of the commitment of the heart. It is a matter of disposition to this or that power, influence or 'master'.

This argument presupposes that there are two balancing, alternative 'masters' which together comprehend the whole, and that the relationship to each can be described as either slavery or freedom. Thus if one is a slave to A then, in the nature of the case, one is free from B (or we might in logical terminology say, from non-A). These two alternatives also indicate the Christian's position and the non-Christian's position, and it is therefore possible to set out the pre-Christian and the Christian position according to Romans 6.

pre-Christian position	Christian position
6:16 *slaves* to death	*slaves* of obedience to righteousness.
6:17 *slaves* of sin	obedient from the heart to the standard of teaching to which they were committed.
6:18	They have been made *free* in regard to sin.
	They are *slaves* in regard to righteousness.
6:20 *slaves* to sin	
free to righteousness	
6:22	they have been made *free* in regard to sin.
	they have become *slaves* to God.

Paul thus accepts the basic slave/free alternative of the Greek tradition, but he develops it in such a way that the important thing is not whether one is free or slave but that to which one is slave or free. Because he develops the imagery in this way, it is possible for him to view any given individual as being at the same time slave and free. The important thing to him is that one should be slave to God or righteousness and free in regard to sin. Thus, that from which one is delivered or free is that which is over against God, and in this sense freedom is not simply political or even restricted to the law, or morals, but is cosmological. Sin and death, the ultimate opposition to God, are the alternative slaveries from which the Christian has been delivered.

From the point of view of fulfilment Paul's use of the idea of freedom and slavery does not mean that the Christian is absolved from any moral obligation. Rather, what is conveyed by means of the idea of freedom is that the Christian is someone who is enslaved to God and thus to God's will, and free from that which stands over against God. The question of the law does not necessarily enter into this discussion. It does come into the discussion in so far as enslavement to the law for the purpose of achieving righteousness or acceptance by God is a slavery from which the Christian is delivered, as he is delivered from the elements of the universe, sin or death.

This way of using the idea of freedom serves to introduce the very important fact that, for the purpose of Christian ethics, the most important way of understanding the Christian is as someone who is a slave to God. The precise terms of this relationship are defined in different ways in different passages, but the fundamental idea of the Christian as someone in relationship with Christ provides not only the best way to see the basis of the Christian's ethical life, but also the form and content of that life.[29]

The position of the Christian

The position of the Christian as someone in relationship with Christ provides the immediate theological statement from which his moral life and obligation is to be understood. The details of the relationship need, however, to be drawn out at this point. It has already been noted that the gospel is not only the good news of salvation which is proclaimed in the New Testament, but also the tradition to which the Christian is committed by his belief. The gospel shows that the Christian's position is, from a theological standpoint, first and foremost a position within the framework of the purposes of God. The purposes of God in this context have a distinct and important eschatological goal, as well as a point of reference in the incarnation which is understood in eschatological terms.

This may be illustrated by reference to Colossians 1:3–8 where Paul records his prayer of thanksgiving for the Colossians' faith and love. They have this because of the hope laid up for them in heaven, that is, their Christian life is orientated towards the future reception of the substance of that hope. But this hope, lying in the future, was part of the gospel message which they heard and believed and learned from Epaphras. Thus the gospel message in this passage is about future hope. The other side of the coin can be seen in Romans 6 where Paul appeals to the Romans on the basis of their relationship with Christ which has been established in the past, and the point of reference to which he specifically draws attention is the death and resurrection of Christ. That is to say, he draws attention to a past event considered to have important ethical implications in the present life of the Christian. The appeal in this argument is to the past achievement of Christ and the relationship of the Christian to him in that achievement. The present ethical life of the Christian is, in terms of the analogy in the argument, parallel to the resurrection of Christ.

These two sides of the picture of the Christian as involved in the purposes of God can be seen together in 1 Thessalonians 5:1–11. The immediate purpose of the passage is to remind the Thessalonians about parts of Paul's teaching with which they were already familiar, about times and seasons. The passage makes use of quite common eschatological images, some of which Jesus had himself used. As the picture develops some imperatives are introduced which are clearly intended to refer to the way in which the Thessalonians, as Christians, should conduct themselves. In verse 6 Paul says, 'So then let us not sleep, as others do, but let us keep awake and be sober.' It is obvious that the terms of these exhortations are drawn from the imagery of the passage, and that they are not to be taken literally. It is perhaps not so obvious that for this very reason the exhortations do not have any substantial content. They do not provide any indication as to how the Thessalonians should conduct themselves. That, however, is not really the point of the exhortations. The point of the passage is to encourage the Thessalonians to persist in doing what they already know to be right. This motivation arises from the eschatological imagery and the conviction that the position of the Christian is correctly understood in this eschatological framework.

It is worth noting that this framework has two principal points of reference. There is the past point of reference by relation to which the Thessalonians can be said already to be not of the night, and there is the future point of reference, the day of the Lord which will come as a thief in the night. The popular aphorism about Christian ethics, that you should become what you are, is thus inadequate. The idea indicated by that aphorism is that the Christian should show in his behaviour the truth of his standing as a Christian, and is a perfectly proper idea which is found in the New Testament. It is not, however, the whole picture, since it does not do full justice to the eschatological position of the Christian.

There is another framework within which the Christian finds himself, and which affects his behaviour; that is a social framework. The behaviour of the Christian occurs in different social contexts, some of which condition his behaviour. For example, in his relations with a weaker brother who has not yet grasped the point that nothing in itself is unclean, and is therefore scandalized by meat-eating, the Christian should not offend his brother. However, the Christian is set in a society and his relations with his fellows continue as before. There is no evidence in the New Testament that the Christians withdrew from normal social intercourse. It would be exceedingly surprising if they had. The problem in Corinth about eating meat that had been offered to idols would never have arisen if the Corinthian Christians had withdrawn from social contact with unbelievers. The Corinthians did misunderstand one of Paul's letters and took him to say that they should not associate with wicked and evil men at all, but Paul is quick to correct this misunderstanding (1 Cor. 5:9–13).

The position of the Christian in relation to God is also critical in the understanding of the motivation and goal of Christian behaviour. The Christian is, by the nature of the case (or by definition), someone who is caught up in, or involved in, and thus committed to, the purposes of God. The position of the Christian can be seen in a number of ways. First is the fact that he is in a relationship to the purposes of God, as they have been revealed in Christ and as they will come to fruition at the parousia of Christ. The Christian is also seen as the recipient of the grace of God, and thus it is appropriate that he should behave in accordance with the character of God. The present position of the Christian is in contrast to the position he held before he became a Christian, and the contrast in the pattern of behaviour is a motive that is appealed to. The appeal is made effective on the principle that it is appropriate to behave in a manner consistent with the Christian profession just as pre-Christian behaviour was appropriate to another, quite different profession. Similarly, appeal is made to be consistent with earlier Christian behaviour. The most fundamental point of the appeal is the nature of the relationship between Christ and the Christian, and the implications of that relationship. In the one passage where the question of motivation is directly discussed (Rom. 6) the argument depends entirely on the fact and character of the Christian's relationship with Christ.

Such things as the Christian's relationship with Christ, the contrast with his previous non-Christian behaviour, or his involvement in the purposes of God, do not provide in themselves a satisfactory basis or motivation for ethical action. There are thus certain principles underlying these considerations which are necessary to make them effective. The most important principle in this respect is that of appropriateness. The principle is expressed in a variety of ways, sometimes by the interrogative 'how', or the simple dative case, or such words as 'worthy' or 'fitting'. Sometimes it is implicit in the passage, or it is reflected in the way in which terms are used to describe the position of the Christian in ethical exhortations.

Some ethical material is expressed in the context of prayer, such as at the beginning of Colossians, and this context must be considered to carry with it a certain motivational force, since it would imply that the ethical material in the prayer must be understood by Paul at least to be according to God's will, or what Paul saw to be God's will for his readers. However, the goal of the ethical activity of the Christian is not simply that he should do God's will. The fact that ethical behaviour is seen as related to the ultimate purposes of God, means that the ethical action of the Christian has a significance far beyond the immediate circumstance of the life of the Christian. This may be illustrated by reference to Paul's prayer in Philippians 1:3–11. The first part of the prayer does not concern us, but in verses 9–11 Paul says that he prays that the Philippians' love might increase more and more in knowledge and understanding, in order that they might discern those things that are significant. That is to say, he wants them to be able to see what is significant and what is not and thus be able to make the correct decisions about their behaviour and so behave as they should. This is for a second, more ultimate, reason, that they might be pure and blameless on the one hand and filled with the fruits of righteousness on the other, for the day of Christ. In other words he wants them so to act now that, at Christ's return in judgment, they might have nothing against them, but rather a record of right behaviour. But even this consideration has a yet more ultimate purpose or goal, that is, the glory of God. The ultimate goal of the day-to-day ethical actions of the Christian is therefore the glory of God. In this way the ethical life of the Christian falls into line with all the action of God, and it is thus not exceptional that Paul should regard the ethical behaviour of the Christian as his worship, as that which praises and glorifies God.

The moral life of the Christian

The bulk of the material which has come down to us from Paul is concerned with the life of his converts. This is particularly the case with the Corinthian correspondence, and even though it is less true of Romans, he nevertheless concerns himself with the same subject in that letter. It is not possible to attempt a full-scale discussion of the teaching of the letters of the New Testament or even of Paul alone, on the subject of the moral life of the Christian. However, we do have a convenient way of seeing what Paul regarded as of importance for his readers since he often records in his letters something of his prayers for them. These prayers are not so similar that they can be regarded as mere stylistic phenomena, although the prayers in Colossians and Philippians are very similar. The prayers contain thanksgiving material as well as intercessory material, and both types of material are relevant to our question.

In Romans Paul gives thanks for the faith of the Roman Christians, and the fact that it is well known. Similarly in 1 Corinthians he gives thanks for the grace of God which has been given to them in Christ Jesus, so that they are enriched in every way. In writing to the Philippians he expresses thankfulness for their partnership in the gospel from the beginning, and he gives thanks for the faith of the Colossians. Pre-eminently then, Paul's thanks-givings are related to the faith of his readers, though in 1 Corin-thians he mentions the gifts which they have for the confirmation of their faith.

Paul's intercessions are more related to the developing life of his readers. He prays that he might visit Rome to impart some spiritual gift to them, and he records his prayer that they might abound in hope. In Philippians and Colossians he prays that they might have more knowledge and discernment for the purpose of making moral judgments. In 2 Thessalonians he gives thanks that their faith is growing, and he prays that they might be worthy of their calling, and fulfil every good resolve, so that the name of the Lord Jesus might be glorified.

In Paul's letters, therefore, the presumption is that Christians will grow and develop in faith and character. They should become more able to make correct moral decisions, they must learn to discern what is important and what is not, and they are expected to develop in character as Christians. Whether we call this sanctification or not does not really matter. It is certainly not exclusively so named by Paul; indeed sanctification means primarily a state or a relationship effected by God, although it does come to have a moral sense because of the moral character of God. While sanctification as such is not referred to very often by Paul, the idea of growth in Christian character underlies the major part of his letters.

The idea of edification is one important way by which this sense of growing to maturity is mentioned. Edification is part of the Christian's responsibility to his fellow Christian. He is to seek the good of his neighbour. All things may be allowable to him, but the criterion for action is whether or not it edifies (1 Cor. 10:23). On the other hand Paul insists that the criterion which is to be applied to congregational activities is edification or mutual en-couragement (1 Cor. 14:26, 31). In both these it is a matter of edifi-cation of individuals, of their being encouraged in the Christian life, of learning and progressing. It is not a case of building up the numbers of the congregation, but of helping the neighbour, or other members of the congregation, to grow in maturity. In the congregation this is achieved by the orderly exercise of different gifts, which have been given for this specific purpose. In the ordinary social contacts outside the congregation, edification is achieved by considerate behaviour in personal relations with fellow Christians.

The reason for this mutual edification has already been mentioned, that the Christians involved might be better able to make moral decisions, and to persist in the Christian life. The backdrop to this is not simply the need for the new Christians to learn about their faith, but the fact that each Christian finds himself confronted with temptation, and a struggle against sin. Because of this 'hostile environment' the Christian needs the mutual encouragement and edification to which Paul refers. Just as the purposes and activity of God are directed against hostile powers, so too the Christian, as someone involved in, or caught up in those purposes and activity, is involved in a struggle against the hostile powers. The battlefield for this conflict is the moral life of the Christian, who, from his position in relationship with Christ, strives to manifest in concrete terms the activity of God.

DISTINCTIVE EMPHASES IN OTHER NEW TESTAMENT EPISTLES

At this point it may be worth considering briefly the distinctive emphases of some other Epistles in the New Testament. This is not meant to be a treatment of the teaching of these letters in any comprehensive way, but simply some consideration of the ways in which a slightly different emphasis is struck in them, while sharing the broad outlines of Paul's teaching on our theme. It is convenient to deal with 1 and 2 Peter, Hebrews and James in that order, since not only are there probably strong similarities in the situations addressed by the letters,[30] but also because in the order given there is a more manifest development.

1 and 2 Peter

Two things are noteworthy in 1 Peter about the pattern of Christian life that is laid before the readers. First there is some reference to inner purity as a condition for brotherly love. This is found in the first chapter, verse 22, where Peter places the purification of the souls of his readers by their obedience to the truth before their love of the brethren. This verse provides something of a summary introduction to the following section, where the readers are said to have been born anew of imperishable seed through the living and abiding word of God; and thus in 2:1 they are to put away all guile and insincerity. Similarly in 2:11 the readers are exhorted to abstain from the passions of the flesh that wage against their soul.[31]

The second characteristic of 1 Peter is what, for want of a better word, we may call his piety. This is not his formulated and habitual practice of certain religious exercises, which is what, today, piety is often mistakenly thought to be. Rather it is his pious and 'faithfull' attitude to life. Thus, for example, he encourages his readers in the first chapter about the sufferings which they experience now, on the grounds of the hope which is laid up for them in heaven. This hope thus enables them to enjoy a certain serenity in the face of present difficulties. In chapter 4 the readers are told that they share in Christ's suffering when they suffer, and therefore they should rejoice. Schnackenburg says, 'The tone of the whole work shows that the First Epistle of Peter does not lack religious warmth. Once, in a reference of a kind rare in the epistles of the New Testament, the author speaks of love for Christ: "Whom having not seen, you love" (1:8). His is a sound, virile and yet profound piety. We may well believe that it embodies the mind of Simon Peter himself.'[32]

In 2 Peter there is much more concern over certain heresies that are bothering the readers. In particular some are challenging the hope of a second advent of Christ, and these charges are rebutted in a number of ways. For our purposes, however, we note that there is here a presupposition that error in religion will lead to error in morals. Thus in 2:1ff. the readers are told that there will be false teachers among them 'who will secretly bring in destructive heresies', and 'many will follow their licentiousness'. The rest of this chapter is taken up with one of the strongest expositions of God's judgment in the whole of the New Testament.

On the other hand, the assurance that the end of the world is certain is a ground for holiness of living (3:11ff.).

Hebrews

The 'letter' to the Hebrews is in fact called a word of exhortation, and this description fits well the kind of picture of Christian life given in the document. That life is one of hope, in following the example of Christ. Within that conception the author refers to the problem of apostasy, the need for growth in Christian life and the importance of mutual encouragement.

That Christian life is a life of hope may be seen from the heavenly call which Christians share, the consecrated way which they are to live and the character of the cloud of witnesses who are their example and encouragement. In 3:1 the readers are said to share a heavenly call, and they are then exhorted to consider Jesus, the apostle and high priest of their confession. Jesus is then contrasted with Moses, and the houses over which they presided. Christ was faithful over God's house, which house the writer and readers are, if they hold fast to their hope.

Similarly in chapter 6:11ff. the author says he desires each of the readers to show earnestness in realizing 'the full assurance of hope until the end'. In this way they will not be sluggish but will imitate those who inherit the promises through faith and patience. The same theme of heavenly calling is found in chapter 10, where the new and living way which Christ has opened up for them enables the readers to embark on that life of hope, which is marked by love and good works. The cloud of witnesses in chapter 11 are witnesses to the life of hope. They saw what was promised, greeted it from afar, and acknowledged that they were strangers and exiles on earth.

The supreme witness, however, is Jesus. The witnesses are there, but the readers are exhorted to look unto Jesus the pioneer and perfecter of their faith. This theme of the example of Jesus goes back to the earlier parts of the epistle where Jesus is described as the high priest who knows and understands the human situation, because he experienced it himself. The themes of hope and following Jesus are drawn together in the last chapter in the exhortation to go forth outside the camp, where Jesus suffered in order to sanctify the people through his own blood. The readers are to go out, and bear abuse for Jesus, because they have no lasting city, but they seek the city which is to come.[33]

It is in the context of this picture of the Christian life that the idea of apostasy is such a terrible thing to the author.[34] The danger arises through unbelief, of infatuation wrought through sin. Rather, the readers are partakers with Christ and should be united to him in following him into the life of the world to come. It is worth noting that the context of the exhortations to go on, and the claims that it is not possible to be re-laying foundations, is not of a problem about intellectual elitism, or special *gnosis* which was being sought by those who fell, but rather the context is that of stultifying gospelism. What is intended is that they should come to a mature understanding of the kind of life to which as Christians they are committed. They are not immature theologians being initiated to some higher *gnosis*, they are immature Christians needing more explication and application of the gospel.

Finally, we note the critical importance that is given in Hebrews to mutual exhortation and encouragement. In chapter 10 the new and living way on which they have embarked is followed by the only New Testament exhortation to Christians to assemble together. The reason for this emphasis in Hebrews is probably that it has been emphasized that the Christian life is a life of hope, which hope is directed to the age to come. It is not a life that is worked out in the present circumstances as if it completely belonged to those circumstances; it does not. There is a constant tension for those on the new and living way which calls for continuing encouragement.

James

The study of this letter has been marked by the criticism of Martin Luther that it is a 'right strawy epistle'. Luther was correct in saying that it had no gospel character to it in the way that the epistles of Paul and Peter did, but that is an altogether different thing from saying that it could not have been written by a Christian, or that it does not have something to tell us about Christian ethics. What James says arises from a true and living faith, and as such deserves our attention. Two things especially deserve our attention here: the trials of the readers, and their group life.

James is perhaps showing a Jewish character in the way he deals with the rich. They are to fade away in the midst of their pursuits, they are to receive all kinds of miseries. The rich seem to be the characteristic agents of suffering for the pious, they oppress them and drag them into court; they blaspheme the honourable name by which the pious are called. But the pious are to endure suffering patiently because they know that the Lord will come, the Judge is standing at the doors. As well as this motive there is the claim that suffering produces steadfastness, and they should let this steadfastness have its full effect so that they may be complete and lacking nothing.

Within the Christian group there is to be no partiality. In their synagogue no special notice is to be taken of the rich; after all, God chose the poor to be rich in faith. But in any case, and more importantly, such partiality is a transgression of the royal law which says that you should love your neighbour as yourself. Presumably this means that to show partiality is not to love your neighbour as yourself, but to love him for the reward or profit that he might give you. This would fit the emphasis of the divine judgment that relates to the royal law which is made in the passage. Thus love of the neighbour is something that flows from a man's faith, not from his hopes of a return from his neighbour. This point provides the introduction to the discussion about dead and living faith which follows in 2:14ff.

The theme of group life is considered again in chapter 5, verses 12–20. There is to be no oath-taking, but the simple statement of the truth. Oath-taking (that is, swearing by heaven or earth or anything else) is really for the benefit of the hearers so that they may be sure the person is speaking the truth. But in a Christian group such assurance should not be necessary, and indeed it is not helpful in that it discourages rather than encourages the plain statement of the truth.

In 5:13–18 there is the most remarkable set of group exhortations, which might well be titled, mutual responsibility and interdependence. Each is to 'do his thing': pray, sing, call the elders for prayer, as is appropriate to his situation of suffering, joy or sickness respectively. The last reference to prayer is widened from petitions for the sick member to prayer for each other generally.

The letter ends with an exhortation to rescue any erring fellow Christians. Mutual care in regard to joys, sorrows and sickness is important and part of James' Christian way of life. Mutual care in regard to faith, sin and right and wrong in Christian living is especially important for 'whoever brings back a sinner from the error of his way will save his soul from death and will cover a multitude of sins' (5 : 20).

These 'minor' New Testament Epistles share the same central convictions as Paul's letters, but they show at times a greater awareness of the importance of the example of Jesus,[35] and at the same time show clearly the centrality of love of the neighbour and the brother, and the divine perspective of Christian hope which characterize the picture of the Christian life in the epistles of the New Testament.

NOTES

1. Other prayers can be found in Rom. 1:8–10; 10:1; 15:5; 16:25–27; 1 Cor. 1:4–9; 2 Cor. 1:3, 4; Phil. 1:3–11; 1 Thes. 1:2, 3; 5:23, 24; 2 Thes. 1:3; 1:11f.; Phm. 4ff. See P. T. O'Brien, *Introductory Thanksgivings in the Letters of Paul* (Brill, Leiden, 1977).

2. One may note the projection into the resurrection of the kingdom given to the saints of the Most High in Dn. 7, and also the way in which during the exile the Jews maintained their moral and religious code within an alien social context. See C. K. Barrett, 'The New Testament Doctrine of Church and State' in *New Testament Essays* (SPCK, 1972), pp. 1–19 and B. N. Kaye, *Using the Bible in Ethics* (Grove Books, 1976). For an interesting discussion of the question generally see H. R. Niebuhr, *Christ and Culture* (Faber and Faber, 1952).

3. It is interesting to note that some of the most significant names used by Christians of themselves are names given to aliens or outsiders in society, *e.g.* strangers, foreigners, aliens, pilgrims and sojourners. See W. H. C. Frend, *Martyrdom and Persecution in the Early Church* (Blackwell, 1965); R. MacMullen, *Enemies of the Roman Order* (Oxford University Press, 1967).

4. *Cf. Theological Dictionary of the New Testament,* II (Eerdmans, Grand Rapids, 1965), pp. 710ff.; *Interpreter's Dictionary of the Bible,* II (Abingdon, New York, 1962), pp. 442f.; *New Bible Dictionary* (Inter-Varsity Press, 1962), p. 400.

5. See P. Feine, *Theologie des Neuen Testaments* (Weicher, Leipzig, 1912), pp. 338ff.

6. See, for example, C. H. Dodd, *The Apostolic Preaching and its Development* (Hodder and Stoughton, 1963).

7. For a discussion of the naturalistic fallacy see P. Foot (ed.), *Theories of Ethics* (Oxford University Press, 1967); W. D. Hudson, *The Is–Ought Question* (Macmillan, 1969).

8. See W. Nauk, 'Das *oun* paraeneticum', ZNW 49, 1958, pp. 134ff.

9. A. Schweitzer, *The Mysticism of the Apostle Paul* (A. & C. Black, 1931), p. 296. Chrysostom's remark is made in his comment on Rom. 6:5; see Migne P. G. 60 Col. 483.

10. This does not mean that it does not matter what you believe, as long as you do the right thing. Rather it means that belief in God involves in its very nature a commitment to right ethical behaviour. But it also means that 'doing the right thing' is so fundamentally a matter of faith that it cannot be done apart from belief in God.

11. On the interpretation of this passage see especially *Römer 7 und die Bekehrung des Paulus* (Leipzig, 1929) and R. Bultmann, 'Romans 7 and the Anthropology of Paul', in *Existence and Faith* (Fontana, 1964), pp. 173–185.

12. This is a much discussed passage and it is impossible here to enter into the debate over the various interpretations. For the discussion see the commentaries, especially Dodd, Leenhardt and Barrett; also C. E. B. Cranfield, 'St Paul and the Law', *Scottish Journal of Theology* 17, 1964, pp. 48–50, who, however, adopts a somewhat strained interpretation, and (perhaps realizing this) offers an alternative on p. 50 n. 1; C. F. D. Moule, 'Obligation in the Ethic of Paul' in W. R. Farmer, C. F. D. Moule and R. R. Niebuhr (eds.), *Christian History and Interpretation* (Cambridge University Press, 1972), pp. 396–406; R. N. Longenecker, *Paul, Apostle of Liberty* (New York, 1964), pp. 144–153; J. A. Ziesler, *The Meaning of Righteousness in Paul* (Cambridge University Press, 1972), pp. 205–208; E. P. Sanders, *Paul and Palestinian Judaism* (SCM Press, 1977). The term 'law' in this verse may well be an abbreviation of the phrase 'works of the law'. This phrase is abbreviated by Paul at Rom. 4:2, 6; 6:15; *cf.* E. Lohmeyer, 'Probleme Paulinischer Theologie: II Gesetzeswerke', ZNW 28, 1929, pp. 177–205.

13. See Strack–Billerbeck I, pp. 907f., III, p. 306. In Lv. 19:18 the injunction is addressed to 'the sons of your own people', but in Lv. 19:34 and Dt. 10:19 it refers to the sojourner (*gēr*, MT and *prosēlytos* in LXX in both verses) who dwells with you.

14. Note the parallelism in Lv. 19:33f.

> When a stranger sojourns with you in your land,
> you shall not do him wrong (*ou thlipsete auton*).
> The stranger who sojourns with you shall be to you as the native among you,
> and you shall love him as yourself.

Compare Rom. 15:2.

15. See B. N. Kaye, *Using the Bible in Ethics* (Grove Books, 1976).

16. G. Delling in *Theological Dictionary of the New Testament*, VI (Eerdmans, Grand Rapids, 1969), p. 293.

17. Discussion of Paul's attitude to the law may be found in the standard works on Paul. The following may be noted: R. Bultmann, *Theology of the New Testament*, I (SCM Press, 1952), pp. 259–269; W. D. Davies, *Paul and Rabbinic Judaism* (SPCK, 1955), pp. 147–176; H. J. Schoeps, *Paul* (Lutterworth, 1961), pp. 168–218; H. Conzelmann, *An Outline of the Theology of the New Testament* (SCM Press, 1969); R. N. Longenecker, *op. cit.*; the comprehensive discussion of C. E. B. Cranfield, *op. cit.* and W. Gutbrod in *Theological Dictionary of the New Testament*, IV (Eerdmans, Grand Rapids, 1967), pp. 106–107B.

18. Note the claim of Cranfield, *op. cit.*, p. 55, that Greek had no ready terminology for legalism.

19. E. Larsson, *Christus als Vorbild* (Uppsala, 1962); A. Schulz, *Nachfolgen und Nachahmen* (Munich, 1962).

20. See O. Cullmann, '*The Tradition*', in *The Early Church* (SCM Press, 1956), pp. 59–99; C. H. Dodd, 'Ennomos Christou' in *More New Testament Studies* (Manchester University Press, 1968), pp. 134–148; *Gospel and Law* (Cambridge University Press, 1951); David L. Dungan, *The Sayings of Jesus in the Churches of Paul* (Blackwell, 1971); E. Käsemann, 'Sentences of Holy Law in the New Testament', in *New Testament Questions of Today* (SCM Press, 1969), pp. 66–81.

21. See, for example, Herodotus, *History,* 7.104.

22. H. Schlier, in *Theological Dictionary of the New Testament,* 2 (Eerdmans, Grand Rapids, 1965), p. 489.

23. Epictetus, *Discourses,* 4.1.63.

24. *Discourses,* 4.1.81.

25. *Discourses,* 4.1.152.

26. Luther, *A Commentary on St Paul's Epistle to the Galatians* (J. Clarke, 1953), p. 518.

27. Lightfoot, *Saint Paul's Epistle to the Galatians* (Macmillan, 1890), p. 210.

28. Compare 1 Cor. 7:22.

29. On the different emphases in Galatians and Romans in regard to slavery and freedom see B. N. Kaye, ' "To the Romans and Others" Revisited', *Novum Testamentum* 18, 1976, pp. 59ff.

30. Compare 1 Pet. 1:1; Jas. 1:1. Hebrews was probably written to a group in Rome which faced some difficulties about their relationship to the synagogue. See W. Manson, *The Epistle to the Hebrews* (Hodder, 1957).

31. Peter probably means by 'soul' something like 'life' or 'self'; see 1 Pet. 1:9; 2:25; 3:20; 4:19, and E. Best, *1 Peter* (*New Century Bible,* Oliphants, 1971), p. 80.

32. R. Schnackenburg, *The Moral Teaching of the New Testament* (Burns and Oates, 1965), p. 371.

33. See W. Manson, *op. cit.*

34. See I. H. Marshall, *Kept by the Power of God* (Epworth, 1969), pp. 132ff.

35. Compare R. Schnackenburg, *Christian Existence in the New Testament,* 1 (University of Notre Dame Press, 1968), pp. 114ff.

5

The New Testament and social order

Bruce Kaye

Introduction

The question of how society should be ordered has occupied man for thousands of years. It is not surprising therefore that it should be asked if the religion which has dominated European civilization for nearly two thousand years has anything to say on this question in its foundation documents. In the first instance we need to apply the question directly to the New Testament documents. Do they say anything about the way in which society is to be ordered? However, we should also ask what the New Testament documents have to say about particular officials of society and their official actions, and what comments are made in relation to the existing social institutions before an overall picture of the attitude of the New Testament documents to the way in which society should be ordered can be attempted.[1]

The New Testament as a political document

There is a long history of ancient documents dealing with social order. While Plato's *Republic* is perhaps the best known to modern readers, there were a number of works nearer in time to the New Testament which fit in to this tradition. Zeno the Stoic wrote a book called *The Republic* which is quoted by Christian and non-Christian writers alike but which has not come down to us. Seneca's *De Clementia* is addressed to Nero and portrays a view of monarchy. Paul's contemporary, Epictetus, touches on the subject, although he does not address himself systematically to it in a treatise. The revolution started by Caesar, and carried on by Augustus, whereby the Roman Republic became the Roman Empire, prompted considerable discussion. In some quarters there was justification of the change and an attempt to show that the change did not mean as much as some people thought it did. Augustus' *Res Gestae* is an example of this, while Tacitus represents a more conservative attitude.

The New Testament writers were thus writing at a period when the way in which society should be ordered was not only a subject of practical politics, but it was also the subject of serious discussion. One might wonder if it was really possible for Paul not to have discussed it. Epictetus, whose writings come down to us not only in a somewhat similar form to those of Paul, but also deal with many of the social and moral questions that Paul discussed in his letters, is certainly aware of this question.

Nevertheless one is forced to say that the New Testament contains no consideration of the ordering of society as a question in its own right. At first sight this is surprising if one is conscious of the Old Testament heritage of early Christianity, and the national self-consciousness that the Old Testament displays. The argument is sometimes put in a form that would suggest that the continuity of the law of the Old Testament as a guide for ethical action has so affected the New Testament that significant elements of the Old Testament idea of how society should be ordered were accepted by the New Testament writers, even if they could not advocate their implementation immediately. However, this overlooks a very important aspect of early Christianity, namely that at the social institutional level there is a radical discontinuity from the Old Testament. With the coming of Christ a new situation has arrived, and the Old Testament structures and institutions are not just reformed, but in certain important respects radically rejected. The Old Testament sense of the nation in close relationship to the land dissolves in the New Testament. Christianity is a universal faith and is not tied to any land. The temple, as the sign of the presence of God with his people, goes, in favour of the presence of the risen Christ, and the kingdom which Jesus preaches and introduces is not of this world. 'The New Testament sees the Old Testament realities of the land, the nation, the kingdom and the temple as fulfilled in Christ. In this process, however, all these realities are given new and personal meaning.'[2] Or to put it more tersely in the words of W. D. Davies, Christianity 'has Christified holy space'.[3]

Rejection of the Old Testament social structures does not at all mean the rejection of society. On the contrary the New Testament consistently indicates commitment to and involvement in society. The details of that involvement and the reflection on it is thus the area of our concern here.

Direct references to particular officials and actions

The references that come under this head relate to John the Baptist, Paul and Jesus. In Mark 6:17–29 (Mt. 14:3–12) the death of John the Baptist is told in such a way as very clearly to imply criticism of Herod's administration of justice. Mark appears to draw out the picture of Herod in a sympathetic way. Matthew portrays Herod as the one who wanted to kill John because he had rebuked Herod for adultery with his sister-in-law, but was not able to do so because he feared the crowd, who took John to be a prophet. In Mark it is Herodias who has the grudge against John, and, although Herod does not appear to have done anything about John's condemnation, he nevertheless sees that he is a just and holy man, and he listened to him regularly even though he was perplexed by what he heard. It is hard to avoid the implication of Mark's account that the real power in domestic and court affairs was Herodias. It is presumably from her that Herod has to keep John safe (Mk. 6:20).

Herod's real fault was his use of executive power in an improper way. It would almost certainly not have been regarded as improper by Herod's guests or by his illicit wife and her daughter. However, the story is told in such a way that the evangelist's view is quite clear. Herod made a foolish promise in front of his guests, and he was manipulated by Herodias. In order to keep face he gives orders for something he has consistently opposed. The point of the story is not so much a comment about unjust action by a king, as the inconsistency between Herod's private views about the impropriety of killing John the Baptist, and his public action in ordering his death.

In Luke 3:12–14 John gives advice to tax collectors and soldiers as part of the advice which he was asked for by the multitudes. The multitudes are told that the fruits of repentance they are to show are those of sharing clothing and food with those in need. The tax collectors and soldiers are then selected as particular groups, and specific advice is recorded for them. Why these two categories were selected is not said. Perhaps it was because they were likely to be regarded as, in some sense, collaborators with the foreign Roman overlords, whereas the crowd appears to have been somewhat self-consciously Jewish (Lk. 3:7-9). John, however, does not question the propriety of their job. Indeed his advice to them that they should do their job honestly and well, in the terms specified, has rather the opposite effect. Thus, neither the story of John's death, nor the advice he gave to public officials about the performance of their job offers substantive advice about how society should be ordered. The existing order is simply accepted, and honesty and consistency are called for within the terms of that order.

When we come to the trial and death of Jesus, the same situation prevails. If we take the Gospel narratives more or less as they stand then it is quite clear that Jesus dies as part of a divine plan for the salvation of all men. This is clear from the prophecies of Jesus' death, and the conscious symbolism in the passion narrative. Professor S. G. F. Brandon thinks that the evangelists have sought to draw Pilate as support for the innocence of Jesus and to show that the Jews were 'solely responsible for his death'.[4] He thinks that the historical reality is that Jesus collaborated with the Zealots in an attack on the temple area as part of an attempt to overthrow the authorities. Thus he was executed by the Romans for sedition. If Brandon is correct then Jesus is clearly a social revolutionary of a violent kind, and the fact has great significance for the theme of this chapter. It does not seem to me, however, that the evangelists have covered over the facts out of embarrassment about the death of Jesus on the cross.[5] If we ask what is the attitude of the evangelists to social order, as seen in their accounts of Jesus' trial and death, then three things can be said. First, Jesus' death was a unique, historical event and does not therefore provide any direct example for the attitude to be taken by Jesus' followers. Secondly, Jesus' death by crucifixion was unjustified in the strictly legal sense, and also in the broader moral sense. He was not guilty of the charge in the sense in which it was brought, nor was he a bad man. Thirdly, such use as is made in the Gospels of Jesus' trial and death for the purpose of moral example, is restricted to personal endurance of suffering in the most general sense, or submission to political or legal interrogation without giving offence.

There are a number of other passages in the New Testament which tend to suggest a somewhat negative attitude towards the social order of the day,[6] and others which tend to suggest a more positive attitude.[7] These passages, however, do not really help us with our question.

If we turn to Paul's experience of the authorities then we have more precise information. There are five principal references: Paul and Silas and the magistrates at Philippi (Acts 16:19–40), Gallio's judgment at Corinth (Acts 18:12–17), the riotous assembly at Ephesus (Acts 19:28–41), Paul's use of his Roman citizenship with the tribune in Jerusalem (Acts 22:25–29), and Paul's appeal to Caesar (Acts 25:11, 12). The more important of these references for us are those where Paul takes an initiative or action, that is to say, the use of his citizenship in Philippi and Jerusalem, and his appeal to Caesar. In the case of Paul's use of his citizenship at Philippi he probably had in mind the position of the infant church which he was leaving behind. It was better for them that the founder should not leave under a legal cloud. In the case of the exchange with the tribune in Jerusalem Paul is using his position for his own protection. It may have been that he was not recognizably a citizen, and he may not have been in the habit of carrying the metal certificates of citizenship often carried by merchants. Claudius Lysias clearly accepts the claim and treats Paul accordingly.

The use of the law for self-protection in this way probably also explains the appeal to Caesar in Acts 25. When faced with the prospect of the charges against him being transferred to Jerusalem, Paul's response is a politico-legal one. He sees that from a legal point of view the matter could go either way. He could be protected by the Roman authorities, or he could, with complete legality, be turned over to the Jewish authorities to be dealt with as an offender against a religious law about the temple in Jerusalem. Paul did not need much political sagacity to see that he would not receive a very sympathetic or even a fair hearing in that quarter. Thus he uses his legal right to appeal to Caesar and keep the matter clearly in the jurisdiction of the Roman authorities. Equally, Festus responds with a politico-legal decision. He probably had a legal right to release Paul even after he had made his appeal to Caesar, but from the point of view of his relations with his superiors and his subordinates this would certainly have been an unwise line of action. Sherwin-White puts it nicely: 'It is not a question of law, but of the relations between the Emperor and his subordinates, and of that element of non-constitutional power which the Romans called *auctoritas,* prestige, on which the supremacy of the Princeps so largely depended. No sensible man with hopes of promotion would dream of short-circuiting the appeal to Caesar unless he had specific authority to do so.'[8]

SOCIAL INSTITUTIONS REFERRED TO

Certain social institutions are referred to in the New Testament which call for brief comment here. The references to the 'powers', to slavery and to the household have received considerable attention from scholars. This is not as true of references to hospitality and commerce, which are understandably often related to references to the household, and also references to certain kinds of sectarian activities.

Politico-legal institutions

In Paul's letters there are many references to the social and legal situations of himself and his readers. It would be surprising if it were otherwise. He touches on his own experience of the social authorities in different places in his account of the trials of an apostle,[9] and Philippians is written from prison.[10] Paul's readers are involved in social hospitality generally (1 Cor. 8:10), situations of marriage and divorce (1 Cor. 7:1–3), slavery (1 Cor. 7:21 and Philemon), and the law courts (1 Cor. 6:1–11).[11] The most important passages in Paul's letters for our purposes are those in which he provides an analysis of the politico-legal situation to which he is speaking, and the two most important of these are Romans 13:1–7 and 2 Thessalonians 2:6–7, though we will need to look also at his comments in 1 Corinthians 6 about civil litigation in the public courts.

Romans 13:1–7

I have argued elsewhere[12] that in this passage Paul is referring to the particular Roman authorities of his day, and that on the basis of his assessment of them he makes the theological statement with which this passage opens. It is not necessary to repeat the arguments for this position here, but it will be useful to make a number of points related to them before going on to the analysis of the argument of the passage.

If the time of writing Romans is to be set within AD 54–59 then the contemporary sources suggest that there was settled government in the empire, and a number of sources particularly draw attention to the humane influence on imperial affairs of Seneca and Burrus.[13] It is quite incorrect to assume that the inadequacies of Nero's later rule are present from the beginning of his reign. When we look at the people to whom some sort of obligation is enjoined in the passage it is not possible to be precise about their identification. *Timē* not only means worship or esteem, but it is also used in the legal sense of damages such as would be settled by a court.[14] *Apodidōmi* is used in this context for the payment of such damages.[15] *Timē* also has a political sense to describe the value at which a citizen's property was rated for taxation.[16] *Phobos* has a range of meanings which includes the respect which one would give to someone with authority, a magistrate, or someone with family or clientele *potestas*. It is not possible to be certain about the precise nuance of *phoros* and *telos*,[17] but they clearly refer to taxes. The picture of the sword most likely is a general picture or one taken from the capitol.

The crucial question is the analysis of the argument of the passage, and it may be of some help to outline the way in which John

Calvin interpreted this passage so as to highlight the issues. Calvin claims that the rulers of the time of writing 'not only hated piety, but also persecuted religion with the most hostile feelings',[18] and it is for this reason among others that Paul seeks to establish the authority of the magistrates most carefully. In doing so Paul 'first lays down a general precept, which briefly includes what he afterwards says: secondly he subjoins an exposition and a proof of his precept'.[19] The general precept is found in verse 1, 'we ought to be subject to the magistrates'. The reason for this is also in verse 1, 'because they are constituted by God's ordination'.

Calvin takes verse 3 as support for the initial exhortation, 'the causative *gar*, for, is to be referred to the first proposition, and not to the last verse', and he also sees this verse as giving a 'ground of utility'. In other words, government is a divine provision 'to provide for the tranquility of the good, and to restrain the waywardness of the wicked'. Calvin is all too well aware that not all governments behave in a manner of which he would approve, but he takes Paul to be speaking of the 'true, and, as it were, of the native duty of the magistrate, from which, however, they who hold power often degenerate'. Bad government does not, in Calvin's view, remove the obligation to submit. On this verse he argues that 'princes do never so far abuse their power, by harassing the good and innocent, that they do not retain in their tyranny some kind of just government; there can then be no tyranny which does not in some respects assist in consolidating the society of men.' This is a pragmatic argument which would be questioned by many. Can a tyranny never reach the point where, on pragmatic grounds, it is better to have a rebellion than the tyranny, with a view to, at least, a more tolerable tyranny?

Calvin sees further support for the basic exhortation of the passage in verse 5. 'What he had at first commanded as to the rendering of obedience to magistrates, he now briefly repeats, but with some addition, and that is—that we ought to obey them, not only on the ground of necessity arising from man, but that we thereby obey God.' In other words, even if the power of the magistrates to punish were removed, the obligation to submit would still be present. At the conclusion to his comments on verse 7 Calvin says, 'Now this passage confirms what I have already said,—that we ought to obey kings and governors, whoever they may be, not because we are constrained, but because it is a service acceptable to God, for he will have them not only feared, but also honoured by a voluntary respect.'

Calvin's understanding of the argument is thus:

statement of basic general principle	13:1
general supporting considerations	13:1
(they are ordained by God)	
supporting argument of utility	13:3
(magistrates, even bad ones, provide	
for the good of mankind)	
repetition of basic exhortation	13:5
supporting argument of conscience	13:5

The logic of the argument as analysed by Calvin is basically deductive. A fundamental proposition is given, and certain consequences developed from it. I would like to suggest that the logic of the argument is quite the opposite to this, that the passage proceeds by way of explanation, and that as the explanation is developed the ground for the initial statement becomes clear. That initial statement is thus the conclusion drawn from the material in the passage, not the premise upon which the rest of the passage is built.

The argument can thus be analysed something like this:

13:1 the basic exhortation—'be subject to the governing authorities'
the basic claim on which the exhortation is grounded—'there is no authority except from God, and those that exist have been instituted by God'

13:2 an implication of this general statement—'those who resist will incur judgment'

13:3 an explanation of this claim—'the rulers are not a terror to good conduct, but to bad'.

This explanation is developed in the second half of verse 3 and in verse 4 by telling the readers that if they wish to have the praise of the ruler, and not to be in fear of him, then they should do good and not evil.

13:5   a repetition of the basic exhortation, with two supporting considerations, wrath and conscience.

13:6, 7   further particular forms of the general exhortation.

The reference to wrath in verse 5 may go back to the statement in verse 2, 'those who resist will incur judgment', and the mention of conscience may go back to the references in verses 3 and 4 to good and evil behaviour. However, verses 3 and 4 are the crux of the problem. Can they really be taken to refer in general terms to 'the state'? Calvin clearly finds this a problem in his exegesis, and he is not alone amongst commentators in this respect. These verses are clearly not intended to persuade the readers to do good, and not to do evil. Rather they are intended to say something about the rulers. The difficulty is that, as a general statement, it cannot stand because it is so manifestly not true, and it is so unconditional. Paul does not say 'the ruler should . . .' or 'if the ruler . . .', he states as a bald, unconditioned fact, 'the ruler is . . .'. Given this, and the historical circumstances at the time of writing, it is difficult to resist the idea that Paul is here speaking about the particular authorities of his day.

If we accept that Paul is referring to the particular authorities of his day in verses 3 and 4 then we have here an argument that combines particular descriptive material and theological evaluation. Because he is able to say the things he does about the authorities of his day, Paul is prepared to speak of them as ordained by God.

This analysis of Romans 13 is therefore very significant because it shows that Romans 13 is a theological evaluation of the politico-legal situation of Paul and his readers. It is therefore very important to identify the criteria by which Paul makes this evaluation.

Paul approves of these authorities because they approve good works, and are a terror to evil. Thus the authority is the minister of God for the good (*eis to agathon*) in relation to the readers. Unfortunately this one general criterion seems to be the only specific thing that we can draw from this passage, in terms of evaluating criteria. However, two other points can, I think, be made. First, Paul treats the politico-legal structure more or less as a whole. He exhorts his readers to pay *all* their due, taxes, honour and respect, as well, of course, as submission. Secondly, Paul draws the idea of conscience into this argument. This means that, involved in the evaluation in which he has been engaged, Paul has had to make some particular judgments. We are thus introduced to the general question of how Paul thinks moral decisions are made. That he presumed his readers should make such moral decisions, and should have such discernment as to enable them to make sound judgments, may be seen from his prayer in Philippians 1:9–11.

2 Thessalonians 2:6–7

These verses come in a passage which is very difficult to interpret with confidence, and there is wide variety of opinion amongst scholars. The passage is relevant to our considerations only if the 'restraining one' in verses 6 and 7 is understood as referring to the empire. At the present time the man of lawlessness is being restrained by the empire (or the emperor), and the parousia of Christ will not be until the man of lawlessness has been revealed. This is part of an argument to rebut the idea that the day of the Lord has come. In the present situation, therefore, the empire, the Roman state, has a positive and restraining role within the purposes of God. That role is here thought of within the framework of eschatology, and is, in this framework, a temporary role.[20]

The interpretation of this passage cannot be settled apart from the interpretation of Paul's eschatology generally, and in the Thessalonian letters in particular. Without going into details here[21] I might be permitted to say that I do not think that there is any connection between ethical laxity and disorderliness at Thessalonica and eschatological interest in the Thessalonian letters, nor do I think that the language of imminence in Paul's eschatological statements necessarily implies chronological proximity.[22]

This passage does contribute one point to our question. The

state, in so far as it maintains order in the body politic, may be seen in that activity as part of the purposes of God which reach their culmination in the day of the Lord. Order, therefore, is a positive criterion, though by no means a sufficient criterion for a favourable evaluation of a particular political situation.

It might be helpful at this point to draw together the conclusions of this survey of Paul's letters. It does not need to be emphasized that the results do not seem very extensive or very specific. Romans 13 yielded to us only the general point that a favourable evaluation of the politico-legal structure was made if it operated for the good, where the good was defined in the quite general terms of Paul's ethical framework. We noted also that he took the situation as a whole, and that the evaluating was to be thought of within the general pattern of ethical decision-making reflected in Paul's letters. We noticed also that in 2 Thessalonians the role of the state fitted in to Paul's general eschatological framework, and that it served to promote order in the present situation.

We can conveniently draw attention to 1 Timothy 2:1–7 at this point, even though the authorship of this document is a matter of some dispute. It seems to me that this passage may be seen as summing up the points just made and elaborating them in one respect, namely the definition of the 'good'. Here what is good and acceptable in the sight of God is that Christians might 'lead a quiet and peaceable life, godly and respectful in every way'. The writer then goes on immediately to say that God 'desires all men to be saved and to come to the knowledge of the truth'. What is generally true in Paul's letters about the good, is here spelled out in close relationship to statements about what is sought, or to be prayed for, by Christians in regard to their politico-legal situation.

Household institutions

In the society in which the early Christians lived, and especially where there was strong influence from the Roman republican tradition, the family was a strong and important social unit. The household contained a wide range of relatives and others and their membership was expressed through various forms and styles of obligation to the family and its commitments. The interrelation of families was an important political factor in the republic, and remained so in the first century AD. This strong household unit is reflected in the New Testament documents, where Christians are members of such households and have domestic responsibilities.[23]

There are a number of passages in the New Testament which are sometimes described as 'household codes' (1 Pet. 2:18 – 3:7; Col. 3:18 – 4:1; Eph. 5 :21 – 6 :9). They are so called because they contain lists of exhortations appropriate to the particular positions which people have within the household structure, and it is sometimes suggested that the form and even the content of these codes have been influenced by non-Christian 'household codes'. It is possible that some confusion may be introduced by the use of such a phrase to describe these passages. They are not codes in the sense of providing a statement of what a Christian's household should look like. Rather they are sets of exhortations addressed to Christians who find themselves set within the household structure of the day. That structure is not itself the subject of either exhortation or direct comment.

This is particularly clear in 1 Peter, where the exhortations come within the context of teaching about social involvement generally. It is also clear that the wives addressed have non-Christian husbands. It is natural that when the husbands are addressed there is a presumption that the family has followed the religion of the head of the house. These exhortations to husbands in regard to their wives do seem to imply an added dignity for the wife in so far as she is to be held in honour and is a fellow heir of the grace of life. The household is to be a place of hospitality (1 Pet. 4:9) and a place for encouragement in the faith. There are no exhortations here for masters, though there are extended exhortations for those who are slaves. Nor are there any exhortations for children in this section.

The sets of exhortations in Colossians and Ephesians are more comprehensive in that they include references to wives and husbands, children and fathers, slaves and masters, in the same order in each letter. There is no reference in these passages to freedmen who were still serving in the household, though they might conceivably be thought of under the heading of slaves. In Ephesians there is a clear argument for the high significance of marriage and thus the relationship between husband and wife, but the other exhortations are best thought of as addressed to those Christians who happen to be in the situations so addressed. It is only in this loose sense that we can regard these passages as household codes. They do not directly provide a theological or ethical foundation for the creation of a family institution, they are rather exhortations addressed to Christians in their positions within the existing social, domestic structure.

Ecclesiastical institutions

Our concern here is not with the institutions of the church as they appear to be developing in the New Testament period: the question of church order, ministry and so on. Rather we are concerned here to note how far there is any indication that the church early set up institutions which took over, or related to, the existing social institutions of the day. It is sometimes thought that there are passages in the New Testament which provide some basis for the establishment of a Christian social order. Most important in this respect are the early chapters of Acts which describe the policy and practice of common property amongst the Jerusalem Christians. However, there are a number of problems attached to this. It is not at all clear how extensive was the group involved, nor is it clear how long the practice persisted. It is clear, though, that the policy is not advocated for general use in Acts, and no other New Testament writers even refer to it. The background to the distribution referred to in Acts 6:1 may simply be that the Christians set up their own welfare distribution along the lines of that which already existed amongst Jews in Jerusalem. It may not imply any kind of communalism at all.[24] There is reference to welfare concerns amongst Christians in the Pastorals in the instructions about widows.[25]

1 Corinthians 6:1–11 is sometimes thought to be relevant to this question in that it might appear to advocate disregard of the courts. Paul is clearly opposed to the Corinthians resorting to the courts in

litigation, which apparently they had been doing. He is opposed to this because it is simply inappropriate for those who will judge the world to be unable to judge between themselves on such small matters. To have disputes at all is, of course, defeat, and they would be better off not contesting matters. It should be noted very carefully, however, precisely what is being referred to here. It is litigation between Christians before the civil authorities who are unbelievers. Paul is not referring to litigation between a Christian and an unbeliever. A Christian might not have opportunity to avoid such proceedings. However, within the limits of the Christian fellowship it was possible to avoid recourse to the magistrates by settling disputes privately. This is in no way a disregarding or undermining of the Roman administration. In fact considerable provision in Roman law is made for private judgment.[26] Paul is saying that there should be no public displays of dispute within the Christian fellowship, and he does that in a legal context which allows for private litigation to be settled privately by arbitration. There is thus no sense here of a church law supplanting the legal framework of the society.

Conclusion

The result of our investigation is that the New Testament gives us no direct answer to the question of how society should be ordered. The institutions of the first century are not attacked or undermined as a matter of deliberate policy. There are some indirect guidelines as to the evaluation of a given society which can be discerned in the analysis of the politico-legal situation of Christians in the first century. The simple acceptance of slaves into the Christian fellowship without the normal social distinctions, together with the failure to examine the system of slavery as a whole is an outstanding and curious feature of the New Testament. Westermann thinks that this lack of concern is 'a direct corollary of the doctrine that enslavement was spiritually meaningless under the all-embracing hope of salvation'.[27] This element may just be present in 1 Corinthians 7, but the attitude of the New Testament writers generally is rather that of simple acceptance of the institution without apparent consciousness of any problem in so doing. From this side of the nineteenth century this may seem a little surprising, and to some perhaps even a little embarrassing. The New Testament writers, however, seem to be occupied with other matters.

NOTES

1. Two very useful collections of essays on this general subject are H. von Campenhausen, *Tradition and Life in the Church* (Collins, 1968) and A. A. T. Ehrhardt, *The Framework of the New Testament Stories* (Manchester University Press, 1964). See also O. Cullmann, *The Early Church* (SCM Press, 1956), and A. Richardson, *The Political Christ* (SCM Press, 1973), pp. 53ff.

2. B. N. Kaye, *Using the Bible in Ethics* (Grove Books, 1976), p. 15.

3. W. D. Davies, *The Gospel and the Land* (Berkeley, 1974), p. 368.

4. *The Trial of Jesus of Nazareth* (Batsford, 1968), p. 139.

5. There is not enough space to undertake a refutation of those major conclusions of Brandon's thesis with which I disagree. Scholarly disputation on Brandon's interpretation of Jesus' trial, and of the origins of Christianity generally, is still going on.

6. E.g. Mt. 5:33–37, 38–42; 6:25–26; 10:17–20; 20:1–16; Jn. 5:10ff.; Acts 2:42–47; 4:32–37; 6:2–6; 2 Cor. 11:23, 32, 33; 1 Tim. 5:3, 4.

7. E.g. Mt. 5:31, 32; 17:24–27; 25:14–30; Lk. 5:13–16; 22:35–38; 1 Cor. 7:12–16; 10:25, 26; Eph. 5:21 – 6:9; Col. 3:18–22; 1 Pet. 2:18 – 3:7.

8. A. N. Sherwin-White, *Roman Society and Roman Law in the New Testament* (Oxford University Press, 1963), p. 65.

9. 2 Cor. 11:23–29. See also the reference to King Aretas in 2 Cor. 11:32–33.

10. Phil. 1:7 and see the reference to the praetorian in Phil. 1:13.

11. He also uses knowledgeably the terminology of adoption and inheritance.

12. *TSF Bulletin* 63, 1972, pp. 10–12.

13. E.g. Dio Cassius, *History of Rome*, 61; Tacitus, *Annals*, 13.11.

14. Aristophanes, *Vespae*, 897; Lysias, 27.16.

15. Plato, Lg. 914c.

16. Plato, Lg. 744e.

17. *Phoros*, meaning direct taxation, Herodotus, *History*, 3.13, and *telos*, meaning direct taxation, Plato, *Republic*, 425d, P.Oxy.1473, 30 (third century AD).

18. J. Calvin, *Romans* (tr. and ed. John Owen, 1849, Eerdmans, Grand Rapids, 1958), p. 478.

19. *Ibid*.

20. See E. Stauffer, *New Testament Theology* (SCM Press, 1957), pp. 84f., and J. D. M. Derrett, *Law in the New Testament* (Darton, Longman and Todd, 1970), pp. 313ff.

21. See B. N. Kaye, 'Eschatology and Ethics in 1 and 2 Thessalonians', *Novum Testamentum* 17, 1975, pp. 47–57.

22. A. L. Moore, *Parousia in the New Testament* (Brill, Leiden, 1966).

23. See especially E. A. Judge, *The Social Pattern of Christian Groups in the First Century* (Inter-Varsity Press, 1960), pp. 30ff.

24. See F. J. Foakes-Jackson and K. Lake, *The Beginnings of Christianity*, V (Macmillan, 1933), p. 149.

25. Compare 2 Thes. 3:10.

26. L. Wenger, *Institutes of the Roman Law of Civil Procedure* (ET, New York, 1940), par. 35.

27. W. L. Westermann, *The Slave Systems of Greek and Roman Antiquity* (American Philosophical Society, Philadelphia, 1955), p. 150.

6

The universality of the concept of law

Robin Nixon

Introduction

The law code of the Old Testament was given to the people whom God had chosen and redeemed. It might therefore be argued that this had little, if any, relevance to other peoples at other times. Similarly the element of law which is to be found in the ethical teaching of the New Testament is largely concerned with the conduct of Christians, whether corporately or individually. It might therefore be argued, again, that the principles of conduct appropriate to Christians have no claim whatsoever on non-Christians. It would therefore be a case of, 'Accept the biblical faith before you can understand or practise the biblical ethics.'

There is a good deal of truth in this approach. It is true that even the Ten Commandments are set in the context of redemption. 'I am the Lord your God, who brought you out of the land of Egypt, out of the house of bondage. You shall have no other gods before me . . .' (Ex. 20:2f.). The redemptive setting supplies both the full reason and the motive for obedience to the commandments. What is true of the old covenant is also true of the new. 'I appeal to you *therefore*, brethren, by the mercies of God, to present your bodies as a living sacrifice, holy and acceptable to God, which is your spiritual worship' (Rom. 12:1). On the other hand, God is shown throughout the Bible as the Creator. He has not only made the universe, but he has revealed many of its guiding principles. In the opening chapters of Genesis we find basic teaching about man's relationship to God, to his fellows and to the created world.[1] All men can have some knowledge, however distorted, of these, and all men are accountable to their Maker for the way in which they have sought to obey them. The fact of God's judgment gives us certainty that in the end his will will be perfectly done, and also gives us purpose and dignity in our lives.[2]

The Old Testament

There is relatively little in the Old Testament which makes reference to the universality of the concept of law. It is, however, relevant to the issue that the early chapters of Genesis deal with mankind as a whole, and redemptive history does not really begin until the appearance of Abraham on the scene. In the first eleven chapters of Genesis we read of the creation and fall of man and of judgment and blessing coming through Noah. The covenant of God with Noah (Gn. 9:8–17) was intended to embrace all mankind and indicated that there would be a basic consistency in God's dealings with his creation. The rabbis understood the Noachian precepts, which they took to preclude idolatry, murder and adultery and the eating of flesh with the blood, to be binding upon Gentiles. The first rabbi known to have referred to this is Chanina ben Gamaliel, *c.* AD 120, but he assumes that this is widely accepted even though the details are disputed. It may be that allusion is made to this in the Apostolic Decree found in Acts 15:29, where certain minimum regulations are laid upon Gentile Christians, so that they may have table fellowship with Jewish Christians.[3]

Most of the Old Testament is written firmly within the context of *Heilsgeschichte,* but the wisdom literature bears witness to the fact that there were general principles about the moral ordering of things which could be cast in the form of maxims applying to all men. The categories of law are not normally used, but the idea of universal principles underlying conduct is easily extended to a concept of duty extending to all. At any rate, we can see that the sins of the heathen are not ignored in the Old Testament. If the climax of the denunciations of Amos is saved for Israel, whose sins are committed in the face of the saving activity of God on their behalf, the nations are also castigated for a series of specific crimes against humanity. Their 'three transgressions and four' must in some way be a breach of laws which they ought to have known (Am. 1 and 2).

The New Testament

As in the Old Testament, so in the Gospels there is little direct teaching upon this subject. The teaching of Jesus is given almost entirely in a Jewish milieu, and sayings addressed to Gentiles are uttered in the context of specific acts of healing (Mk. 7:24–30). What is perhaps more significant is the way in which, even in his evangelistic preaching to Jews, Jesus can apparently expect truths to commend themselves to their consciences. This is done frequently in the parables, without any explicit reference to truths which have been revealed in the Old Testament. A parable such as that of the unforgiving debtor (Mt. 18:21–35) is manifestly intended to rouse his hearers to indignation, because they know these things ought not to happen, since they offend against principles of justice which they have learnt either from the law or from common human experience.

There is an interesting passage in Luke's Gospel where Jesus explains that the people have become good weather forecasters, because they have come to understand the principles which govern the climate. They are therefore condemned for not applying their understanding to the principles of God's action in Christ. 'And why do you not judge for yourselves what is right? . . .' There are truths which ought to be discernible if only men are willing to discern them (Lk. 12:54–59). There is also a sense in which greater responsibility lies upon those whose position is most privileged (Mt. 11:20–24).

One of the most important references in the Gospels is the description of the Word as 'the true light that enlightens every man' (Jn. 1:9). In its context ('coming into the world' almost certainly referring to the light rather than to every man) the main emphasis of this expression is upon the illuminating mission of Jesus. But behind it there lies the assumption that light was already being shed upon mankind. In John's Gospel the great sin for which men are condemned is the failure to believe in Jesus as the Revealer and Redeemer. But such condemnation is closely associated with fear of the light and the exposure it brings, which must spring from some sense of wrong (Jn. 3:16–21).

The main teaching on this issue is found in the writings of Paul and in particular in the Epistle to the Romans. In passing we may note the speech in the Areopagus attributed to Paul (Acts 17:22–31). In this speech the apostle seeks common ground with his Athenian listeners, who, he says, worship God as unknown. But he also shows that God has issued a universal call to repentance in the face of coming judgment. Here he seems to be appealing partly to a sense of sin in his audience, based upon their failure to keep the universal laws of God.

Romans

One of the most important factors in the understanding of Pauline thought which has been brought out in recent scholarship, is the Adam–Christ motif.[4] This has implications connected with the universality of the redemption which Christ brings. It also inevitably has implications about the relationship which all men have to their Creator and therefore to the ordinances of creation. In the Epistle to the Romans it is possible to discern the influence of this thought at a number of places where it is not made explicit in the way that it is in chapter 5. E. Käsemann has suggested that this theme underlies chapter 7.[5] Romans 7:7b–12 deals with the temptation and the fall of Adam. The command to him not to eat of the tree of the knowledge of good and evil could be called a command not to covet, and in that sense it was a *nomos* which summed up the substance of the later, written *nomos*. Romans 7:13–24 represents the state of man after Adam's transgression. If this is correct, we see how Paul conceived of the universal nature of law. If the first three chapters of Genesis also underlie the first three chapters of Romans, this universal element will be further strengthened.

In Romans 1:18–32 the Gentiles in particular are condemned for their ungodliness and wickedness, and their suppression of the truth. If the pattern of creation in Genesis 1 and 2 showed man to be related as it were upwards to God, downwards to the rest of the created order and on the same level to his fellows, particularly the opposite sex, this passage demonstrates how all these relationships have gone wrong. Men worship the creature rather than the Creator and all their human relationships, especially the sexual ones, have been perverted. It is quite clearly stated that God has revealed to them certain basic facts about his own nature and the sort of moral response which that requires in men.

After rounding upon those who are critical of others, because they do the same things themselves (2:1–11), Paul then comes on to the question of the Gentiles and the law. He shows that sinners without the law are under the same condemnation as sinners under the law. But in verses 14 to 16 he refers to Gentiles doing what the law requires. As the interpretation of these verses has been disputed it will be appropriate to examine some representative views of their meaning.

Among recent commentators there appear to be three main views concerning the meaning of verses 14ff. Dodd takes what might be called the normal 'natural law' view. He asserts that, 'Pagans have in "natural religion" both a knowledge of God through His work in creation, and also a knowledge of the eternal principles of right and wrong, a law written on their hearts . . .' He finds that this is similar to the views of the Greek moralists, Plutarch and Aristotle, and the Stoics. He draws the parallel: for the Stoic the law of nature, for the Jew the law of Moses, for the Christian the law of Christ. 'For Paul the Mosaic Law is the most complete revelation of the will of God there is in terms of precepts and prohibitions; but the "law of nature" is not a different law, but only a less precise and complete revelation of the same eternal law of right and wrong. Thus the pagan's obedience or disobedience to the law of nature is on all fours with the Jew's obedience or disobedience to the Law of Moses.'[6] It seems that Dodd, while rightly stressing the unity of the divine law, is suggesting wrongly that it may be possible to live by the light of 'natural law' in a way that is generally pleasing to God, and is therefore an adequate, though inferior, substitute for the law of Moses and even for the law of Christ.

Barth,[7] in his shorter commentary, bases his interpretation on the fact that the reference to the requirements of the law being 'written on their hearts' is an allusion to Jeremiah 31:33 and Ezekiel 11:19 and 36:26. He compares this with Romans 2:26f., which refers to those who are circumcised without circumcision, and concludes that they must be Gentile Christians. There is, after all, no moral law of nature, and Paul has shown in 1:19-32 what the Gentiles are and what they do. It seems that Barth the theologian has got the better of Barth the exegete, and it is highly unlikely that in this context the verses could be interpreted in this way.[8]

Most helpful is the view of Nygren,[9] who seems to have the general support of Bruce and Barrett.[10] He asserts that the passage has nothing to do with *lex naturae*. When Paul talks about their doing what the law requires, he is referring to particular instances when they happen to act in this way, rather than producing a general theory about the heathen. 'God has not written "the law" on the hearts of the Gentiles, in the sense that they have by nature a universal principle to which to subject life and from which to draw conclusions as to how they ought to live. He has written "the works of the law" in their hearts, so that, if they do otherwise in the concrete situation, they are aware that they have done evil.' There are, he says, three witnesses: the act, showing that what the law requires is written in the heart; conscience; and accusing or excusing thoughts. These show that the Gentile is without excuse when he does evil. 'They are a law to themselves'—their good deeds are made, in the doing of them, into the law which condemns themselves. 'In the last analysis, whatever can be said positively about Jew and Gentile turns into something negative. About the Jew, the position is that he knows the law; but that very fact becomes the basis of his condemnation. About the Gentile, the position is that he is a law to himself; but for that very reason he is without excuse before God, since he is also a sinner.'

There are basically then, these three views: that the Gentile may to some extent keep the natural law; that there is no such thing as natural law, and the Gentile Christian is here being referred to; and that the fact that the Gentile sometimes does keep the law serves to act as a condemnation of him for not always doing so. The context of the chapter suggests strongly that the last view is the right one. Paul is leading up to 3:19f., where he shows that the whole world must be held accountable to God. It is only against the background of the universal condemnation of Jew and Gentile alike that he can reveal the wonder of the gospel, which brings new life to all who believe.

Conclusion

It seems that the law of God is one, and has universal significance. It calls for perfect relationship between man and God, between man and his fellows, and between man and the creation. This is the picture presented by Genesis 1 and 2. Genesis 3 shows how these relationships were all disrupted. The Mosaic law was essentially a bringing into focus of the demands of God, and giving them a particular expression in the life of those who by election had become his people. Jesus interpreted the Torah as being the living out perfectly of the relationship to God and fellow men, in the perfect attitude of love(Mk. 12:28–31). The law of Christ was a fulfilment (in the sense of giving the full meaning to it) of the Mosaic law, extending it from the part to the whole, and from the act to the motive. It was also a fulfilment of God's purpose for all men in creation. (The temptation story in Matthew 4:1–11 and Luke 4:1–13 can be seen as a reversal not only of Israel's sin but of Adam's.)

If this is a correct understanding of the position, let us turn back to Romans again. In 1:18–32 it seems that the condemnation of the Gentiles is based on their failure to live as they were created, that is in the perfect relationship to God, man and the creation, outlined in Genesis 1 and 2. The Jews are condemned on the same basis, though they are more easily shown to have sinned because they have had the law of God revealed to them through Moses, and the form in which it is cast makes their offences clear. But 'all have sinned and fall short of the glory of God' (3:23). In its context this must surely mean that they all fall short of man as he was created and as he was meant to be—the image and glory of God (1 Cor. 11:7; *cf.* Gn. 1:27). The non-Christian is therefore to submit to the one law of God, the Creator and moral Governor of the world. His failure to do so is a failure to attain true humanity. This one law has been perfectly obeyed only by Christ, the new Adam, and it is only through him that there is salvation. Only in the new covenant which he has made, and in the power of his Spirit, can men begin truly to keep the law which has claims upon them all (Rom. 8; *cf.* Gal. 6:2).

NOTES

1. See John Murray, *Principles of Conduct* (Inter-Varsity Press, 1957), pp. 27–44.
2. See Leon Morris, *The Biblical Doctrine of Judgment* (Inter-Varsity Press, 1960), p. 72.
3. C. H. Dodd, 'Natural Law in the Bible', *Theology Reprint* 17, 1946, p. 7. See also Part 1, chapter 3 of this book.
4. C. K. Barrett, *From First Adam to Last: A Study in Pauline Theology* (A. and C. Black, 1962); R. Scroggs, *The Last Adam* (Blackwell, 1966).
5. E. Käsemann in a lecture given in the University of Durham, 15th May, 1972.
6. C. H. Dodd, *The Epistle of Paul to the Romans* (Fontana, 1959), pp. 61f.
7. K. Barth, *A Shorter Commentary on Romans* (SCM Press, 1959), pp. 35–37.
8. See also C. E. B. Cranfield, *The Epistle to the Romans* (*International Critical Commentary*, T. and T. Clark, 1975), pp. 155–163.
9. A. Nygren, *Commentary on Romans* (SCM Press, 1952), pp. 124–130.
10. F. F. Bruce, *The Epistle of Paul to the Romans* (Inter-Varsity Press, 1963), pp. 90f.; C. K. Barrett, *The Epistle to the Romans* (A. and C. Black, 1962), pp. 48ff.

Part 2

Christian Moral Reasoning

1

The nature of Christian morality

Oliver Barclay

To many people Christian ethics seem to be an arbitrary set of rules imposed by a remote God for no very good reason. What has been written in the first part of the book makes it plain that that is not the biblical view of the matter. The law was, for instance, always given for certain reasons and towards certain goals (see chapter 1). But we now want to ask what kind of a thing Christian morals are when viewed from 'outside'. Are they arbitrary? Are they essentially a rational or empirical system? What do they profess to be? The Christian gets his ethics primarily from the Bible. He does not claim to have thought it all out from first principles alone. If he did, he would have to admit that before he started on that process he had a fairly full idea of where he wanted to go. Does this mean that, basically, Christian ethics are simply a systematization of largely unrelated biblical texts? Are they purely the household rules of the church?

It is popular today to describe Christian ethics as 'alien' to the non-Christian. To many writers it seems that Christian ethics are unrelated to reality—a set of norms imposed on the Christian by virtue of his obedience to Christ, and for no other reason than that God says so. 'Theirs not to reason why; theirs but to do and die' is presumed to be the responsibility of the believer. But for that very reason the unbeliever has no obligation whatsoever to follow Christian standards, and it is thought that the believer ought to accept this situation and say that he does not expect the non-Christian to pay any attention to Christian ethics. In that view, the non-Christian has to build up an entirely independent ethical system if he admits that any such thing is possible.

The traditional answer to this view of Christian ethics has been in terms of a doctrine of 'natural law'. This is, unfortunately, an ambiguous term, but basically the 'natural law' approach argues that Christian ethics are firstly, 'natural' to man (or correspond to man's true nature), and secondly, can be shown to be so by a process of natural reason, that is, unaided by revelation. The concept of what is 'natural' (or what is a 'natural law') is, we believe, a bad basis for the discussion and is particularly confusing today. We propose to tackle the problem another way, though what we say will overlap to a considerable extent with what some of the 'natural law' enthusiasts are saying. We have to ask ourselves how far we should claim that Christian morals are rationally justifiable and should, for that reason, be observed by all men, whether Christian or non-Christian. To cut a long argument short, we are not going to maintain that, *because* they can be shown by reasoning to be correct, Christian morals are for all men. We are nevertheless claiming, on another basis, that Christian morals are for all men. In addition we are saying that, if our knowledge of the world and of human nature were complete, which it is not, we should be able to provide a rational justification for Christian morals.

The rational status of Christian morals

The whole 'natural law' theory is in disrepute today largely because, rightly or wrongly, it is thought to depend essentially on a rationalistic method. It is thought that the 'natural law' theorists are seeking first to establish certain self-evident truths on a purely rationalistic basis, and then to develop their whole ethical system from these truths by deductive thinking. It is felt that this is no longer possible because there is so little today that will be generally accepted as self-evident. We want to approach the question in a different and, we believe, a more biblically based manner, and to place the whole argument in a different context.

There are broadly speaking three different approaches to a justification of the Christian faith. The first is the deductive approach, whereby the Christian position is argued towards from certain basic assumptions, which are either self-evident truths or which in some other way provide an agreed starting-point for discussion. The second is inductive, in which, starting with the whole range of human experience and knowledge, general principles are induced from the facts. The third is conceptual. By this we mean the approach which first explains the Christian position as one frankly arrived at from divine revelation, and then goes on to argue that this framework is uniquely convincing as an explanation of the phenomena of life, both intellectual and experimental.

These three approaches are, of course, not mutually exclusive. It is, for instance, almost impossible to think in an exclusively deductive or inductive manner. But historically the 'natural law' approach has been associated most with the deductive tradition and that seems to be the fundamental reason why it is no longer so convincing today when the necessary assumptions are in doubt. Humanist ethics would claim to follow a largely inductive approach, and we would here wish to argue more in terms of a conceptual approach than any other.

The best analogy is found in the methods of those natural sciences which have not become almost pure mathematics. In science of course the raw data is provided by sense experience. Advances have sometimes come by sheer induction (that is, working out generalizations from a collection of facts), sometimes they have come by deduction, or a mixture of induction and deduction. But the big advances have frequently come when someone has suddenly (and sometimes without a clear, logical basis) produced a fresh hypothesis which has far greater explanatory value than any that went before; many more bits of information are related and given a significance by it. Kekule's hypothesis that the benzene molecule is basically a ring of six carbon atoms was a brilliant idea (or intuition, or piece of luck) and is a good example. It fits the facts superbly, but it was not arrived at in the first place by logical argument. He visualized six snakes in a ring each chasing the tail of the next one. Darwin's idea of the origin of species by natural selection was another such hypothesis which, because it seemed to co-ordinate and 'explain' so much otherwise unrelated knowledge, had a rapid success in scientific circles and beyond. Often such hypotheses cannot be proved to be true by any deductive argument, but they are widely accepted because they fit so many of the facts.

Medical diagnosis provides another example. Some diagnosis can be broken down into detail and solved by computer, but the doctor with a gift for diagnosis is often one who sees a whole 'Gestalt' and has the art of distinguishing one 'picture' of ill health from another. The process of seeing a picture may lead to an altogether new idea, as in the discovery of penicillin. Certain familiar observations were seen as possibly expressing a new principle of great therapeutic value.

We are not suggesting that the Christian faith is just a sort of philosophical or scientific hypothesis. What we are saying is that, from the point of view of a purely logical method, the conviction that Christian doctrine or Christian ethics are true, comes more by realizing the overwhelmingly convincing nature of the Christian position as it fits and explains and co-ordinates experience, than by building up a system in a mathematical or traditional, deductive, philosophical way. On the other hand the concepts and the scheme of Christian thought are not developed inductively or by guess-work or by intuition, but are given to us in the Bible 'ready-made'. Our task is to show how convincingly they fit. This is not proof in the traditional, philosophical sense but it is often more compelling than such proof. The given biblical framework fits and explains reality. To the unbeliever it opens a new world of reality and gives new tools for handling life.

The man who comes to accept the Christian position will very often say that he now 'sees it'. This phrase is significant. He is very unlikely to say that he has been argued into it or had it proved to him. The Christian himself does not start from scratch in a rationalist tradition, neither is he following a basically empirical approach to the experiences of mankind. The honest truth is that his views on ethics, as on other aspects of the Christian faith, are framed by the biblical revelation, and that he seeks rational justification and elucidation *afterwards*.

For many purposes, therefore, it is best to follow the argument in the way in which it is built up in the Christian's experience. He is first confronted with a whole understanding of the world and human life as expressed by the teaching of Jesus and his disciples. A part of this is an approach to ethics and certain fixed points of right and wrong. The Christian then has a duty to try to show at least that the framework is by far the best available, and that the fixed points, which are a consequence of that framework, make excellent sense. But when he has done his best his argument will often be in the form: 'The framework of Christian ethics fits the thinking and experience of man as nothing else does. It therefore has a uniquely convincing explanatory value.' At least that is how it is best presented to the non-Christian. Quite often we can also show that, in its details, it is the best for mankind or that it has better rational justification than the alternatives. This gives confidence that it can be trusted at those points where no full justification is available, either rationally or in other ways, at least in our present state of knowledge. Apart from anything else, moral issues are not often so tidy as to allow neat demonstration.

Creation ethics

The Christian approach we want to make is in terms of what may be called *creation* ethics as opposed to *natural* law. Natural law has to start with experience—what is—and to try to get from there to what ought to be. This almost always commits the 'naturalistic fallacy' (*i.e.*, it is; therefore it ought to be). Creation ethics start with God and his will for living in his creation. Whatever its weaknesses it need not fall into that same error. Natural law starts with the world and tries to work to moral imperatives. Creation ethics start with God and his revelation and, looking at the world as his creation, works towards moral imperatives that are both divine commands and also good sense.

It is sometimes debated whether the good is good because God wants it or alternatively God wants it because, in some absolute sense, it is good. If the word 'absolute' were removed we would answer that it is not an either–or but a both–and. God's will at the same time creates and defines the good (for he alone is the measure of good) and also, because he is Creator and providential Ruler of his world, he commands only what is good in the sense that it corresponds both to man's God-given moral sense and to the good (benefit) of mankind. Only if God were not who he is, could we set the one against the other by making the good some absolute (uncreated?) principle to which God has to conform because he is good. We discern to some extent what is good 'by nature' because a good God made us like that. The same could be said about truth and beauty, but that does not exalt any of these into abstract principles independent of the Creator, even though we may discern them in a way that we think is our own independent vision.

A vital part of the intellectual framework of the Christian is the belief that this is a created world. God, the infinite, all-wise and all-loving God created it, set man within it and has now given to men outlines of ethical principles and a few fixed points which give teeth to these principles. The Bible often stresses that Christian ethics are for our good. This was true of the Old Testament law[1] and it is equally true of New Testament teaching (see below). But one of the main reasons for this is that the God who commands is also our Creator. He knows exactly how human nature works best. It is his world and he cares how it is used.[2] Because he loves us and is a holy God he commands only what is good. But it is good not merely in an abstract, moral sense, it is good also in the sense that all God's gifts and our enjoyment of the creation are good. That is how he made the world to work; that is his creation at its best. To take only one example (Dt. 5:29): 'Oh that they had such a mind as this always, to fear me and to keep all my commandments, that it might go well with them and with their children for ever!' Christian ethics are given 'that it may be well with us' and we maintain that, by and large, it can be shown that adherence to Christian ethics will have that result.

This of course does not imply any one-to-one relationship between doing right and human benefits. We are to love in a self-sacrificing way whatever the consequences may be. Particular acts of virtue do not always pay off. I may be drowned when I try to rescue a child being washed out to sea. I may be maimed for life trying to help an old lady attacked by thugs. The Christian contention is, however, that the observance of what is good is in the long run, and in the community as a whole, for our own good. A society in which no-one goes to rescue a drowning man will be the worse for it. There is this utilitarian side to creation ethics, and the appeal of secular utilitarianism is due in part to the fact that it has emphasized this undoubted truth, though it has tried to make too much of it.

The utilitarian ideal, the 'greatest good of the greatest number', is, so long as it does not overlook the individual, a Christian concern also, and Christian ethics, if they are truly creation ethics, will serve that end in society as a whole. We cannot, however, start at the other end with the greatest good of society as our aim, without either assuming too much or distorting the whole picture. We need to know first, for instance, what is the greatest *good*. The Christian perspective is also distinctly different, in that for the individual there is included the eternal dimension. Like the man who cheerfully deprives himself now for the sake of passing an examination and what lies beyond, the Christian knows that his own personal good is not just in terms of this life. What matters to him and, much more important, what matters to God, has other dimensions that cannot be exhausted in terms of the present, this-worldly, good of society. But that fact is too often used to escape the issue. If Christian ethics are creation ethics *they will work best.* They must be the best for society in this life also. That is one of the major reasons why God gave them. He wants us to enjoy his gifts in the best ways (1 Tim. 6:17). His service *is* perfect freedom (Gal. 5:13). The Christian way brings love, joy (not just happiness) and peace (Gal. 5:22). Jesus brings life and life abundant (Jn. 10:10). We are enabled to live as near as possible to the way in which we function best (the way we were created to live) when we follow God's law.

If we apply this to sexual morality the issues are probably clearer. Certain people are claiming that marriage as an institution can be dispensed with. They say that there is no particular reason to play the game of sexual morality that way. It could be played any way so long as there is an agreed convention between those involved. There is nothing sacrosanct, they say, about mono-gamous or lifelong marriage. Some societies are polygamous, others like much of the West today follow a pattern of serial polygamy and polyandry (changing partners at intervals) and a few others pursue a more promiscuous pattern. What reasons could there be for following one pattern rather than another?

The Christian replies that, first of all, man is not infinitely plastic. Some things do violence to human nature as it is. Certain chemicals are poisonous and will kill or injure you; certain actions are poisonous too. We have a definite psychological and biological make-up as well as a definite chemical make-up. So far most people would agree. The Christian, however, goes on to say that man is not as plastic as some people think, and God, because he sees the limits and the ideals, has set us certain limits and ideals. Monogamous, lifelong marriage is a creation ideal. Man is so made that he works best like that. Jesus himself appeals behind the permissions of the Old Testament law of divorce to what was 'in the beginning' (Mt. 19) and says that God wants us to have, and therefore commands, what he created us to enjoy: lifelong partnership. The Christian, therefore, would argue that the biblical ideal is the best and will prove to be the best for men, because it is the ideal of creation—or as near to that ideal as man's sinfulness allows. He will expect this to be to a substantial extent demonstrable, but not necessarily capable of proof beyond doubt.

The point is well developed in terms of Patrick Nowell-Smith's illustration of the game of marbles.[3] Following some work of Piaget he notes that young children have strict rules for the game handed down from their elders. Any departure is heresy. When they get older, however, they invent new rules and new games. So long as they agree about the rules they can play it any way they like. All adherence to traditional rules in ethics, he says, is merely infantilism—an inability to try out new and better ways of playing the old game in changing circumstances.

To this we reply that, even in marbles, the structure of reality limits you—you can't play hockey or rugger with marbles and you can't play it in the middle of Oxford Circus. But ethical conduct is not really like marbles; it is vastly more complex, and there are many more hidden factors needing to be taken into consideration. God has been kind enough to give us certain basic rules (*e.g.* the Ten Commandments) which correspond to the way we are made. We would reply to Nowell-Smith that because we believe the moral law corresponds to creation, we believe it is always best, and to play the game (*e.g.* of sex) any other way is to court disaster in the long run even if it cannot yet be proved psychologically. Hence the 'law of the Lord' leads us not only to righteousness, but also to wisdom (Ps. 119:97–104 and Ps. 19:7–11): that is to say, to an understanding of how human nature and the world actually are and how life should be lived in relation to that.

Creation ordinances and structures

The idea of a creation base for ethics is associated with the concept of creation ordinances. It is important to see these also not as mere divine artefacts imposed upon an amorphous humanity. They are rather the divinely given structures which are a part of God's creation.

Thus marriage was part of the original creation. It is in itself a benefit because it creates relationships which are capable of so much good. In view of man's sinfulness it is more than ever necessary. Who could have thought of such an effective means of curbing human selfishness so that two selfish people actually live together in harmony for sixty years or more and give self-sacrificing service to one another and to maddeningly self-centred children? It is perhaps the most astonishing social achievement in the whole of creation. But it is not merely expedient, or in a general sense a 'good thing'; it is one part of the way in which man is made to function, and any departure from it is a second best and an injury to the created order. The result is that marriage has to be thought of not only as one possible, even the best, solution to the problems and the potential of sex; it is also part of the ideal structure of society. The Christian is bound to doubt very much whether it is possible ever to get away from it altogether, and to regard any attempt to do so as a very sad deprivation—like settling for accepting malaria or bilharzia as diseases endemic or extremely common in the population. There is a realizable ideal of better health than that!

In the same way the Christian cannot accept anarchist ideals. The 'powers that be' are a part of the providential order. The state may have a wide variety of forms within certain limits but the

Christian is asking what are the best forms and is not asking whether we can dispense with the state altogether.[4]

Ephesians 4:25–30 provides another example of a created structure. Here we are told that everyone is to 'speak the truth with his neighbour' (*i.e.* with non-Christian as well as Christian) and then two reasons are given. Firstly, because 'we are members one of another' (*i.e.* because of the social community to which we belong and its solidarity. If this phrase is taken only to apply to the Christian community it gives no reason for ceasing to lie to non-Christian neighbours. That is clearly not what he is intending). And secondly, because we are not to 'grieve the Holy Spirit of God'. Similarly we are to work and not steal because of (1) a social reason and (2) our relationship to God. Whether we like it or not we are in a society. To lie or to steal injures all social relationships. It is possible to have a society that does not respect truth but it is a sadly deprived community. God has made us 'members one of another' and intends us to respect that fact of creation and live accordingly.

For this reason we should not lie in order to try to accomplish good unless we absolutely have to: as we might for instance in a 'just' war. To lie in order to get Bibles into Russia is to work against the very kind of mutual trust and respect which is necessary if our talk about biblical 'truth' is to be credible. We must beware lest we destroy or weaken *the structures* of society, because we need to use them to be God's witnesses; and they are in themselves positively good things for the community. If we believe Communism to be wrong we must show that we are not anti-social (as lying is) and that we do not lie when we offer the truth of the Bible. The duty to spread the truth does not overrule creation-based responsibilities but has to be worked out within that creation framework (see also 1 Tim. 5:8 and Mt. 15:5–6).

In the same way a number of other basic commandments are related to the way we are made: 'The sabbath was made for man . . .' *i.e.* related to his actual needs. 1 Corinthians 6 implies that fornication is an insult and injury to the personality ('sin against his own body' where body means the person). Murder is forbidden and amongst other, greater reasons is: 'Whoever sheds the blood of man, by man shall his blood be shed' (Gn. 9:6), which seems to involve the fact that violence begets violence (*e.g.* 'all who take the sword will perish by the sword' Mt. 26:52).

Basic values

We have asserted that to break these moral commandments is to offend against a created order, and the points we have mentioned are to a considerable extent open to observation. A school, a family or a wider community in which you cannot rely on people speaking the truth is, as we all know, impoverished. At best, it is extremely inconvenient and destroys good personal relationships as well as wasting a lot of time and effort. Nevertheless it is not always possible to show so convincingly the positive value of Christian morality. In the area of sex ethics, for instance, people in the West have not lived long enough with the alternatives to a Christian view to see as clearly as Christians believe they will in time, how alarmingly inferior the modern, secular alternatives are. But the truth begins to emerge increasingly clearly.

We are not therefore claiming that the Christian case can be proved in a knock-down manner. What we are saying is that, on examination, Christian morals are seen to be extraordinarily fitting to the way things really are. Far from being alien, or arbitrary, they are exactly fitted to the creation as we find it. In this sense they correspond to what is truly natural—not necessarily to what men like to do or find it 'natural' to do. This explains why many aspects of Christian ethics are also held by other religions and philosophies—they are after all a result of a right understanding of human society and can be seen to be so to a considerable extent by any wise man. Any rational reflection on man and society produces some of the same 'obvious' points: there must be a basic morality; it must include things like justice, truth and respect for life.

The Christian can *recommend* these things without reference to revelation, but he can go much further on the basis of revelation. He knows that they are *commanded* but he can also relate them all in terms of an understanding of the world and of man as he is and is intended to be and to live. The Christian has *insight* into reality that should enable him to apply the commands properly. The commands have a different and far richer aspect when they are known to be 'wise' and not merely expedient, *i.e.* to embody true insight and to be set in a context of which that insight is a part.

But there is a further possibility of fundamental criticism of the Christian position. The advantages of the creation ideal will not be convincing if there is real disagreement as to what counts as an advantage. To take a crude example, if you do not value the status of women or the rich partnership of a lifelong marriage then you will not value two of the greatest advantages of monogamy. It is at this level of a whole scale of values that the differences between the Christian and the non-Christian may in fact appear. The Christian has therefore both to justify his scale of what is valuable in society and then to show that biblical ethics are the best way to attain them. The non-Christian could attack at either level. On the question of basic values there is, however, often far more agreement than one might expect. There are certain basic values which almost everyone respects if they are forced to think about them. It is almost impossible, for instance, to justify regarding women—or children —as less important to society than adult men. They are different, of course, but once you accept that equality you have one rough sort of measuring rod for what kind of social morality works best.

Christian morals and the Fall

It could be argued that the Fall (or equally the present sinfulness of man) has so messed things up that the ideal is now unrealistic. The ideal, it is argued, now has little significance and may have to be abandoned because of 'your hardness of heart', as Moses did in the matter of divorce (Mt. 19:8, 9). But our Lord makes it plain in that very context that God's ideal does stand firm: 'from the beginning it was not so'; *i.e.* the *creation* ideal is still the ideal to which we should seek to adhere, even if public legislation (the law of Moses) no longer enforces the ideal.

Sin in the world and in human nature has chiefly the effect that we have to have an order of priority of moral values because the ideal cannot always be reached. We are sometimes faced with a decision as to what is the *lesser evil* of the choices now left open to us. One weakness of legalism is its failure to provide any priorities. Christian ethics, however, do provide just that. When asked what is the *greatest* commandment Jesus had no difficulty in giving a straight answer for the first two priorities.

Sin and the indirect effects of sin do not really alter the ideal fundamentally. They make it much more complex and much more difficult to get anywhere near the ideal. They make it necessary for us to introduce certain functions that would otherwise have been unnecessary, so that the state, for instance (which would have been necessary in any case), cannot concentrate exclusively on its positive tasks but has to spend a great deal of its time in restraining and punishing evil. But when all these and other effects of sin have been mentioned, the creation ideal is still the ideal for the whole of God's creation. We still want to get as close to it as we possibly can and Christian morals are the way to do just that. Complex problems arise. No-one should suggest that it is all easy. But we should know what we are aiming for and have confidence that following the revealed will of God is the best way of attaining it. This is not altered by the eschatological ideal. We are here talking about the present world where states, marriage, families, sabbath, *etc.,* are a God-given way of life in a way that they will cease to be in heaven.

It is of course true that from another point of view the effects of the Fall are dramatically matched and overcome by the gospel and the work of the Holy Spirit. If the discussion so far might give the impression that we did not think the Fall a catastrophic disorientation of life, and the gospel a more than adequate and altogether unexpected answer to the devices of the devil, that would be because we are not here discussing the whole outworking of Christian life, but are simply discussing what is the nature of morality and how the ideals and structure of Christian ethics are affected by the Fall and the gospel. In these respects we have suggested that the change is not revolutionary, but see the further section on pages 144–149.

Christian morals for all men

We would claim, then, that the basic creation ethics are for *all* men.

That is to say first of all that they are for the good of all men. The Christian, when he tries to show that this is so, has usually to abandon arguing from the revealed basis and to show, as far as he can, that their outworking in society supports the claim that they have this creation basis and that they do work out better than any other. As we have said this can only be done up to a point but such demonstration goes a lot further than some people think.

We have also a right to argue that Christian ethics are to a considerable extent a package deal. They are a consistent and inter-related whole. If they can be shown to be extremely good sense in many areas it can be argued that they should be accepted by non-Christians in other areas also, unless and until there have been found very powerful reasons against. Certainly it can be argued that it is not *un*reasonable to accept them as a whole even if one is uncertain about their divine origin. This of course has been, and still is, the position of millions of people. They are not Christians in any personal sense, but they firmly believe in Christian ethics, and believe in them as a whole. This they do in spite of the fact that they know that at some points rational justification is very thin, and despite acknowledging that they don't keep all the standards themselves. They at least wish that everyone else did, and accept the package as an ideal—or nearly all of it.

The situation of the Christian is like that of an intelligent child in relation to his (ideal) parents. Certain things are commanded or forbidden. A certain amount of sleep (or at least time in bed) is commanded; dangerous drugs are forbidden. Occasionally the parent will give reasons: 'If you don't go to bed soon you will be so bad-tempered', or 'you will find your work difficult'. But at other times the command will appear merely arbitrary; no reason has been given, none is obvious, but the children who have confidence in their parents will know that there is good sense behind it, even if they cannot altogether understand the reasons. The parents have a wider experience and, at least up to a certain age, can be trusted.

We have been speaking of the Christian. The non-Christian may reply that he doesn't like God's ideal plans for us. Whatever his attitude may be to his own parents, he is not willing to trust other people's parents! The whole of Christian ethics, he may argue, is only rational *within* a Christian framework. In the same way Marxist ethics are rational within a Marxist framework. But that is only partly true. Ethical systems overlap to a surprising extent.

The Christian contention is that in several ways you come up against objective factors which force you into a pattern which has basically similar features almost wherever you start philosophically. The non-Christian, on the whole, realizes the importance of truth and honesty in society. Even Communist societies have become quite 'puritan' about such things and are often more strict on sex ethics than so-called Christian societies. Their reasons are utilitarian, but even the seven-day week, which seems exceedingly arbitrary, has not been successfully improved upon in spite of experiments after the French Revolution and later.

By and large the basic set of principles which the specific, Christian commands protect, is recognized as in practice the best, though only after other policies deduced from their philosophy have been tried and found wanting. The attack on the family as too 'bourgeois' for instance was soon given up in Russia. Even when people are advocating the abandonment of marital fidelity it is often because they say that occasional immorality or pre-marital 'experience' will make marriage more stable. In this they are wrong, but their ideal is not so contrary to the Christian ideal after all. This is part of what Paul refers to in Romans 2 (see Part 2, chapter 6).

Nevertheless it must be admitted that a situation could arise in which most of what is valued by the Christian was deplored by the non-Christian and vice versa. Theoretically an outlook could arise that applauded murder, dishonesty, untruthfulness, indiscriminate sex, the dissolution of family life, and despised work and concern for others. In practice we believe it would be self-destroying. Life is not infinitely plastic. As an aberrant minority group you can practise such views within a wider community that lives by the moral law, but you cannot put these views into practice as a majority or life becomes unbearable. As soon as it is tried even up to a point, people are driven back to the old fixed points, as has happened to a remarkable extent in Russia. If you did not care about the position of women, monogamy would be less obviously important, but very few people would seriously propose a return to polygamy once they have seen monogamy working well in practice.

Even to the non-Christian, therefore, we believe that we can show that Christian ethics are not arbitrary but are related to the way we are made. We will need to work hard, however, to demonstrate that the specifics of Christian ethics are good and health-giving commands which all men, whether Christian or non-Christian, will benefit from observing, and which will enhance any society in which they are truly practised.

There is another very important point. The non-Christian usually accepts many more positive, ethical standards than his theories would justify. His morality is better than his theories. This is also exactly what the New Testament teaches us to expect. The fact is that man is not a morally neutral being whose mind waits to have morality imposed upon it by rational argument. As Pascal puts it in another context: 'The heart has its reasons that the reason knows nothing of.' When the Christian appeals to the non-Christian, puts before him the Christian ethic and invites him to admit that it is incomparably the best for all men, he does not find that he has to start from nothing and build up by pure reasoning. There is in the other man's consciousness an awareness of moral truth, and moral truth which already corresponds in some degree to the Christian revelation. If it doesn't already correspond in any articulate sense, Christian ethics are often quickly acceptable to a surprising degree once they are properly understood. They are seen to be creation ethics, exactly tailor-made for man as he is.[5]

At the beginning of this section we said that creation ethics are for all men in the sense that they are for the good of all men. We can now go further than that. They are for the good of all, but they are also the outline of the ethics which claim to come from God for all men. The Ten Commandments express succinctly, though in largely negative form, the ethical rules that the Christian regards as basic, because they illustrate and define practically the basic ethical principles. The Ten Commandments did not just happen accidentally, or evolve. They were given by revelation as a package deal. It is true that they overlap with other ethical codes, but if what we have said about creation ethics is true, that is what one would expect. No-one could be 100% wrong in a serious ethical code, and the wiser they were, and shrewder in observing the ways and nature of men, the nearer they would come to the right conclusions.

Christian ethics, therefore, are for the good of all men and can be seen in considerable detail to be so. They are also part of a package deal of revealed ethics and finally, as we have argued, they are to a remarkable extent the same in detail as the ethics that even the nations without the Christian revelation acknowledge, this being particularly true of those people who have thought out an ethical system most carefully. The result is that a very large number of people, when they are faced by Christian ethics, have a realization of a moral obligation towards these standards. The influence of Christian ethics on Hindu thought is an example. This may not be very articulate or very profoundly rational. It needs to be constantly reinforced because conscience can be de-sensitized, but even in the most secularized community there is usually far more moral awareness, and therefore often more moral nobility, than the ethical theories in circulation would allow. Even if it has had no Christian or other explicit moral teaching, we are not dealing with a population that starts from scratch, and the moral awareness that we find and seek to evoke is 'on our side', as it were, even if it is very little honoured in practice. The alternative theories are often too bad to be true from the standpoint of the remains of moral sense which God has left even in the most morally depraved of men.

Finally, the Christian is bound to declare that Christian morals are for all men just because all men are made by God in his image and Christian morals are his prescription and his loving command for all his intelligent creatures.[6]

Fixed points and principles

It is sometimes objected that Christian ethics in the form of mere commands (or certain fixed points) come to us in a far too complex flux of difficult decisions and relationships. Life, it is said, is just too complicated to be dealt with like that. The Ten Commandments are really just a few rules and Christians have tended to follow their pattern and elaborate their morality in sets of rules, while they lose sight of the principles.

This, however, is not to be fair to the biblical view, as earlier chapters have shown. God has given us some rules (*e.g.* 'Thou shalt not commit adultery') but a reading of both Old Testament and New Testament soon shows that these are specific applications of wider principles. If it were left at the level of principles many of us would find it hard to apply at all. If it were left at the level of rules we should easily fall into legalism. Jesus' treatment of the matter in the Sermon on the Mount is, because of who he was, the last word on the subject. He quotes a number of rules, some from the Old Testament and some from the 'traditions'. All had been treated legalistically (see Mt. 5:21-48): swearing had been divided into binding and not so binding oaths; angry words had been divided into punishable and not punishable; a rule for the law courts (an eye for an eye) had been turned into a practice of limited personal revenge, *etc.* Our Lord cuts through this accumulation of tradition and says that all our words should be totally reliable, all our attitudes should be humble and loving, *etc.* He takes us back to a principle of truth and a principle of love. On adultery he takes us back to purity in sex relations. He does not deny the rules; he says we must do far better than that. 'Unless your righteousness exceeds that of the scribes and Pharisees, you will never enter the kingdom of heaven' (Mt. 5:20; see also Part 2, chapter 3).

The rules are fixed points which give teeth to the principles. A principle of truth does not always mean much unless we express it in one or two rules. Then we see what it means in other areas. But the Sermon on the Mount forbids our ever treating the rules as if they exhausted the principle. We need both, and the Bible gives us both and shows us how to relate them. When looked at carefully the number of New Testament rules is very small and we run into grave danger when we multiply them far beyond the canon, though traditions have their value when they are accepted as traditions and not made of equal authority with biblical rules or principles.

Romans 13:8–10 provides another classical example of the relation between rules and principles:

'Owe no one anything, except to love one another; for he who loves his neighbour has fulfilled the law. The commandments, "You shall not commit adultery, You shall not kill, You shall not steal, You shall not covet," and any other commandment, are summed up in this sentence, "You shall love your neighbour as yourself." Love does no wrong to a neighbour; therefore love is the fulfilling of the law.'

Having the cake and eating it?

The Christian may give the impression of trying to have his cake and eat it. He is not in principle a utilitarian. He does not believe that Christian ethics have to be proved to be the best for society. Yet he believes that they *are* the best and can show enough evidence that that is true to use this as a reason for commending them for all men. The Christian, equally, is not an intuitionist. He does not believe that our moral intuitions are a final moral authority, but he claims that there is enough 'intuition' of true ethical principles and ideals for Christian ethics (which are creation ethics) to commend themselves intuitively to the majority of people to a large degree. Christian ethics correspond remarkably to intuitive ethics. Finally, the Christian is not a rationalist. He does not believe that Christian ethics depend on being capable of rationalistic proof, but he believes that if the matter is thought out rationally the result will correspond to an impressive degree with basic Christian ethics.

All this, the Christian claims, is because Christian ethics are the duties that are man's in view of his being a creature in God's world. Because man is fallen he does not *reliably* detect his moral responsibilities either rationally, intuitively or sociologically, but in all three ways he is left with enough to do more than hint at the validity of Christian ethics as being of universal application. The Christian accepts them as authoritative because they are revealed, and will seek to defend them rationally and sociologically even when at a particular point in history they come under fire as not obviously the best for men. He believes that if we knew enough we could show that they were the best and the most rational.

The Christian, however, escapes to some extent the criticisms that are rightly levelled at intuitionists, utilitarians and rationalists. His position does not depend on being able to prove his case in any one direction. He argues that, man being what he is, no fool-proof demonstration is possible. But he still holds that there is something in all three approaches and that together they add up to a powerful argument, which fully justifies the common man when he acknowledges an obligation to the major tenets of Christian ethics, even while the philosophers point out the weaknesses of each of the major approaches in turn.

Man himself is a most noble ruin; his ethical senses are in the same state. They are sufficiently ruined for no absolute proofs to be available but they retain sufficient of the basic structure for it to be possible to trace out convincingly the original plan and order of the building, and to glimpse something of its superb qualities.

This is particularly reinforced because the three main philosophical approaches mentioned do in fact converge to such a degree on *one* pattern of practical principles and rules and these coincide with at least the rudiments of Christian ethics. It seems that ethics are more than just a matter of culture and opinion. There are ethical truths which are part of the way in which things are made. They are part of the reality of life, of creation. We can't altogether escape them unless we throw out so much that we are reduced to almost complete scepticism. Even if philosophically there remains much debate, the Christian can with confidence ask all men to accept that the basic ethical duties are some of the 'facts of life' and should be personally accepted by all men as a result.

The metamorphosis of creation ethics

At first sight it looks as if it would be outrageous to talk about New Testament ethics as if they were just an elaboration of the themes of creation ethics. Creation ethics are far more than a legalistic system but it seems impossible to squeeze New Testament ethics altogether into the creation ethics mould. New Testament ethics are to creation ethics what the butterfly is to the caterpillar. There is an essential continuity. Its blood and genes are the same but its character and mode of operation look totally different. The promise which the caterpillar had, though rather obscurely, is realized in the adult butterfly. This is part of what the Bible means when it talks about the law being fulfilled in Christ. The metamorphosis, indeed, is of such a far-reaching kind that it is dangerous all the time to emphasize the 'law-fulfilment' theme, because it can suggest that we are merely expanding the law. The New Testament, apart from the Sermon on the Mount and Ephesians 4:22 – 6:9, usually starts at the other end with the demand that Christians should be like Christ. That seems at first sight to be an altogether different kind of ideal from fulfilling the law.

On further examination, however, it becomes clear that these two poles of biblical ethics—creation and likeness to Christ—are not so far apart or so different as they appear to be on the surface. Creation ethics in the Old Testament are crystallized out in terms of the law of Moses, and the moral law of the Old Testament could be described as an expression of creation ethics aimed to restrain evil and encourage good in all men within the very mixed community of Israel. But the very word creation takes us back to Genesis 1 and the creation of man in the image of God. Jesus, as has been pointed out, appealed to the creation ideal of Genesis 3, behind the permission of the law of Moses, when he was asked a question about divorce (Mt. 19). The biblical ideal has always been in both Old and New Testament to get as close as possible to that creation order—of man in God's image. The idea of the image of God is used very little in the Old Testament but it stands behind Old Testament ethics and is developed much more in the New Testament.

The Old Testament is more concerned with the ideal of the community of Israel as the covenanted people of God who are to be holy because God is holy. That community ideal is in the New Testament of course, applied to the church with many of the identical phrases carried over and applied in a fresh way. We are saved so that we shall be God's people as Israel was intended to be.[7] In the New Testament, however, there is presented to us a new ideal: the character of Christ, who is the fulfilment of the Old Testament ideal, both as the head of the body (*i.e.* in a corporate sense) and as the 'measure' (Eph. 4:13) of Christian maturity in a personal sense.[8] The Old Testament ideal lacks this personalization. Perhaps the Old Testament ideal is best expressed in terms of the man who loves and obeys God's law. He *loves* the law because it is the expression of God's character and his ideal for man, and because it has endless blessings in that it enables us to live a truly human (creation ideal) life.[9]

New Testament ethics go further, and they go further because the experience of new birth into eternal life, and the continued renewal of the Holy Spirit as well as an assured personal relationship with God, are now open to *every* ordinary, individual Christian. The result is repeatedly spoken of, not as conformity to law, but *renewal* into the likeness of Christ.[10] In 2 Corinthians 3:15 to 4:6, for instance, the Christian experience is contrasted with experience under the law. To us the beholding of the glory of the Lord in the face of Jesus Christ (4:6) results in our being changed into his likeness. Personal fellowship with God transforms us as the law never could.

The same passage in 2 Corinthians, however, goes on to emphasize (in 4:4) that Christ is 'the likeness of God'. This brings us back full circle to the idea of the image of God, in which man was first created. Jesus Christ is, after all, himself the true image of God in a sense vastly greater than Adam or any other man could be. In Colossians also the same theme appears. In Colossians 3:10 it is said that the Christian's new nature 'is being *renewed* in knowledge after the *image* of its creator'. That is the creation ethics theme plus the New Testament emphasis on spiritual new birth and renewal by the indwelling Holy Spirit. But if we ask how should we envisage the 'image', the same Epistle a little earlier has told us that Christ is the 'image of the invisible God'.

The concept of the creation original to which we ought to conform and to which creation ethics should lead us, is expressed in the New Testament, therefore, not in terms of the law but in terms of the person of Christ, who perfectly expresses the image of God. It is true that he perfectly obeyed and indeed fulfilled the law but he is more than an ideal of obedience to law. He is the ideal man, the perfect expression of the image of God, both in the sense that he perfectly and uniquely represents God in human terms and also that he is the one and only example of the perfected ideal of the original creation of man in the image of God (Gn. 1:26f.).

New Testament morality, therefore, holds out the ideal of man as restored (or rather being continually restored) into the likeness of the ideal which is expressed in Christ. This is a personal, warm, living ideal, not a dead, legal one. This contrast is often made in the New Testament. Love, and not mere obedience, is the life-blood of New Testament ethics. Love fulfils the law which by itself can be deadly.[11]

Pharisaic legalism, as our Lord made plain in the Sermon on the Mount, was a tragic restriction of morality to a few bare constituents of morality. He did not deny these constituents, but stressed that this had never been how morality was intended to be understood by those who belong to God. The moral ideal can never be adequately expressed by a mere set of rules and this the whole New Testament makes clear. *Christ is our ideal and likeness to Christ is our aim.*

Why then, we may ask, was the law elaborated to such a vast system of regulations as we have in the Old Testament? Paul answers this in 1 Timothy 1:9–11, where he says that the trouble is that people misuse the law:

'The law is not laid down for the just but for the lawless and disobedient, for the ungodly and sinners, for the unholy and profane, for murderers of fathers and murderers of mothers, for manslayers, immoral persons, sodomites, kidnappers, liars, perjurers and whatever else is contrary to sound doctrine, in accordance with the glorious gospel of the blessed God.'

(Note the implied references to several of the Ten Commandments.) That is to say, the creation ideal was elaborated in terms of law for

Law, morality and the Bible

those who are not obedient. The Christian, alas, may be in that category, and there are times when the plain 'Thou shalt not . . .' or the positive 'Thou shalt . . .' are exactly what is needed even for the Christian. Certainly the New Testament writers do not hesitate to give plain, crisp commands of this kind for the church. To the non-Christian, talk of likeness to God was (and still is today) neither very compelling, nor very intelligible. The same truth was set out for them in legal form which was both compelling and meaningful. But the true believers in the Old Testament always saw beyond it. They rejoiced in God's gifts of the law for themselves and for their society.[12] But their morality was one of personal relationship to God, and was far more subtle and personal than mere obedience to law. This is often expressed in the Psalms.

We are to 'put on the new nature, created after the likeness of God in true righteousness and holiness' (Eph. 4:24). That is one of the most concise summaries of the Christian ethical ideal. In the same way, in the Sermon on the Mount Jesus stresses that we must go far beyond a morality that stops at mere obedience to a few rules. Equally, he warns us of the damage of taking aspects of social law (an eye for an eye and a tooth for a tooth), and making them into a kind of personal code. Such rules, we are told in 1 Timothy, were enunciated for the *un*godly, not to enable the children of the household to feel self-satisfied.[13] The result is that Christian morality goes down to the level of our character as well as our habits; to love as well as action. It is therefore insufficient, though true as far as it goes, to speak of Christ as the supreme fulfilment of moral law. Christ is God incarnate and so he also shows us what the moral law looks like when it is *incarnate*; but that in itself shows that mere rules and regulations were intended to express a reality of a far greater kind, with all those dimensions of the image of God which cannot be adequately captured in terms of laws.

If, like the Pharisees, you start with law, then the next step is to see Jesus as the one who *fulfils* it. If, like the Greeks, you think of moral duties, then Paul leads us on to love as the *fulfilment* of all such codes. But that is not the whole story. We must not forget that fulfilment is not just a development or elaboration of rules. Fulfilment is a metamorphosis. Its goal is in a person, Jesus Christ, and as far as we are concerned, therefore, our ideal is a Christ*like* character and nature. But this is not unrelated to the creation image of God, which Jesus incarnates, and often, in practical terms, the general truth of likeness to Christ has to be broken down into the nitty-gritty realities of creation ethics, as Paul does in the more practical parts of his Epistles.

The relationship between these two—the ideal in the person of Christ, and the practical command—is worked out in Ephesians 4:22 onwards. Paul gives a marvellous picture of the Christian ethical ideal when he says 'created after the likeness of God in true righteousness and holiness'. But that is not a starting-point for a devotional treatise on the subtle characteristics of the spiritual man. It leads immediately into a very practical discourse in which each of the Ten Commandments is mentioned, at least by implication. It starts immediately with 'speak the truth' and goes on through anger, stealing, work, speech, forgiveness, immorality, idolatry, covetousness, drunkenness, marriage, to honouring of parents and employer–employee relationships. The work of salvation, as Paul remarks in Romans 8:4, is that the 'just requirement of the law might be fulfilled in us, who walk not according to flesh but according to the Spirit'.

NOTES

1. *E.g.* Dt. 5:29, 33; 6:2, 18, 24. It is perhaps significant that Israel was placed in an ecologically marginal environment. Departure from a right use of resources quickly brought disaster. Obeying God's law brought ecological stability, because God's law corresponds to the best use of resources. (See Part 1, chapters 1 and 2.)

2. See A. N. Triton, *Whose World?* (Inter-Varsity Press, 1970).

3. M. Knight (ed.), *A Humanist Anthology* (Barrie and Rockliff, 1961), pp. 182–188.

4. 1 Peter 2 is even clearer than Romans 13 because it is written under persecution. Bruce Kaye's view on Romans 13 (Part 1, chapter 5) cannot apply to 1 Peter 2.

5. See the section on legislation below, Part 2, chapter 6, and B. Mitchell, *Law, Morality and Religion in a Secular Society* (Oxford University Press, 1970).

6. Those who wish to make the kingdom of God the basis of ethics cannot show how to relate it to the non-Christian. The kingdom of God is an important biblical theme. In a Jewish context, especially in the Gospels, it is sometimes a synonym for the gospel because the Messiah is 'King'. It often has a powerful ethical connotation because we are to obey the King. In the Epistles, however, the theme is very rare indeed. It is often 'the kingdom of Christ' and its place is usually taken by the idea of the Lordship of Christ. Both the kingdom of God and the Lordship of Christ relate to the believer. The non-Christian is not in the kingdom and must be made to realize that fact, as Jesus stressed to Nicodemus.

Law, morality and the Bible

The ethical impact of the kingdom/Lordship of Christ theme, however, while it is very powerful, is, in the nature of the case, general. In the Epistles it does not come down to the particular. Creation ethics can be and are specific as well as general because they are related to specific needs and limitations of man (*e.g.* Eph. 4:25–29 and 1 Cor. 6 where the 'sin against the body' gives the specific part to the general argument). Creation ethics have a shape and can relate to the Ten Commandments in a way that kingdom ethics have difficulty in doing. The result is that, as G. E. Ladd points out in his very full treatment of the kingdom of God, *Jesus and the Kingdom* (SPCK, 1966), no-one has yet shown satisfactorily (without straying into an unbiblical view of the kingdom as including non-Christians) how kingdom ethics relate to non-Christians or to social ethics in a mixed society.

The kingdom ethics enthusiasts, of course, do not wish to deny the creation theme, and this paper does not intend to imply that the kingdom theme is totally irrelevant. There are also other doctrines that bear on the moral life of the Christian: for example, in Ephesians 5:21–29, the doctrine of Christ and the church. But creation ethics provide the basic theme that lies behind all the others in much the same way that the truth that God is Creator lies behind the truth that he is Saviour.

The creation approach therefore gives us many things that the other approaches do not. It shows us the fundamental nature of Christian ethics. It shows how and why to apply Christian ethics to the unbeliever and to society in general, and it gives biblical guidelines for its outworking in practical terms, since the New Testament works out many particular applications in these terms. See A. N. Triton, *Salt to the World* (Inter-Varsity Press, 1978), Appendix 1.

7. See for instance 1 Peter 1:14ff., and 1 Peter 2:9, 10; and the recurring theme 'they shall be my people and I will be their God', referred to, *e.g.,* in Tit. 2:14.

8. The Eph. 4:11–16 passage has a marvellous combination of personal and church ethics which shows that they must not be divorced, and that indeed their ideal and goal is the same: 'the measure of the stature of the fullness of Christ'. This cannot be limited, in the context, to a purely corporate meaning.

9. *E.g.* Ps. 119:14, 20, 24, 35, 40.

10. In Old Testament times some people clearly shared this experience. Psalm 51, for instance, shows a perfectly clear understanding that holiness is a matter of character and not only of deeds and that this is to be realized by God's work.

11. See for instance Rom. 13:8–10. In a list of Christian duties Paul repeats four of the Ten Commandments; but he prefaces them by saying that they are fulfilled by love.

12. See for instance Ezra's prayer in Ne. 9:13, where amongst all God's great mercies to Israel he includes, 'Thou didst come down upon Mount Sinai, and speak with them from heaven and give them right ordinances and true laws, good statutes and commandments. . . .'

13. See also Gal. 3:23 and 4:7, and the contrast between the morality of young children under rules and regulations (the law) and the morality of mature sons who are now heirs of the inheritance and call God 'Father'.

2
Situations and principles
James Packer[1]

The most obvious challenge to Christian morality today comes from a view of Christian morality itself which, if accepted, would sweep away most of the approach and conclusions for which this book contends. It is time for us to take a long hard look at it. 'Situation ethics' is its name.

'Situation ethics', 'situationism' as we shall call it, burst with a shower of sparks on the English-speaking Christian world in the 1960s and is clearly here to stay for some time yet. Its best-known expositor has been J. A. T. Robinson; its most incisive spokesman the American, Joseph Fletcher.[2] It has a good deal going for it. It offers itself as a seemingly simple method of solving complex problems about what to do. It claims to correct the legalism and remove the artificiality which have in the past disfigured much Christian thinking about conduct. It endorses the modern (and, we might add, ancient and Edenic) disinclination to treat any external rules as unbreakable. Its exponents have a lot to say about sex, which to most people is a very interesting subject, particularly when handled in a way that sounds permissive.[3] In its rhetoric, situationism seems to endorse the hunch which popular music and pulp writing so often express, that love will justify anything and that in seeing this we are both wiser and more humane than our fathers were.

Not surprisingly, therefore, situationism allures as common ways of stating Christian morality do not. Frequently today the old formulations are dismissed as a bad brew of Victorianism and Puritanism, two outlooks which we are urged to abhor as unholy and oppressive blends of narrow-mindedness, pomposity, prejudice and hypocrisy—all law and no love, and dull as ditchwater into the bargain. The moral pendulum has swung with a vengeance, so that creative freedom in structuring caring relationships is now 'in' while the conscientious rigour of law-keeping is 'out'.

It could at once be objected that since loving action is what the Decalogue and the law of Christ are all about, the antithesis is false, just as are the proffered descriptions of Victorianism and Puritanism. Granted; but since situationism sees loving as the only prescribed duty and denies that there are any other, more specific, divine laws to keep, we cannot leave the matter there. Situationist claims must be examined on their merits. As we saw, this viewpoint owes much of its attractiveness to its identifying with what Fletcher called 'the whole mind-set of the modern man, *our* mind-set';[4] an outlook which Paul Ramsey correctly if turgidly summed up as 'prejudice in favour of individualistic freedom, normlessness, traditionless contemporaneity, and modern technical reason'.[5] So, too, when J. A. T. Robinson calls for a recasting of Christian ethics, with Christian faith, on the ground that man today has 'come of age', he is appealing to our un-self-critical conceit in the same way that Fletcher does. No doubt, favour is gained this way. But the rights and wrongs of situationism cannot be settled at the murky level of popular prejudice, whether for or against. There are arguments to be weighed—complex and sophisticated arguments, as it turns out.

What is situationism ?

First, let us note that though 'situationism' is usually thought of as a term referring specifically to one view of Christian morality, it is actually an umbrella-word for all views which reject the idea that the way to decide what to do is always to apply rules, positive and negative, concerning types of actions (*e.g.* keep your promises, do not steal, do not rape, do not torture). The situationist does not regard such rules as *prescriptive, i.e.* as having absolute and universal authority, but as at best *illuminative,* in the sense of being relative, provisional and violable indicators of what behaviour may (though it may not) be right here and now. Thus, 'situationism' is a term of negative classification, clear only in what it excludes and covering many positive conceptions that are intrinsically different.

The word 'existentialism' is similar; it, too, is an umbrella-word for all views, Christian and non-Christian, which reject the idea that one can achieve authentic personal existence without total commitment, and it, too, in practice covers a wide range of outlooks. Now as a view about the way to determine what one should do, situationism can be part of an atheistic existentialist or humanist position no less than of a Christian one. The mark of existentialist situationism is its requirement that one should always act wholeheartedly, in conscious personal freedom (meaning by this, openness to variation from all one's actions hitherto). The mark of humanist situationism is its quest in all circumstances for the realization of personal values as it sees them. The mark of Christian situationism is its conviction that general moral rules applied to the matter in hand will not always lead you to what the command of God and the calculations of neighbourly love (which two things some identify and others distinguish) actually require.

The claim traditionally made for Christian morality is that love can be, and indeed has been, embodied in rules, so that in using the moral principles of Scripture prescriptively a Christian will always be expressing love, never frustrating it, and so will always be doing the will of God. Situationism diagnoses this claim as legalistic and declines to accept it, insisting that love itself requires one to go further and do more: namely, to pay fullest attention to the situation itself, which may be an exceptional set of circumstances requiring, for the fullest expression of love, an exceptional way of acting. Action which the rules would call wrong will yet be right if analysis shows it to be the most loving thing to do. For no types of action, as such, can be said to be immoral; only failures of love in particular situations can be called immoral or thought of as forbidden, inasmuch as the fullness of loving action is the whole of what God commands.[6]

How, then, should we decide what to do in a given situation? Here the ways part. The *rational* situationism of the Anglo-Saxon Anglicans Fletcher and Robinson offers us a method of calculation; the *existentialist* situationism of the big Bs of continental neo-orthodoxy—Barth, Bonhoeffer, Brunner, Bultmann—takes the line of attuning us for particular self-authenticating commands from God which will reach us via Scripture, though they will not be identical with, nor will they be simply applications of, moral principles stated in Scripture. Neither position (be it said) is intentionally lax or antinomian (that is, opposed to law); both think they achieve what the law in Scripture is really after; the differences between them, and between them both and Christian ethical stances which would not call themselves situationist, are theological. This chapter is most concerned with the former type of situationism, but we shall grasp it better by comparing it with the latter, and this will be our next step.

Pure situationism

Neo-orthodox situationism may be called 'pure' as distinct from 'principled'. Its main thesis is that as I face each situation, taking its measure and noting its complexities, God will speak, in some sense of that word, directly. The determining factor here is the dynamism or 'actualism' of the neo-orthodox conception of God: that is, the insistence that the Creator-God, who is transcendent, sovereign and free, is known to us and reveals his command to us only in the particularity of the present moment. So the generalized ethical injunctions of Scripture are understood not as formulae embodying the fullness of God's will for all time, but as so many indications of the lines along which, or within which, particular commands of God may be expected to come. God's revealed will never takes the form of a universally valid rule for us to apply to all relevant cases, but only of particular summonses. 'God's commanding can only be this individual, concrete and specific commanding,' says Karl Barth.[7] Formally, then, the Christian ethic is obeying God in a most direct way; and materially it is neighbour-love, in whatever mode God's self-authenticating command specifies here and now. Thus Brunner writes: 'Nothing is good save obedience to the command of God, just because it is obedience. No reasons of determination from content here come under consideration. The "form" of the will, obedience, is all. But to be obedient means: "love your neighbour!" '[8]

Bonhoeffer says this most starkly, forbidding us to ask 'What is the will of God for this particular case?' because the question embodies 'the casuistic misinterpretation of the concrete. The concrete is not achieved in this way . . . The will of God is always concrete, or else it is not the will of *God* . . . the will of God is not a principle . . . which has to be applied to "reality".'⁹ These negations sound startling; but the guidance that Bonhoeffer takes away with the one hand, by denying that God reveals principles, he effectively restores with the other, by his teaching on the 'mandates'—church, government, labour and culture, and marriage and the family, spheres of delegated divine authority which the Reformers also recognized. 'Mandate' (which term Bonhoeffer preferred to the more usual 'orders', because it denoted a God-given task) meant for him 'the conferment of divine authority (*i.e.* the right to command obedience as God's representative) on an earthly agent', and 'the formation of a definite earthly domain by the divine commandment';¹⁰ and the mandates themselves, conservatively conceived, define closely the limits within which God's concrete will is expressed and encountered. Barth and Brunner speak similarly. Barth also affirms that, while God's demand cannot be anticipated in abstraction, his constancy of character revealed in Christ means that like demands will be made in like situations: for Jesus Christ, who is the same yesterday, today and for ever, is 'the ground, content and form of God's command'.¹¹

In all this neo-orthodoxy is polemicizing against what Barth calls a 'theoretical casuistry' which assumes that the whole of God's command consists of a legacy of general principles left us in the Bible, to be applied by our own best wisdom. Their motive—a proper one—is a desire to display Christian obedience as direct response to God's present, personal address. But as anyone with a ripe doctrine of the Holy Spirit can and will make that point without denying that in what God says today he applies what he has said in Scripture once for all, so the 'pure' situationism to which these men resort seems to turn God's command, at least in its details, into an uncheckable private revelation every time.¹² Nor (to their credit!) do they sustain in practice the daunting notion which they profess. Thus, Bonhoeffer's concept of the command of God, which if it is not 'clear, definite and concrete to the last detail . . . is not God's command', receives a crippling qualification when he admits that God's will 'may lie deeply concealed beneath a great number of available possibilities', so that 'the whole apparatus of human powers must be set in motion when it is a matter of proving (*i.e.* discerning, as in Romans 12:2) the will of God'.[13] These admissions, and the whole excellent section on 'proving' from which they come, recognize realistically the perplexities which ethical choices involve, but hardly square with 'clear, definite and concrete to the last detail'. And Barth's treatment of areas of ethical decision in terms of God's work in Christ (which, he holds, is the basic subject-matter of ethics) differs little from the kind of casuistical reasoning which he professes to abhor.

The most problematical version of neo-orthodox situationism is Rudolf Bultmann's. Here the existentialist motif is strongest (for man's existence consists wholly in his possibility of existence, and he is always seeking authentic selfhood by choosing who he is); here, too, God and his will are most elusive, for God is silent, and 'Jesus teaches no ethics at all in the sense of an intelligible theory valid for all men concerning what should be done and left undone',[14] and obedience itself must be understood in a 'non-objectifying' way, not literally, that is, as response to God's command, but in a Pickwickian, that is, private and unnatural sense as decision in the situation, whereby authentic existence is achieved. The whole ethical process in man is reduced to successive crises of new decision each present moment. 'A man', Bultmann insists, 'cannot in the moment of decision fall back upon principles, upon a general ethical theory which can relieve him of the responsibility for the decision . . . man does not meet the crisis of decision armed with a definite standard; he stands on no firm base, but rather alone in empty space.'[15] Newness of decision is called for each new moment, for each new moment the situation itself is new.

So how should we act? First, we must realize the necessity of meeting the demands of the moment, for it always carries eschatological, that is, ultimate, significance for our existence; second, we must realize that each moment calls on us not just to do something but to be something—namely, persons who love their neighbours as themselves. We know how we love ourselves and how we want others to love us, so we already know how to love others. Jesus and Scripture do not therefore tell us what things love should make us do (that, if attempted, would be legalism); all we are told is that we should love, and that is all we need to be told, for 'if a man really loves, he knows already what he has to do';[16] and he knows it, 'not on the basis of any past experience or rational deductions, but directly from the immediate situation.'[17]

General strictures on situationism will come later, and general criticisms of Bultmann on God, Christ and Scripture would not be in place here, but some particular shortcomings of his ethic may be noted at once. First, he takes an over-optimistic view of *man*. Does one who 'really loves' thereby always know what to do? Does real love keep us who are naturally daft from speaking and acting in character? Second, Bultmann takes an over-simplified view of *situations*. Do not most perplexities in moral decision stem, not from lack of loving intention or will to obey God, but from ignorance of past and future facts, so that one cannot with confidence calculate consequences? Is it not daunting to note, with Thomas Oden, that Bultmann lacks 'realistic understanding of the intense and endless *conflicts of values* and interests and obligations that characterize human existence'?[18] Is it not disastrous that Bultmann neither will nor can develop a social ethic? Third, Bultmann gives an over-simplified account of the moral life, reducing it to a series of isolated decisions and allowing no significance to factors like character, habit, aspiration and growth (all of which find a place in the New Testament!). Fourth, Bultmann gives an unrealistic account of moral decision itself, speaking as if there never need be—indeed, never should be—any doubt in a Christian's mind as to what he should do this moment, for if his heart is right God will have made the right course clear to him. I do not always find that, nor do you; who does?

Principled situationism

Set beside this, now, the 'principled' situationism of Fletcher and Robinson—'principled' because it offers a constant method of deciding in each case what love demands. We may state it thus:

(a) Neighbour-love is God's absolute and only demand in each situation. God does not require invariable performance of particular types of action, as such, whatever the simple reader of the Decalogue and the ethical parts of the New Testament might think; he calls simply for love, first as a motive (good will) and then as beneficent behaviour, of whatever form the situation requires. 'Love is both absolute and relative by its very nature. An unchanging principle, it nevertheless always changes in its concrete application.'[19]

(b) 'Old' Christian morality lapses into Pharisaic legalism and so sins against love, because in determining how to act it 'begins from the deductive, the transcendent and the authoritative. It stresses the revealed character of the Christian moral standard . . . (and) starts from Christian principles which are valid "without respect of persons".'[20] The 'new' morality, by contrast, starts from persons rather than principles and from experienced relationships rather than revealed commandments, and in and from the situation itself works out, by reference to personal claims and probable consequences, what is the most loving thing to do. Fletcher, stressing that love maximizes good for all, assimilates love and justice and affirms a Christianized utilitarianism[21] so calculating that one reviewer called his book 'blood-chilling' and asked: 'Does this "calculus" of love not, in effect, dehumanize love?'[22] Robinson, by contrast, seems to think that the discerning of love's demands will occur spontaneously, through intuition rather than calculation. 'Love alone,' he writes, 'because, as it were, it has a built-in moral compass, enabling it to "home" intuitively upon the deepest need of the other, can allow itself to be directed completely by the situation. . . . It is able to embrace an ethic of radical responsiveness, meeting every situation on its own merits, with no prescriptive laws.'[23] At all events, it is part of the optimism of situationist faith that, by one means or another, love will be able to see what the personal claims in each situation require, without needing to run to God's law for guidance.

(c) Love may dictate the breaking of accepted moral rules of the 'do this', 'don't do that' type. These rules, both in Scripture and in life, are no more than rules of thumb ('maxims', Fletcher calls them; 'working rules' is Robinson's phrase); they give preliminary guidance as to how love will normally be expressed, but sometimes for the sake of persons different action will be called for. This, however, presents no problem theoretically, for what the rules forbid is forbidden only because it is ordinarily unloving, and nothing that actually expresses love in a particular situation is actually wrong. 'Apart from (love) there are no unbreakable rules.'[24] Love as the end justifies its means; nothing is intrinsically evil, since what makes for good in a situation thereby becomes good in that situation. Fletcher notes that Paul rejects all thought of doing evil that good may come (Rom. 3:8), but sees Paul as here 'victimized' by 'the intrinsic theory', that is, the false notion that things are good or evil in themselves.[25]

(d) No situation ever faces us with a choice of evils; the traditional view to the contrary is one more product of the mistaken 'intrinsic theory'. *'The situationalist holds that whatever is the most loving thing in the situation is the right and good thing.* It is not excusably evil, it is positively good.'[26] To illustrate, Fletcher is ready with blandest aplomb to justify— not as lesser evils, but as positively good—such acts as killing one's baby (p. 125), abortion (pp. 37ff.), therapeutic fornication (pp. 126f.), patriotic prostitution (pp. 163f.), adultery to induce pregnancy (pp. 164f.), pre-marital sexual intercourse (p. 104), sacrificing lives on your own side in time of war (p. 98), suicide and euthanasia (pp. 66, 74, 165f.), and distribution of contraceptives to unmarried women (p. 127; *Moral Responsibility*, pp. 139f.). He also insists on saying that 'in principle, even killing "innocent" people might be right', and 'in some situations lying and bribery and force and violence, even taking life itself, is the only righteous and good thing to do in the situation'.[27] It is Fletcher's use of 'good', 'right' and 'righteous' that secures to situationism its well-known reputation of being desperately lax; here the 'new morality' and the old immorality do seem to speak in identical terms.

Situationism evaluated

Christian situationism claims to distil essential biblical teaching about decision-making. This claim must now be tested.

Let it first be said that fair dealing with situationism is not easy, for it is a very mixed bag. Viewed as a reaction of protest against the all-too-common legalism which puts general principles before individual persons and whose zeal for God ousts neighbour-love from the heart, it commends itself as making a healthy biblical point, namely that only by love and care for others can we acceptably serve God (*cf.* Rom. 13:8–10; 1 Cor. 13:1–3; Gal. 5:14). But viewed as a method to guide us in choosing our behaviour, it appals, particularly when Fletcher cracks it up as the panacea for all moral perplexity, delivering us from centuries of Christian ethical error.[28] When situationists detect provincialism, shallowness, negativism, thoughtlessness and lovelessness in our ethical thought and practice, we must humbly take the criticism, and be grateful for it. But when they treat God's revealed directives as working rules only, and invite us to hail as good what God calls evil, a different response is called for.

Situationists are right to stress that each situation is in some respects unique, and that only by concentrating intensely on it shall we ever see what is the best we can make of it. Rightly too do they stress that love always seeks the best for all parties, and is betrayed if we settle for mere formal correctness, or avoidance of wrongdoing, without asking whether we could not do something better. Insistence that real love is creative, enterprising and unwilling to settle for the second-best in relationships is a substantial grain of truth in situationism, as is its further insistence that the lovingness of loving action should be thought out and spelt out in terms of the relationship itself. Robinson's casuistry of pre-marital sex, for instance, runs thus: 'To the young man asking in his relations with a girl, "Why shouldn't I?", it is relatively easy to say "Because it's wrong" or "Because it's a sin"—and then to condemn him when he, or his whole generation, takes no notice. It makes much greater demands to ask, and to answer, the question "Do you love her?" or "*How much* do you love her?", and then to help him to accept *for himself* the decision that, if he doesn't, or doesn't very deeply, then his action is immoral, or, if he does, then he will respect her far too much to use her or take liberties with her. Chastity is the expression of charity—of caring, enough.'[29] Though weakened by Robinson's unwillingness to declare sex relations apart from the full bed-and-board commitment of marriage wrong as such, this is surely right-minded. No; it is only in its denial that any particular action is intrinsically immoral, evil and forbidden that situationism goes astray. Unfortunately, this one mistake is ruinous.

Whence does it spring? Partly, from an unbiblical habit of defining actions externally, in merely physical terms, abstracted from their motive and purpose;[30] partly, from misconceptions about the place of the law of God as such. The New Testament says that while our relationship to God is no longer determined by law (Rom. 6:14), Christ having freed us from law as a system of salvation (Rom. 7:1–6; 10:4; Gal. 3:23–26), we are 'under the law of Christ' (1 Cor. 9:21; *cf.* Gal. 6:2) as a standard of sanctification; Robinson, however, seems to infer from the end of the law for salvation that it has no place in sanctification. The continentals, conceiving God's command as essentially specific and concrete, deny that the Bible's moral teaching, which was specific and concrete for its own situation, can be directly applied to ours.

The effect of denying that there are universal God-taught prohibitions is to enmesh love (good will, the commanded motive) in perplexities. How am I to love my neighbour now? By attending to the situation, I am told. But how should I define 'the situation'? Any circumscription of it will be arbitrary and open to challenge; I could always have included more, or less. And however I define it, how can I be sure what is really the most loving thing to do in it? By trusting my 'built-in moral compass'? I do not know whether Robinson risks trusting his, but I dare not rely on mine. My love is often blind, or at least goofy, partly through sin, partly through natural stupidity (two factors with which situation-ism fails to reckon). Also, I know by experience that in moments when I have to make decisions the factors that ought to count most, and the long-term implications of this or that way of handling the situation, are often far from clear to me. So am I to calculate my way through all possible alternatives, both those which stick to the rules and those which break them? But time, brains and factual knowledge fail me; and in any case it is plain that, whatever I do, whether I keep the rules or break them, uncertainty about the consequences I calculated will leave me still unsure whether I did the most loving thing. James Gustafson observes that ' "love", like "situation", is a word that runs through Fletcher's book like a greased pig'[31]—how does one catch and tie down such slippery items? Fletcher's method, which in intention makes things easy and, as Gustafson notes, 'omits any possibility of a bad con-science',[32] actually makes it impossible for me to know whether I have ever done what I should, and so leaves me with an anxious conscience every day. The way of relating love to law which re-quires the former to do duty for the latter does not make the life of Christian obedience easier for anyone.

But how are love and law related in the Bible itself? As follows:

First, no doubt ever appears about the universal applicability and authority of laws commanding and forbidding particular things—promise-keeping, payment of debts and care of one's children, for instance, in the one case; murder, adultery and theft, for instance, in the other—and John tells us 'this is the love of God, that we keep his commandments' (1 Jn. 5:3; *cf.* 2:3–5; 3:21–24, and Jesus' words, Jn. 14:15, 21; 15:10). In 1957, before the situa-tionist storm broke, John Murray wrote: 'It is symptomatic of a pattern of thought current in many evangelical circles that the idea of keeping the commandments of God is not consonant with the liberty and spontaneity of the Christian man, that *keeping* the law has affinities with legalism. . . .' He then quotes the passages referred to above, beginning with John 14:15, 'If you love me, you will keep my commandments', and ending with 14:21, 'He who has my commandments and keeps them, he it is who loves me', and concludes: 'When there is a persistent animosity to the notion of keeping commandments the only conclusion is that there is either gross ignorance or malignant opposition to the testimony of Jesus.'[33] It is hard to see how this can be gainsaid.

Second, love of God has priority over neighbour-love. Jesus categorizes love of God as the great commandment, which comes first (Mt. 22:37f.). Scripture is full of instruction on how to trust, fear, praise and serve the Lord, and for this we may be grateful—no utilitarian calculus could possibly take its place! It is odd that situationists regularly write as if love of God is wholly a matter of loving one's neighbour, but in Scripture it is certainly not so.

Third, neighbour-love is to be directed by law. So far from seeing an antithesis and possible clash between the claims of persons and of principles, Scripture assumes that we can only meet the claims of persons as we hold to the God-taught principles in dealing with them, and the principles take the form of directives as to what should and should not be done to them. The theology, in a nutshell, is that God our Maker and Redeemer has revealed the unchanging pattern of response that he requires, and that man needs if he is to be truly himself. The pattern is both an expression of God's own moral character, an indication of what he approves and disapproves, and also a clue to man about his own nature and that of his neighbour. By adhering to the pattern we express and further our own true humanness on the one hand, and true love for our neighbour on the other. Our fellow man is always something of an enigma to us, just as we are something of an enigma to ouselves, but our Maker who knows our true nature and needs has told us how we are to do ourselves and each other real good. So love and law-keeping are mutually entailed, as Paul shows in Romans 13:8-10. The sixth, seventh, eighth and tenth commandments prohibit particular actions and attitudes (murder, adultery, theft, covetous jealousy) and Paul quotes them to make the double point that when we keep these commandments we love our neighbour as ourselves, and when we love our neighbour as ourselves we keep these commandments. The point is confirmed by John's striking reasoning in 1 John 5:2: 'By this we know that we love the children of

God, when we love God *and obey his commandments*.' Neighbour-love fulfils the law.

Biblically, then, there is no antithesis between the motive of love and the divine directives which tell us what kinds of action on man's part God approves and disapproves. Situationism is, after all, gratuitous.

The lesser evil

But if God's laws, and the actions which they prescribe and prohibit, have fixed intrinsic values, as expressing God's unchanging will for mankind, what are we to think and do when we find ourselves in situations where we cannot move at all without transgressing a divine prohibition, so that the best we can do is evil from one standpoint? Briefly, love's task then is to find how to do the most good, and the least evil; doing nothing is rarely the answer! Rightly, different principles come out on top in different situations: two Christians armed with 'honour your parents' and 'do not steal' might well act differently if one could only prevent his parents dying of hunger by stealing, while the other was being told to steal by his heavily gambling father. We may agree with the situationist that love for persons must arbitrate between the conflicting claims of moral principles, that doctrinaire decisions in such cases will not make the best of the bad job, and that unwillingness to face the situation's full complexities, and insensitivity to the variety of rules and claims that apply, will lead straight into ironclad Pharisaic legalism. But we shall reject Fletcher's grotesque idea that in such situations adultery, fornication, abortion, suicide and the rest, if thought the *best* course (which arguably in Fletcher's cases they might be—we will not dispute that here), thereby become *good*: which valuation, as Fletcher himself emphasizes, leaves no room for regret at having had to do them. Instead, we shall insist that evil remains evil, even when, being the lesser evil, it appears the right thing to do; we shall do it with heavy heart, and seek God's cleansing of our conscience for having done it.

In the film of Nicholas Monsarrat's novel *The Cruel Sea,* a destroyer commander had to decide whether to drop a depth-charge that would kill dozens of desperate seamen struggling in the icy North Atlantic, but might also (*might*—there was no certainty) destroy the U-boat waiting on the sea floor to ravage the rest of the convoy. The alternative was to stop and pick up the swimmers. He headed through the men in the water and dropped the depth-charge. One of his men yelled, 'Bloody murderer!' He did not know if he hit the U-boat. The experience temporarily shattered him. He said: there are times when all we can do is guess our best, and then get down on our knees and ask God's mercy. This is the most painful form of the lesser evil situation, that in which knowledge is limited and one does the evil that seems best knowing that it may not turn out best at all. The poignancy and justice of the commander's words need no underlining. The most distressing feature of Fletcher's often distressing book (in which, incidentally, there is a reference to this episode) is that, if he knows what Christian men feel at such times, he keeps quiet about it, and writes as if a dose of situationist casuistry will make them proof against it. One can only say: God help them if it does. Yet this is where situationism logically leads; Fletcher is only being clear-headed in pointing it out.

Cried Mr Hardy to Mr Laurel, not once nor twice, 'Here's another fine mess you've gotten me into!' Might not one have to say the same to any teacher who won him over to situationist ethics?

NOTES

1. This chapter is indebted to three unpublished papers by Gordon Stobart.

2. J. A. T. Robinson, *Honest to God* (SCM Press, 1963), chapter 6; *Christian Morals Today* (SCM Press, 1964); *Christian Freedom in a Permissive Society* (SCM Press, 1970); J. Fletcher, *Situation Ethics* (SCM Press, 1966); *Moral Responsibility: Situation Ethics at Work* (SCM Press, 1967); 'Reflection and Reply', in Harvey Cox (ed.), *The Situation Ethics Debate* (Westminster Press, Philadelphia, 1968), pp. 249–264; 'What's in a Rule?: A Situationist's View', in Gene H. Outka and Paul Ramsey (eds.), *Norm and Context in Christian Ethics* (SCM Press, 1969), pp. 325–349.

3. Unfortunately, Fletcher really did write: 'Sex is not always wrong outside marriage, even for Christians' (*Moral Responsibility*, p. 138). No less unfortunately, H. A. Williams, on this showing a situationist fellow-traveller, dabbled in his essay in A. R. Vidler (ed.), *Soundings* (Cambridge University Press, 1962) with the Freudian fancy of therapeutic and therefore valuable fornication. Of an episode in the film *Never on Sunday* he wrote: 'The prostitute gives herself to him in such a way that he acquires confidence and self-respect. He goes away a deeper fuller person than he came in.' And of something similar in *The Mark*: 'Will he be able to summon up the necessary courage or not? When he does, and they sleep together, he has been made whole. And where

there is healing, there is Christ, whatever the Church may say about fornication' (pp. 81f.). All else apart, however, is it safe to assume that real life will be like what you see at the movies?

4. *Situation Ethics*, p. 58.

5. *The Situation Ethics Debate*, p. 202.

6. Fletcher writes: 'As a "Scripture" for the open-endedness of situation ethics turn to Romans 14:14. When Paul said, "I know . . . that nothing is unclean of itself", what he meant by "unclean" (once we step out of the situation in and to which he spoke), and what he could well have said, is "immoral". Nothing is immoral in itself, intrinsically. What love is, what morality is, always depends on the situation' (*Norm and Context in Christian Ethics*, p. 349). The text does not prove Fletcher's point, for Paul's 'nothing' denotes foodstuffs, not types of action, whereas Fletcher's 'nothing' signifies, apparently, types of action viewed formally and externally without reference to their motive and purpose (*e.g.* shaking hands, or signing one's name, or speaking, or keeping silent, or copulating). Nor in any case is Fletcher's external concept of an action always adequate; some types of action, *e.g.* rape and torture, are only definable in terms of an unloving and therefore (for Fletcher, as for everyone else) immoral motive and volition, so that to say that rape and torture are not 'immoral . . . intrinsically' would be self-contradictory. Robinson, trying to have it both ways, achieves this self-contradiction explicitly, affirming *both* that 'nothing can of itself always be labelled as "wrong"' *and* that there are actions of which 'it is so inconceivable that they could ever be an expresssion of love—like cruelty to children or rape—that . . . they are . . . always wrong' (*Honest to God*, p. 118; *Christian Morals Today*, p. 16 and also *Christian Freedom in a Permissive Society*, p. 16): which, as Paul Ramsey notes, is simply saying that that they are '*inherently* wrong, wrong in themselves, . . . because of the lovelessness that is always in them' (*Deeds and Rules in Christian Ethics*, Oliver and Boyd, 1965, p. 28). For clear discussion with a situationist, the first question one should ask is how he defines an action.

7. K. Barth, *Church Dogmatics*, II.2 (T. & T. Clark, 1957), p. 673. Barth continues: 'We must divest ourselves of the fixed idea that only a universally valid rule can be a command.' See the whole section, pp. 661–708; *op. cit.*, III.4, pp. 1–23; and D. Bonhoeffer, *Ethics* (Fontana, 1964), pp. 278, 285.

8. E. Brunner, *The Divine Imperative* (Lutterworth, 1937), p. 59.

9. *Op. cit.*, p. 285.

10. *Op. cit.*, p. 287.

11. H. Hartwell, *The Theology of Karl Barth: an Introduction* (Duckworth, 1964), p. 162.

12. This brings 'pure' situationism into line with the position of sixteenth-century Anabaptists and seventeenth-century Quakers who relied on what they took to be immediate promptings of the Holy Spirit, not related to the Word in any direct or testable way. A similar tendency appears on occasion in charismatic circles, and in *Knowing God* (Hodder, 1975, pp. 263f.) I cite three horror stories along the same line from the 'fanaticism papers' which Hannah Whitall Smith compiled from her experience among American evangelicals a century ago. The doctrine of the Holy Spirit which underlies expectations of immediate guidance by private revelation is not so much ripe as overripe, and can be expected to produce ethical instability.

13. Bonhoeffer, *op. cit.*, pp. 278, 38, 40.

14. R. Bultmann, *Jesus and the Word* (Nicholson & Watson, 1935), p. 84.

15. *Ibid.*, p. 85.

16. *Ibid.*, p. 94. 'The demand for love needs no formulated stipulations; the example of the merciful Samaritan shows that a man can know . . . what he has to do when he sees his neighbour in need of his help. The little words "as yourself" in the love-commandment pre-indicate both the boundlessness and the direction of loving conduct' (*Theology of the New Testament*, I, SCM Press, 1952, p. 19).

17. *Jesus and the Word*, p. 88.
18. T. Oden, *Radical Obedience* (Epworth, 1965), p. 123.
19. P. Tillich, *Morality and Beyond* (Fontana, 1969), p. 37. Tillich was a situationist of a kind, but he anchors morality in a private doctrine of 'Being' which sets him apart from Trinitarian Christianity.
20. J. A. T. Robinson, *Christian Morals Today*, p. 34, and also *Christian Freedom in a Permissive Society*, pp. 31f.
21. 'Justice is Christian love using its head . . . coping with situations where distribution is called for. On this basis it becomes plain that as the love ethic searches seriously for a social policy it must form a coalition with utilitarianism,' taking over 'the strategic principle of "the greatest good of the greatest number" ' (*Situation Ethics*, p. 95).
22. Norman F. Langford, in *The Situation Ethics Debate*, p. 63. Amazingly, Fletcher's reply is: ' "All right, we accept that. Cold calculation for love's sake is indeed the ideal model . . ." . . . the "warmer" love's calculations are, the more apt they are to be only interpersonal or even individualistic' (p. 261). Comment seems superfluous!
23. *Honest to God*, p. 115.
24. *Christian Morals Today*, p. 16, and also *Christian Freedom in a Permissive Society*, p. 16.
25. *Situation Ethics*, p. 123.
26. *Ibid.*, p. 65; Fletcher's italics.
27. *Situation Ethics*, p. 75; *Moral Responsibility*, p. 181.
28. Fletcher the situationist is a convert turned evangelist. 'After forty years', he wrote in 1963, 'I have learned the vital importance of the contextual or situational —*i.e.* the *circumstantial*—approach to the search for what is right and good. I have seen the light; I know now that abstract and conceptual morality is a mare's nest' (quoted in *The Situation Ethics Debate*, p. 113; *cf. Situation Ethics*, p. 41). Robinson, by contrast, is concerned to claim that 'this "new morality" is, of course, none other than the old morality, just as the new commandment is the old, yet ever fresh, commandment of love' (*Honest to God*, p. 119).
29. *Honest to God*, p. 119.
30. See note 6 above.
31. *The Situation Ethics Debate*, p. 81.
32. *Ibid.*, p. 80.
33. J. Murray, *Principles of Conduct* (Inter-Varsity Press, 1957), pp. 182f.

3

Conscience, choice and character

James Packer[1]

There are two crucial areas where anyone venturing today to write on Christian ethics takes his life in his hands: namely, the understanding of man's nature and the analysing of moral thought. In both areas, Christian views face strong secular attack, and in neither are Christian minds always clear. But clarity here is necessary if ever we are to see how God's law should order our lives, and how law-keeping perfects our nature. The territory may not be by-passed just because it is disputed. This essay, which is a theoretical (though not on that account unpractical) study of how individuals come to discern and do God's will, takes us straight to both battlefields, and our first step must be to set up our flag on the ground we intend to occupy.

Human nature

'What a piece of work is man!' said Hamlet. 'How noble in reason! how infinite in faculty [capacity]! in form, in moving, how express and admirable! in action how like an angel! in apprehension how like a god! the beauty of the world! the paragon of animals!' Bang on, as a modern groundling might say. The words which Shakespeare puts into Hamlet's mouth reflect with dazzling vividness the classic Christian vision of man: namely, as a cosmic amphibian, having a body which links him with animals below him but being in himself a thinking, loving, choosing, creative, active person like God and the angels above him. It is the horse that is usually called the noble animal, but on the Christian view the description is better suited to the rider. There is no such created grandeur as that of man.

I am a man; what, then, am I? Not, as philosophers and gnostics ancient and modern would tell me, a soul that would get on better without a body, but a complex psycho-physical organism, a personal unit describable as an ensouled body no less than an embodied soul. Bodilessness is not a welcome prospect; after physical death I shall be incapable of that full self-expression which belongs to full personal life till a new body is given me (as, praise God, one duly will be). I am at once the highest of animals, since no other animal shares my kind of mental life, and the lowest of rational creatures, for no angel is bounded by physical limitations as I am. Yet I, as a man, can enjoy the richest life of all God's creatures. Mental and physical awareness meet and blend in me, fearfully, wonderfully and fascinatingly. There is far more to me than I can know or get in touch with, at least in this preliminary, probationary life, and I never reach the limits of wisdom, goodness and depth of relationship with others that open out before me. But I must keep my head. My task is not to dizzy myself by introspecting or speculating to find, if I can, what lies at the outer reaches of consciousness, nor to pursue endless, exquisite stimulation in hope of new, exotic ecstasies. It is, rather, to know and keep my place in God's cosmic hierarchy, and in that place to spend my strength in serving God and men.

A cool head, however, is hard to find. Having within me something both of ape and of angel, I can all too easily lose my cosmic balance, so to speak, and lapse into incoherent oscillation beween seeing myself as no less than God, a spirit having absolute value in myself and settling the value of everything else by its relation to me, and seeing myself as no more than an animal, whose true life consists wholly in eating, drinking, rutting and seeking pleasures for mind and body till tomorrow I die. I often catch myself slipping one way or the other; I look around, and see my fellow men in the toils of this crazy oscillation all the time; I read my Bible, and find that it has been so everywhere since the Garden of Eden. Such is life in a fallen world.

The image of God. The human animal, we said, is noble. What makes him so? Not his ambitions or achievements, which, as we have hinted, are rarely admirable and often downright discreditable, but his personal constitution. The most mysterious yet glorious truth about human nature is this: that each individual, male or female, old or young, sophisticated or rough, handsome or ugly, brilliant or slow of mind, outstanding or ordinary, bears God's image. We learn this in the first chapter of the Bible, Genesis 1, which is a majestic introduction of the Creator by means of a review of his work. The thrust is this: 'Think of all that makes up the world you know—day, night, sky, sea, sun, moon, stars, trees, plants, birds, fish, animals, insects, big things, little things, and most of all yourself and other human beings of both sexes; now meet their Maker! and gauge the excellence of his wisdom and power from the marvellous complexity, order and goodness which you see (and he also saw) in his work.' (There is a parallel argument in Job 38–41, where God leads Job to acknowledge the fathomlessness of divine wisdom by reminding him of the wonders of the animal kingdom, especially Behemoth the hippopotamus and Leviathan the crocodile.) 'And realize too,' Genesis 1 in effect continues, 'that you, the admiring observer, were made like your Maker in a way that none of these other things are, so that you might manage the lower creation for God, as his steward, and enjoy its riches as his gift to you. That is your calling, so go to it!'

The key statements here are in verses 26 and 27: 'God said, "Let us make man in our *image,* after our *likeness* . . ." So God created man in his own *image.*' The image of God in which man was and is made (*cf.* Gn. 5:1; 9:6; Jas. 3:9) has been variously explained in detail. It has been identified, for instance, with rationality (*e.g.,* by S. R. Driver), with moral capacity (*e.g.,* by J. Laidlaw), with knowledge of God in righteousness and holiness (*e.g.,* by Calvin), with dominion over the lower creation (*e.g.,* by H. Thieliecke), and with the man–woman relationship in marriage, corresponding to the inner relationships of the Three-in-One (by Karl Barth). Von Rad urges that the phrase must refer to each human individual as a whole, in the psycho-physical unity of his being, not just to 'higher' mental and moral qualities in abstraction from his body; and F. D. Kidner, standing it seems on von Rad's shoulders, writes thus: 'When we try to define the image of God it is not enough to react against a crude literalism by isolating man's mind and spirit from his body. The Bible makes man a unity: acting, thinking and feeling with his whole being. This living creature, then, and not some distillation from him, is an expression or transcription of the eternal, incorporeal creator in terms of temporal, bodily, creaturely existence— as one might attempt a transcription of, say, an epic into a sculpture, or a symphony into a sonnet. Likeness in this sense survived the Fall, since it is structural. As long as we are human we are, by definition, in the image of God.'[2] This line of thought seems to win increasing scholarly assent. But however expositors differ on the nuances of the phrase, the broad theological implications of asserting that each man is made in God's image are matters of general agreement, thus:

Dignity. The assertion shows each man's true *dignity* and *worth*. As God's image-bearer, he merits infinite respect, and his claims on us (which are really the claims of God's image in him) must be taken with total seriousness. No man should ever be thought of as a mere cog in a machine, or a mere means to an end.

Destiny. The assertion points also to each man's true *destiny*. Our Maker so designed us that our nature (the mass of potencies, urges and needs of which each man is made up) finds final satisfaction and fulfilment only in a relationship of responsive Godlikeness— which means, precisely, in that state of correspondence between our acts and God's will which we call *obedience*. Living that is obedient will thus also be teleological, in the sense of progressively realizing our *telos* (Greek for 'end', 'goal') as the Shorter Catechism classically defined it—'Man's chief end is to glorify God, and [in so doing] to enjoy him for ever.' By contrast, to live disobediently is to forfeit fulfilment and to sentence oneself to a life which, however pleasure-filled, is Godless and ultimately joyless.

Freedom. Finally, the assertion confirms the genuineness of each man's *freedom*. Experience tells us we are free, in the sense that we make real choices between alternatives and could have chosen differently, and theology agrees. As the Creator is free within the limits of his own nature to choose what he will do, and as his praise springs from recognition that what he chose was good, so also with us. Self-determining freedom of choice is what sets God and his rational creatures apart from, say, birds and bees, as *moral* beings. Any suggestion that this freedom is illusory and unreal, so that my choices, being somehow programmed in advance, do not matter, and I do not need to work at them, must be squashed as satanic. Granted, predisposing factors influence our choices (much more, in fact, than they should!); granted, God is sovereign in and over our choices (this is part of the mystery of the creature's dependence on the Creator); none the less, it is one aspect of God's image in us that the choices we make are genuinely ours, and are no less decisive for our future than God's choice to create and redeem was decisive for his.

Behaviourism. The modern attack on the biblical view of man comes from a standpoint mainly determined by expertise in the sciences, biological and human. Sometimes this standpoint claims the name of scientific humanism, though its appeal to speculative extrapolations beyond the evidence, and its denial of man's glory as bearer of God's image, would suggest 'unscientific brutism' as a more appropriate name. Purposing to affirm and exalt man, this view actually negates and demeans him by assimilating him entirely to the lower animals. It sees him as a 'naked ape' and an animated computer, wholly programmable by external conditioning once it is known how he works. Concentrated, not to say mesmerized, study of physical, psychological and social factors that condition human action has bred doubt as to whether free (that is, self-determined) moral choices occur at all, and whether, if they do, it is not best to try and stop them, and train people instead into automatic behaviour patterns, by methods comparable to Pavlov's with his dogs or the brainwasher's with his victims. The pipe-dreams of popular Marxism, Aldous Huxley's *Brave New World*, George Orwell's *1984*, C. S. Lewis' *That Hideous Strength* (a flawed fairy-tale, but a brilliant analysis), and B. F. Skinner's *Beyond Freedom and Dignity*, show from different angles what the manipulations of a behaviourist utopia might amount to. Space forbids proper discussion of this viewpoint, but two quick comments can be made.

First, the basic mistake which this view makes is to overlook something quite essential to our humanness, namely our sense of being accountable (worthy of praise or blame) for what we do, and therefore answerable to anyone who has the right to take account of us. A mature person wants to be recognized as morally responsible for his actions, and as he resents refusal to give him credit for what he says and does right, so he does not refuse blame for saying and doing what he knows was wrong. He is clear that though external factors may have conditioned his action, his own decision was its direct cause—and so, we think, he should be, for that is how it really was. We are repelled by one who says he should not be blamed because he is mentally sick, or society's helpless victim, for however much we incline to say these things about him in extenuation, we know that when he says them about himself he is making excuses and being morally dishonest, just as you and I would be if ever we acted this way. To accept accountability for one's choices is part of what it means to be truly human, and any proposal to ignore or change this, or to destroy people's awareness of it (as if we could!), is not humanizing; just the opposite! It is the most radical and grotesque dehumanization that can be imagined, as the novels of Huxley, Orwell and Lewis mentioned above make very plain.[3]

Second, the mistake comes of not distinguishing between two levels of language (two 'logical grammars', or simply two languages, as philosophers would say) which we regularly use side by side when talking of human behaviour. They correspond to the difference within our own self-consciousness between 'me' and 'I', the object-self I observe, and I the subject-self who do the observing. They are, first, impersonal objective language, to which belong all scientific accounts of historical, social, physical, chemical and psychological factors which condition people's acts; and, second, personal subjective language, in which all statements have to do with the individual subject-self thinking, feeling, acting, reacting and making choices. To this latter language belongs all talk about morality (moral goodness and badness, moral judgments and moral responsibilities). The two languages cannot be reduced to one, nor can statements made in either be translated into, or explained without remainder in terms of, the other. They are distinct and complementary, and for full understanding we need both, the first supplementing the second; for the correlations between our external conditioning and our personal choices and decisions are many, and we should abuse our minds if we ignored them.

Scientific humanism, however, tends habitually to go beyond noting the correlations, and to offer explanations of what is said in the second language in terms of the first, thus in effect explaining *away* moral realities as being something else. For example, it might well explain a man's choice of burglary as a way of life in terms of a sociological description of his early life in the slums, and go on to suggest that by changing his environment and reconditioning him we can make an honest citizen out of him. This is to treat a criminal as an invalid needing cure, rather than as a responsible wrongdoer —a patronizing and dehumanizing fancy, guyed as it deserves in that blackest of black comedies, *A Clockwork Orange.* The mistake occurs, as we said, because we so love using impersonal, objective, 'scientific' language that we treat as unreal, or less than ultimate, any realities whose nature it cannot express. A moment's thought, however, will convince us that the realities of personal motivation and purpose in our choices are quite distinct from any external factors which condition them. Should the scientific humanist invoke at this point that full-blown theoretical behaviourism which views all our conscious mental life as the accidental by-product of physical changes in our bodies and brains, the reply would be that in that case his very invoking of the theory is the accidental by-product of physical changes within him, and thus has no rational validity for him or anyone else. This is the *coup de grâce* for all reasoned denials of the validity of reasoning: he who takes them seriously thereby forbids others to take him seriously.

The best response to naive utopian behaviourism, with its simple animalist view of man and its simple optimism about the possibility of retraining him by skilled manipulation, will be to urge that each individual is infinitely mysterious, both to others and to himself, so that no man-made formula can in principle be adequate to produce the desired effect. Anyone who thinks and feels at all deeply finds himself a mystery to himself, fascinating and frustrating by turns, and comes to see that only omniscience would in principle suffice to sort him out.

Conscience

One specific aspect of God's image in us is our conscience, classically defined by Thomas Aquinas as man's mind making moral judgments. As God's mind passes judgment on moral issues, so does man's, and as God's moral judgments should control our acts and will actually settle our destiny, so our conscience functions in the style of a voice within actually addressing us to command or forbid, approve or disapprove, justify or condemn. Conscience does not feel like the spontaneous working of my mind which it actually is; it feels, and is divinely intended to feel, like a monitor from above. The description of conscience as a voice from God highlights the unique character of this particular mental operation. (It should not, however, be taken to imply that divine finality attaches to all the deliverances of conscience; conscience needs educating by Scripture and experience, and to the extent that it has not been thus educated its deliverances will be deficient. From the standpoint of standards, it is truer to say that conscience is a capacity for hearing God's voice, rather than an actual hearing of it in each verdict that conscience passes.)

The experience of conscience is universal, and the operation of it, particularly when condemnatory, has an emotional dimension ('pangs'). It is not perhaps surprising that attempts should have been made to analyse conscience in emotional terms simply, as nothing but feelings of liking and disliking, on the model of my reactions to curry, which I like, and coconut, which I loathe. Critics labelled this analysis the 'Boo—hurrah' theory ('coconut? murder? *boo!* curry? promise-keeping? *hurrah!*').[4] Were the analysis true, moral reasoning designed to persuade to, or dissuade from, particular courses of action would be comparable to 'try this, you'll like it' and 'don't eat that, it's horrid', and no universal moral standards could ever be agreed, any more than it could ever be agreed that henceforth everyone shall like curry and dislike coconut.

But conscience itself tells us that morality is essentially a matter, not of taste, but of truth; not of feeling, in the first instance, but of judgment, based on principles which are in themselves universally valid, and claim everyone's assent.

Traditionally, and surely correctly, conscience has been held to involve two faculties, ability first to 'see' general moral truths and second to apply them to particular cases. Aquinas called the first capacity *synderesis* and kept *conscientia* for the second; Peter Martyr the reformer, followed by many seventeenth-century writers, spoke of theoretical and practical understanding, different words for the same distinction. It was unquestioned among both Protestants and Roman Catholics till this century that the workings of conscience take the form of *practical syllogisms, e.g.* 'Stealing is wrong; taking the umbrella would be stealing; therefore taking the umbrella would be wrong', or 'Bank robbers deserve punishment; I robbed a bank; therefore I deserve punishment'; and, despite some latter-day hesitations based on doubt as to whether God really reveals universally binding moral truths, the historic doctrine seems true, as anyone who checks his own moral reasoning will soon see. Though conscience pronounces on particular actions and cases, it does so on the basis of general principles, which, though not always explicit in the initial pronouncement, will be explicitly cited in justification if the pronouncement is at any stage questioned. And if no such universal principle could be produced to justify a particular pronouncement, the right conclusion would be that here is no genuine deliverance of conscience at all, but a neurotic symptom (guilt, or an obsession, in the psychiatrist's sense of those words) masquerading as the voice of conscience, and needing to be relieved and dispelled, if possible, by professional therapy.

In *Conscience in the New Testament* (SCM Press, 1955), C. A. Pierce argued that the New Testament writers who refer to conscience (Paul, Peter, Luke in Acts, and the writer of Hebrews) used the word in the limited sense that it bore in everyday secular Greek, namely a capacity for feeling pangs of remorse about past actions now seen as wrong, as distinct from a power of direction and vindication of oneself in moral matters. But even were this true, which seems doubtful (note Rom. 2:15, where conscience excuses; 9:1, where it attests a right desire, expressing good will; 2 Cor. 1:12, where it approves; and Acts 23:1; 1 Tim. 1:5, 19, where conscientious obedience produces a 'good' conscience; *cf.* Acts 24:16; Heb. 13:18), the point would be verbal only. For Scripture is clear on what we have already affirmed from experience, namely that man's 'heart' (in biblical usage the dynamic centre of his personal existence, including his self-conscious intellect, emotion and will) will not only 'smite' and 'reproach' in conviction (the bad conscience: *cf.* 1 Sa. 24:5; 2 Sa. 24:10; Jb. 27:6), but also both prompt and attest integrity (the good conscience: *cf.* Gn. 20:5f.; Dt. 9:5; 1 Ki. 3:6; 9:4; Ps. 119:7). The mental operation called *conscientia* in Latin and *syneidēsis* in Greek (both words meaning 'co-knowledge' and signifying a second level of awareness accompanying one's primary awareness of an impulse, thought, act or possibility of action) directs (Rom. 13:5) as well as recording (2 Cor. 1:12) and judging (Rom. 2:15; *cf.* 1 Jn. 3:19ff.), and does all three as, structurally speaking, God's monitor in the soul.[5] Yet its judgments may fall short of God's (1 Cor. 4:4; *cf.* 1 Jn. 3:19ff.); when possessed by false principles of judgment it will be 'weak' and mis-direct (Rom. 14:2 and *passim*; 1 Cor. 8:7–12, *cf.* 10:25–29); and when moral and spiritual light has been resisted it may become 'seared' (*i.e.* cauterized, rendered insensitive) (1 Tim. 4:2; *cf.* Eph. 4:18).

Being God's voice in and to us structurally, our conscience binds us and must always be conscientiously followed; but when through ignorance or confusion its dictates are not God's voice substantially, our conscientiousness will not lead to our pleasing God. (Did Jephthah please God by sticking conscientiously to the vow of Judges 11:30f. when this meant killing his daughter?) So a Christian with an uninstructed conscience is in fact, whether he knows it or not, in a cleft stick; he cannot please God by either disobeying his conscience or obeying it. This fact shows how vital it is that Christians should study biblical morals as well as biblical doctrine, and also what a nightmare our lot would be did we not know God's daily forgiveness on the basis of his once-for-all justification of us, through the blood of Jesus Christ who is the propitiation for all our sins, known and unknown.

Freud's view of conscience has had great influence in this century, and some reference to it is desirable before we move on. Freud gives the name of conscience to the various neurotic and psychotic phenomena of obsessive restriction, compulsion and guilt to which we referred at the end of the last paragraph but two. His model of man, hypothesized on the basis of clinical work with the mentally ill in *fin-de-siecle* Vienna, pictures the psyche as like a troubled home, where the ego on the ground floor (that is, the self-conscious self, with doors and windows open to the world) comes under pressure both from the id (aggressive energy rushing up from the cellars of the unconscious) and from the super-ego (an unnerving voice of command from upstairs, whereby repressed prohibitions and menaces from parents and society are 'introjected' into conscious life in portentous disguise, and with disruptive effect). The super-ego, each man's tyrannical psychic policeman, is the culprit to which neuroses and psychoses are due, and the goal of psycho-analysis is to strengthen one's ego to unmask the super-ego and see it for the hotch-potch of forgotten traumas which it really is, thus winning freedom to discount it. Since Freud's view equates the super-ego with conscience, it might seem to us, as it certainly did to him, directly to undermine any concept of conscience as God's voice; but in fact what Freud talks about is what Christian pastors have learned to recognize as the 'false conscience'—a more or less irrational scrupulosity which shows the mind to be not so much godly as sick. The right comment here is Ronald Preston's: 'Whether, therefore, Freud's theories are sound or not they do not contradict Christian teaching. Indeed they throw light on the well-known phenomenon of the "scrupulous conscience". He has confused the terminology by being unaware of the usual Christian understanding of the term.'[6] In other words: what Freud calls conscience is precisely not conscience on the Christian view, and what Christians mean by conscience (practical moral reason, consciously exercised, growing in insight and sureness of guidance through instruction and use, and bringing inner integration, health and peace to those who obey it) is not dealt with by Freud at all.

Standards

Whether Christians always draw from Scripture the standards whereby they judge of moral good and evil is open to question, but it will not be disputed that this is what they should do. What criteria, then, does Scripture give for judging the morality of deeds done, and for making choices which are not merely legitimate but the best possible in each situation? By what rules should conscience go in these matters?

The first criterion that Scripture yields concerns *the nature of the action*. God loves some types of action and hates others. 'I the Lord *love* justice, I *hate* robbery and wrong' (Is. 61:8). 'Speak the truth to one another . . . do not devise evil in your hearts against one another, and love no false oath, for all these things I *hate*, says the Lord' (Zc. 8:16f.; *cf.* Je. 44:6; Am. 5:21; Rev. 2:6). In the Decalogue God forbids various types of action which he hates: disrespect and distrust towards himself, in a number of forms; disrespect for parents (and by parity of reasoning other bearers of God-given authority); disrespect for human life, for the marriage bond, and for property; and disrespect for truth, especially truth about other people. Most of the Bible's ethical teaching in both Testaments is elaboration and enforcement of these principles, buttressed with theological reasons why some types of action are unfitting and only their opposites can be right.

We should note that the nature of actions, as Scripture and common sense view them, can only be made clear by speaking of them directionally, that is, in terms of their object—that at which the physical movement is aimed, and in which it naturally results. Thus, any physical movement, of whatever sort, which puts me in possession of what belongs to someone else, without his permission and against his presumed will, but of set purpose on my part, would be theft. Actions have to be defined not abstractly, in terms that are physical alone, but concretely, in terms of the agent's aim and object, to which his physical movement is the means. (This assumes, of course, that the agent is rational, and knows what he is doing.)

We should note too that when Jesus linked Deuteronomy 6:4f.

with Leviticus 19:18b as the two great commandments, on which all the specific ethical teachings of the law and the prophets depend (Mt. 22:36–40), he was focusing positively the two proper overall purposes of actions, which the Decalogue illustrates negatively. The Decalogue said, in effect: do nothing which in any way dishonours your God, or your human neighbour who bears his image. Jesus' formula, in effect, says: do everything that expresses the purpose of pleasing and exalting your God, and benefiting your neighbour (which is what 'love' for God and neighbour means). That this is no cancellation of the Decalogue appears both from the rubric Jesus gave for interpreting all his teaching (Mt. 5:17: 'Think not that I have come to abolish the law and the prophets; I have come . . . to fulfil them'), and also from Paul's exposition of loving one's neighbour in terms of keeping the second table (Rom. 13:8–10: 'He who loves his neighbour has fulfilled the law. The commandments . . . are summed up in this sentence, "You shall love your neighbour as yourself" '.) So when good Samaritans bind up the wounded, it is proper to speak of acts of healing (healing being their object) which express a purpose of love (others' welfare being their designed goal). Healing is the object of the action, love the purpose of the agent. Clarity requires the distinction.

Third, we should note that God's law in both Testaments, full as it looks, is actually quite open-textured. It is not a minutely-detailed code of practice for all our actions every moment (the sort of code which Jewish expository tradition produced); it is, rather, a set of broad guiding principles with sample applications to set us going (case law for the courts in the Pentateuch, actual or imaginary examples for individual guidance elsewhere). Some of the applications are couched in typical Eastern hyperbole—for instance, Jesus' 'If any one would sue you and take your coat, let him have your cloak as well; and if any one forces you to go one mile, go with him two miles' (Mt. 5:40f.)—and this shows their purpose: they are not so much models for mechanical imitation as cartoons of required attitudes, which we must learn by experience spontaneously to express. Cartoonists' drawings make their point by simplifying and exaggerating, and such parabolic sayings of Jesus as I have just cited work the same way. The cartoon is there to give us the idea, but most of the detailed applying of the principles is left to us, to manage as creatively as we can. Four aids are given us in Scripture for this task.

First, there is the calculus embodied in Jesus' so-called 'golden rule': 'Whatever you wish that men would do to you, do so to them; for this is the law and the prophets' (Mt. 7:12). The last clause, compared with Matthew 22:40, shows that what the 'rule' is telling us is how to work out the way to love our neighbour as ourselves. The method is, first to recognize that naturally, necessarily and by God's will as Creator, you do love and care for yourself, seeking your own well-being, and to think of all the treatment from others that you feel would conduce to this end; and then to make that the standard for your treatment of them. Christ's matter-of-fact appeal to self-love as setting a standard (an appeal which Paul also makes in Ephesians 5:28f., when teaching husbands how to love their wives) should not shock us; self-love is not sin till it becomes inordinate, and in fact a proper self-love is a further facet of God's image in us, for he too seeks his own felicity. The assertion, common nowadays, that one cannot robustly love either God or one's neighbour unless one robustly loves oneself is, both psychologically and theologically, a deep truth. Meantime, by starting from our self-love as it is, with all its inordinate elements, the 'golden rule' vastly expands our sense of what love we owe to our neighbour. If, for instance, I find myself longing to be listened to more and understood better, there may well be sinful self-pity in my attitude, but that is not relevant here; what matters is that the 'rule' makes me realize, from my own feelings, how much more in the way of attentive patience and imaginative identification love to my neighbour requires of me than I had first thought—and so across the board.

Second, there is the scriptural teaching on man's nature and destiny. This is clear and emphatic. We are told that, being the creatures we are, we can only find full happiness in making appropriate response to the love of God; that each man's highest good lies in conscious fellowship with God beyond this world, for which our present life is a kind of preparatory school and training-ground; and that the path to this prize is discipleship to Christ, whereby through faith we die and rise with him, and live as those for whom the world is not home, but a vale of soul-making where our own decisions sow all the seeds of future joy or sorrow. This teaching instructs us not only to see and live our personal lives as a homeward journey, and to look straight ahead as we travel, but also to relate to others in a way that will help them to know their dignity and potential as God's creatures, and encourage them to embrace eternal life as their destiny too, and puts no stumbling-block in their way at either point: which gives us a strong lead on very many issues, from human rights and business management to family ideals and the priority of evangelism.

Third, there is the summons to imitate God, who says, 'You shall be holy, for I am holy' (1 Pet. 1:16, referring to Lv. 11:44f.; *cf.* 19:2; 20:7, 26), and Jesus Christ, who washed his disciples' feet as 'an example, that you also should do as I have done to you' (Jn. 13:15), and spelt out the message of his action by saying, 'Love one another as I have loved you. Greater love has no man than this, that a man lay down his life for his friends' (15:12f.). The feet-washing symbolized the shedding of Christ's atoning and cleansing blood, and so John elsewhere writes: 'He laid down his life for us; and we ought to lay down our lives for the brethren' (1 Jn. 3:16). God's call to be holy, as he is holy, is a general summons to live by his revealed precepts and prohibitions, as embodying the loves and hates which make up his character and which his ways with us will always express; Christ's call to follow his example is a specific summons to unlimited self-humbling, and giving of ourselves without restraint, in order to relieve others' needs and make them great, which is what true love is all about. Paul, too, charges Christians to imitate Christ's costly and self-forgetful love (Phil. 2:1–8; 2 Cor. 8:9; Eph. 5:25–33, a word to husbands); and Christ's submissive but resilient patience in enduring human hostility is elsewhere held up for imitation as well (1 Pet. 2:21; Heb. 12:1–4). It is striking that all these references focus on Christ's cross, where the glories of his moral perfections are seen most clearly. It is striking too that the concern of each passage centres not on particular routines to be gone through, but on the spirit and attitude which our whole lives must express. Once again, the divine method of instruction is to 'tune us in' on the right wavelength and then leave the details of the application largely to us.

Fourth, there is the principle expressed in Paul's prayer for the Philippians, 'that your love will keep on growing more and more, together with true knowledge and perfect judgement, so that you will be able to *choose what is best*' (Phil. 1:9f., GNB). The principle is, of two goods choose the greater; don't let the good be the enemy of the best. It is the positive counterpart of the principle that, where one faces a choice of evils, the least evil should always be preferred. Here calculations of consequences must be attempted: for the best course, other things being equal, will always be that which promises most good and least harm. But since our capacity to foresee results is limited, differences of opinion here are inescapable, and so on policy decisions the most devoted Christians will not always be able to see eye to eye. We find this in the New Testament itself. Acts 15:37ff. tells how Paul and Barnabas differed as to whether to take with them John Mark, Barnabas' nephew, on missionary service. Barnabas knew his record but clearly expected him to make good; Paul 'thought best not to take with them one who had withdrawn from them in Pamphylia, and had not gone with them to the work'. Each of them insisted on making the best decision, and was not prepared to settle for anything less, but they differed as to what the best decision was. Being disagreed as to whether Mark was likely to prove an adequate colleague, they concluded that the best decision open to them was to split up, and each take the associate he judged best for the task; so Barnabas took Mark to Cyprus, and Paul went with Silas on a trip that ended in Europe. Some are embarrassed that Paul and Barnabas should ever have been involved in passionate disagreement, but there is no reason to regard this as a moral failure, any more than there is to see their parting as a strategic disaster. We can be sure that, God being who he is, no Christian forfeits blessing for parting company with his brother when both want the best, and only calculation of consequences divides them.

Should it be asked where the Holy Spirit's ministry in the conscience comes in, particularly in cases like this where Christian friends conscientiously differ as to what is wise and right, the answer is that as we pray and lay ourselves open to God, the Spirit quickens our minds and imaginations so that we are able to make the fullest use of the four aids listed, without either confusion of thought or perversion of purpose. But no man, no matter how saintly and devoted, is blessed with infallible perfection of judgment in this world, and (*pace* some charismatics) the idea that God will ordinarily give us experiences of being told, as by a human voice, exactly what to do is an unbiblical will-o'-the-wisp.

It is apparent that all these four aids to right conduct have the effect of maximizing the imaginative and creative element in morality, and of encouraging a spirit of enterprise and even opportunism in serving God—the spirit which so marked Paul (*cf.* Acts 16:35–39; 17:22ff.; 23:6–10). Within the boundaries set by God's specific commands, applications can vary and be better or worse, just as chess openings vary within the limits set by the pieces' permitted moves. And the best course will always be that which promises most in the total situation, just as the best first moves in a chess game will be those which promise most in the total situation, bearing in mind the game's importance, whether one is playing black or white, whether one should go for a win or a draw, the known strengths and weaknesses of one's opponent, one's own skill with this or that opening or line of defence, and so on. Proper Christian obedience is thus as far away as possible from the treadmill negativism of the conscientious conformist, whose main concern is never to put a foot wrong and who conceives the whole Christian life in terms of shunning doubtful things. To be sure, a tender conscience which trembles at God's word (*cf.* Is. 66:2; Ezr. 10:3) and fears to offend him, 'hating even the garment spotted by the flesh' (Jude 23), is a Christian grace, and should never be frowned on as an introspective morbidity; but, just as one cannot maintain health on a diet of disinfectants only, so one cannot fully or healthily obey God just by trying to avoid defilements, evading risks, and omitting to ask what is the *most* one can do to glorify God. For that is the question which the Bible forces us to face all the time.

Motives

The second criterion that Scripture yields for assessing choices is *the motive of the agent*. In Christian obedience the motive must be right as well as the action itself. The object of the action and the motive of the agent are distinct; the former we defined as the effect of successfully completing the action (healing, for instance, being the object of binding up a man's wounds), the latter is that in a man which moves him to attempt the action in the first place. Most motives are either reactions to situations or people, determined from without (*e.g.* fear, or gratitude), or they are personal goals determined from within (*e.g.* achieving wealth, or reputation). Love, however, is a complex motive involving both these elements; it can be both a reaction of good will, occasioned and energized by appreciation of the beloved, and also a purpose of conferring benefit and happiness, irrespective of whether the recipients deserve it and of what it costs one to carry the purpose out.

That the Christian's supreme motive must always be the glory of God (*cf.* 1 Cor. 10:31), and that seeking his glory is the truest expression of love to him, will not be disputed. But love to men for the Lord's sake should motivate us also, and this has been an area of keen debate in recent years. How should love determine my behaviour towards my neighbour? It is necessary to reject the situationist idea that biblical rules of conduct are only rules of thumb, and that sound calculation of consequences can in principle make transgression of any of them right and good;[7] but at the same time it is important to realize that the more strongly neighbour-love operates as a motive, other things being equal, the more enterprising and skilful we are likely to be in devising, within the limits that the law sets, the most fruitful ways and means of doing others good. And when one finds oneself shut up to 'lesser-evil' choices, love to God and neighbour will enable us to see the best that can be made of the bad job, and to choose in the least destructive way.

The role of love in our ethical decision-making is comparable to that of the referee in football. The referee's purpose is to apply the rules in a way which secures the best possible game, which is of course what the rules themselves are for. So he does four things. First, he takes pains to familiarize himself with the rules and the proper way of interpreting them. Second, throughout the game he takes care always to be in the best position to make a decision. This requires close observation of all that is happening on the field, and anticipation, born of experience, as to how each situation may develop. Third, in order to get his facts straight, he will where necessary consult his linesmen, who are better placed to observe some things than he is himself; though he will pay no attention to the crowd, which is partisan and not well placed. Fourth, he will when appropriate invoke the difficult 'advantage rule', which allows him to keep the game going though an infringement has occurred, if continuance is to the advantage of the wronged side.

Now, love to God and neighbour requires us to behave like the referee. Our purpose is to live in a manner that is as pleasing to God and as beneficial to our neighbour as possible, within the limits that God has laid down; and to this end love prompts a parallel fourfold procedure. First, it directs us to gain thorough knowledge of the whole range of obligations that Scripture requires us to meet. Without this basic knowledge, good decisions will be impossible. Second, love directs us in each situation to get into the best position for decision-making, by securing as much relevant information about actual causes and possible consequences as we can. The legalistic mentality, from which so many of us suffer, is always in danger of pronouncing (negatively!) too soon, before the necessary minimum of information is to hand; we have to guard against that. Third, love directs us when we are not well placed for decision, either from lack of specialist knowledge or through a personal involvement biasing our judgment, to turn to others who are better qualified to suggest what should be done, while at the same time declining to be swayed by loud noises from persons who are passionate but not well informed.

Fourth, love directs us on occasion to apply the Christian equivalent of the advantage rule, by not jeopardizing a greater good through needless enquiry into doubtful details. Thus, on the question of meat offered to idols, Paul writes: 'Eat whatever is sold in the meat market without raising any question on the ground of conscience. . . . If one of the unbelievers invites you to dinner and you are disposed to go, eat whatever is set before you without raising any question on the ground of conscience. (But if someone says to you, "This has been offered in sacrifice", then out of consideration for the man who informed you, and for conscience' sake—I mean his conscience, not yours—do not eat it)' (1 Cor. 10:25-29). Paul's point is that though Christians should eschew any social activity of which sacrifices to pagan gods form part (verses 14-22), they need not ask, or bother their heads, whether food offered them in pagan homes was offered to idols first. If a 'weak' brother raises the issue, responsible Christians will then practise abstinence for his sake, but otherwise the question should be allowed to lie dormant, while Christians eat freely. As it is neither God-honouring, nor edifying, nor safe (says Paul) to join in sacrifices to pagan deities (for, after all, they really are demons), so it is not necessary in principle nor best in practice to spurn a pagan's hospitality in the interests of a thoroughgoing dietary witness against pagan beliefs (for, after all, ' "the earth is the Lord's, and everything in it" ' (verse 26), and what is on the table, whatever has been done with it, remains God's gift). Knowing the overall value and potential importance of friendly social links with unbelievers, Paul counsels Christians to use their God-given liberty by waiving the idolatry issue, and thus in effect to play their own advantage rule in the situation.

But as referees, however experienced and well-intentioned, can still on occasion make bad decisions, so Christians from time to time have to acknowledge, looking back, that they missed the best course of action, either because an unnoticed cooling of their love left them in a particular situation or relationship thoughtless and apathetic, or else because love made them too eager and sympathetic to be truly prudent, so that they invoked the advantage rule inappropriately. Such acknowledgment is deeply humbling. But Christians live by the forgiveness of their sins; so they can afford to fail, and in humility they will learn from their mistakes.

Choosing

So what is involved in making a moral choice? and how should it be done? The matter may be summed up thus. A moral choice is one involving standards (right and wrong) and values (good and bad). It presupposes a rational agent, that is, one who is free in the relevant respects to act rationally (not a demoniac, then, or a madman, or a baby, or a sufferer from an irrational behaviour pattern like kleptomania or agoraphobia). It presupposes too a field of freedom within which the agent sees that more than one course is open to him. The making of the choice involves, first, thinking out possible lines of action; second, envisaging their consequences; and third, measuring both action and consequences thus envisaged, by the moral standards and scale of values that one recognizes as binding.

The Christian accepts the moral standards which are set forth in the Bible, acknowledging them as standing in a 'maker's handbook' relation to his own nature and as circumscribing the only way of life that can lead him to ultimate fulfilment and felicity. His moral values, too, are determined by theology. They are, on the one hand, the characteristic qualities of those types of actions which God loves and delights in, and, on the other hand, that longed-for state of affairs in which God is being praised for his great glory and men whom he made and loves are being benefited according to their need. He knows that the best choice will always be choice of the best option, and that the way to choose between options is not by reference to rules apart from consequences, as if consequences were morally irrelevant, nor by reference to consequences apart from rules, as if rules had no intrinsic moral value, but by reference to both together. In his choosing he is constantly exercised with the question: 'Is this the *best* I can do?'

It is a law of life that our values become our motives, so that motive, where known (for we do not always admit our motives, even to ourselves), is the clearest indication of character that exists. It is possible, as we all know, to make a right choice from a wrong motive, and equally a bad choice from a good motive. The Christian's aim, however, in his game-plan for living, will always be to do the right thing for the right reason—that is, always to be found applying biblical standards for his guidance from the two-fold motive of the glory of God and the good of men, understanding 'good' in terms not simply of currently felt need, but of godliness and glory (*cf.* the meaning of 'good' in Rom. 8:28). The Christian knows that only when his motives are right will his choices, however good in themselves, be the choices of a morally good man, who truly pleases God.

Is God's promise of a reward a motive, in the sense of a spur to right choice? Strictly speaking, no. The Christian's reward is not directly earned; it is not a payment proportionate to services rendered; it is a Father's gift of generous grace to his children, far exceeding anything they deserved (see Mt. 20:1–16). Also, we must understand that the promised reward is not something of a different nature tacked on to the activity being rewarded; it is, rather, that activity itself—that is to say, communion with God in worship and service—in consummation.[8] God's promise of reward, thus understood, may well be an encouragement to action and a source of strength and joy in it, but the motive must be love to God and neighbour, as we said. We serve our God, not for reward, but because he is our God, and we love him. Francis Xavier's well-known hymn focuses this.

> My God, I love thee—not because
>   I hope for heaven thereby,
> Nor yet because who love thee not
>   Are lost eternally.
>
> Thou, O my Jesus, thou didst me
>   Upon the cross embrace;
> For me didst bear the nails and spear,
>   And manifold disgrace.
>
> And griefs and torments numberless,
>   And sweat and agony,
> And death itself—and all for me,
>   Who was thine enemy.

189

> Then why, O blessed Jesus Christ,
> Should I not love thee well?
> Not for the sake of winning heaven
> Or of escaping hell;
>
> Not with the hope of gaining aught;
> Not seeking a reward;
> But as thyself hast lovèd me,
> O ever-loving Lord.
>
> E'en so I love thee, and will love,
> And in thy praise will sing;
> Because thou art my loving God
> And my eternal King.

C. S. Lewis compares our position, as we move on in the Christian life, to that of a schoolboy learning Greek.[9] The enjoyment of Aeschylus and Sophocles to which he will one day come is the proper consummation of all his slogging at the grammar, just as the enjoyment of God in that glory compared to which, as Lewis elsewhere says, the raptures of earthly lovers are mere milk and water is the proper consummation of discipleship here. But at first the boy cannot imagine this enjoyment at all. As his Greek improves, however, enjoyment of Greek literature begins to come, and he begins to be able to desire the reward that awaits him (more of the same, at an intenser level), which capacity for desire, says Lewis, is itself a preliminary reward. Meantime, however (here I make a point complementary to Lewis's), it is the increased enjoyment in the present which sends him back to work at his Greek with increased energy and excitement; and so it goes on. I like this illustration, both because it is true to life (for when I learned Greek it happened to me) and because is shows the truth about Christian motivation so clearly.

The last and most important thing to be said about moral choice is that our choosing is a function of our character, just as our present character is largely the product of our past choices. Sin, that irrational, self-centred, anti-God surd in the soul, distorts character most fundamentally at motivational level; grace restores character there, but in a way that brings tension and struggle. 'I do not understand my own actions,' writes Paul. 'For I do not do what I want, but I do the very thing I hate. Now if I do what I do not want, I agree that the law is good. . . . I can will what is right, but I cannot do it. For I do not do the good I want, but the evil I do not want is what I do. Now if I do what I do not want, it is no longer I that do it, but sin which dwells within me' (Rom. 7:15ff.). What is going on here? New motivation, supernaturally restored by the coming of the Holy Spirit into a man's heart, is manifesting itself. This is Paul the Christian (the present tense, and the flow of the argument, prove this) testifying to the fact that now by grace he loves God's law and wants to keep it perfectly to God's glory. His reach, however, exceeds his grasp, and his qualified success feels like failure. Sin within him, dethroned but not yet destroyed, is fighting back. The intensity of Paul's distress at being less than perfect by the law's standard is, however, the index of the strength of his new motivation, and it is from this source that character grows and moral energy derives through the inward working of the Holy Spirit. When elsewhere Paul says to Christians, 'Work out your own salvation with fear and trembling [awe and reverence]; for God is at work in you, both to will and to work for his good pleasure' (Phil. 2:12f.), what he means them to do is precisely to keep their motivational channels clear and work against whatever opposition indwelling sin may raise to make and follow out right choices, trusting in the Spirit's power. And as we do so, our capacity for so doing will increase; and thus God's work of grace within us will go on.

NOTES

1. This chapter is indebted to material by Gordon Stobart and Dennis Winter.
2. *Genesis* (*Tyndale Old Testament Commentaries,* Inter-Varsity Press, 1967), p. 51. On the relation between 'image' (*ṣelem*) and 'likeness' (*deₘûth*), Kidner rightly comments: 'The words *image* and *likeness* reinforce one another: there is no "and" between the phrases, and Scripture does not use them as technically distinct expressions, as some theologians have done, whereby the "image" is man's indelible constitution as a rational and morally responsible being, and the "likeness" is that spiritual accord with the will of God which was lost at the Fall' (pp. 50f.).
3. For further development of this point, see C. S. Lewis, 'The Humanitarian Theory of Punishment', in *Undeceptions: Essays on Theology and Ethics* (Collins, 1971).

Law, morality and the Bible

4. The best-known expositions of the 'Boo—hurrah' approach are by A. J. Ayer in *Language, Truth and Logic* (Gollancz, 1936), chapter 6, and by C. L. Stevenson in *Ethics and Language* (Yale, New Haven, 1944). For a candid philosophical criticism of it, see A. C. Ewing, *Ethics* (English Universities Press, 1953), chapter 7, especially pp. 115–126.

5. The Puritan, Richard Sibbes, expounding 2 Cor. 1:12, gave striking substance to this thought by picturing conscience as God's court within us, thus:

'To clear this further concerning the nature of conscience, know that God has set up in a man a court, and there is in man all that are in a court. 1. There is a *register* [registrar] to take notice of what we have done. . . . The conscience keeps diaries. It sets down everything. It is not forgotten, though we think it is. . . . Conscience is the register. 2. And then there are *witnesses*. "The testimony of conscience." Conscience doth witness, this have I done, this I have not done. 3. There is *an accuser with the witnesses*. The conscience, it accuseth, or excuseth. 4. And then there is the *judge*. Conscience is the judge. There it doth judge, this is well done, this is ill done. 5. Then there is an *executioner*, and conscience is that too. . . . The punishment of conscience, it is a prejudice [pre-judging] of future judgment. There is a flash of hell presently [in the present] after an ill act. . . . If the understanding apprehend dolorous things, then the heart smites, as David's "heart smote him", 1 Sam. 24.5. . . . The heart smites with grief for the present, and fear for the time to come.

'God hath set and planted in man this court of conscience, and it is God's hall, as it were, where he keeps his first judgment . . . his assizes. And conscience doth all the parts. It registereth, it witnesseth, it accuseth, it judgeth, it executes, it doth all' (A. B. Grosart (ed.) Sibbes, *Works*, James Nichol, 1862, III, pp. 210f.).

6. Ronald Preston, 'Conscience', in John Macquarrie (ed.), *A Dictionary of Christian Ethics* (SCM Press, 1967), p. 68.

7. See Part 2, chapter 2.

8. 'There are different kinds of reward. There is the reward which has no natural connection with the things you do to earn it, and is quite foreign to the desires that ought to accompany these things. Money is not the natural reward of love; that is why we call a man mercenary if he marries a woman for the sake of her money. But marriage is the proper reward for a real lover, and he is not mercenary for desiring it. A general who fights well in order to get a peerage is mercenary; a general who fights for victory is not, victory being the proper reward of battle as marriage is the proper reward of love. The proper rewards are not simply tacked on to the activity for which they are given, but are the activity itself in consummation' (C. S. Lewis, 'The Weight of Glory', in *Screwtape Proposes a Toast*, Fontana, 1965, p. 95).

9. *Ibid.*

4

Motivation in Christian behaviour

Dennis Winter

Introduction

Saints[1] rather than theologians give the clue to the innermost heart of Christianity. This is not, however, to say that behaviour rather than belief is the core of true religion, but rather that the saint goes significantly beyond the conventions and standards of his own time, and so gives us a glimpse of the inner springs of his religious life rather than the words which express that life. The saint's behaviour is frequently so different from that of his age that he, or she, is an outcast from society. Like Jesus himself he may even be thought of as immoral. Because he clashes with the established ways of his time, it is only the voice of history that proclaims him a saint: it is only the eye of history that can look at his deeds and see that they are 'more righteous' than the righteous deeds of his contemporaries. Such a man or woman has come nearer to the well-spring of Christian morality than the majority who have merely conformed to the accepted standards (albeit 'Christian' standards) of the age.

But in examining motivation in Christian behaviour we have to make sense not only of the saint, but also of the 'average' Christian. We have to treat seriously the fact that some Christians, both past and present, have acted on a double standard of morality—one for the average Christian, and the other for the more 'serious'. At the end of the chapter we shall see that there is indeed something in the structure of Christian morality which could give rise to such a misunderstanding. But before reaching that point we have to find out what the structure is and the various ways in which concepts such as reward and punishment are used in that structure, often by giving them a distinctive change of emphasis.

Innovation rather than conformity has been the distinctive path along which Christian ethics has frequently travelled. Not just any innovation, however. Change for the sake of change may be part of the pattern for modern living, but it has no place in biblical morality. Neither is the direction of innovation random. The many New Testament references to a revolutionary change in the life of the believer may reject aspects of the conventional morality of the time, but they reject even more strongly the conventional immorality of the time. An extended quotation from the letter to the Ephesians shows several features of this aspect of Christian morality:

'I want to urge you in the name of the Lord, not to go on living the aimless kind of life that pagans live. Intellectually they are in the dark, and they are estranged from the life of God, without knowledge because they have shut their hearts to it. Their sense of right and wrong once dulled, they have abandoned themselves to sexuality and eagerly pursue a career of indecency of every kind. Now that is hardly the way you have learnt from Christ, unless you failed to hear him properly when you were taught what the truth is in Jesus. You must give up your old way of life; you must put aside your old self, which gets corrupted by following illusory desires. Your mind must be renewed by a spiritual revolution so that you can put on the new self that has been created in God's way, in the goodness and holiness of the truth.

'So from now on, there must be no more lies: You must speak the truth to one another, since we are all parts of one another. Even if you are angry, you must not sin: never let the sun set on your anger or else you will give the devil a foothold. Anyone who was a thief must stop stealing; he should try to find some useful manual work instead, and be able to do some good by helping others that are in need. Guard against foul talk; let your words be for the improvement of others, as occasion offers, and do good to your listeners, otherwise you will only be grieving the Holy Spirit of God who has marked you with his seal for you to be set free when the day comes. Never have grudges against others, or lose your temper, or raise your voice to anybody, or call each other names, or allow any sort of spite-fulness. Be friends with one another, and kind, forgiving each other as readily as God forgave you in Christ.

'Try, then, to imitate God. . . .'
(Eph. 4:17 – 5:1, JB).[2]

Ethics in the New Testament

Several instructive features of New Testament ethics are found in this passage, and to some extent in all the passages cited:

1. The rejection of immorality. Underlying this rejection is a basic acceptance of the morals of the Old Testament. In the above passage two of the ethical instructions are direct Old Testament quotations. Elsewhere, explicit references to the Ten Commandments as well as the inclusion in lists of sins to be avoided of such items as usury, idolatry and sorcery, all indicate a basic dependence on the Old Testament. A case could be made out for saying that the *moral* code of the Old Testament is never contradicted, but only extended, in the moral code of the New Testament. A saint is not one who blatantly disregards the moral code, but one who goes beyond it. Such a case ignores, however, the distinct possi-bility that neither Old nor New Testament morality is at root a code of rules.

2. The adoption of a strenuous, new morality that extends beyond the conventional morality. Thus the thief is not only to cease stealing, he is also to work so that he will have enough to help those who are in real need. The foul-mouthed is not only to stop his foul talk, but is to replace this by words which lead to the improvement of others.

3. Ethical instructions are frequently linked to theological assertions. Because the Holy Spirit lives in the Christians they are not to grieve him by their foul talk and failure to do good to others. 1 Corinthians 6:19 uses a related argument to show that fornication should not be possible for the Christian. God's forgiveness in Christ is cited as the reason why Christians should be friendly and kind to each other.

4. The change in moral stance between a man apart from Christ and the same man after he has become a Christian, although sometimes spoken of as something which is learnt (verse 20) is more frequently spoken of as spiritual revolution (verse 23). The revolution is described in terms of a changed personality (verses 22–24), linked to the presence of the Holy Spirit.

Passages such as the above are not to be understood as the presentation of a code of moral behaviour; rather they are the outworking of a spiritual revolution in the life of each individual Christian (and indeed, in the life of the whole Christian community). This revolution is nothing less than the coming of the Holy Spirit. It is the presence of the Spirit which gives Christian morality its dynamic quality. Obedience to a code of law might travel the first mile, but by its very nature it cannot travel the second mile. This going beyond the accepted code of morality has always been a hallmark of dynamic Christianity. The inward spring of Christian character is not law-keeping but allowing the Spirit of God to possess and control. The fruit of the Spirit (Gal. 5:22f.) is largely understood as moral excellence, and yet it is a morality that a code of law cannot prescribe or touch (Gal. 5:23). The Spirit is not amoral, as would be expected if he were a power to be harnessed (for power can be used for good or ill according to the man who uses it), but rather the Spirit leads in only one direction. He leads in the direction of Christ-like behaviour, in the direction of pleasing God.

It is only the presence of the Spirit which can prevent the slide of Christian morality into another code of law. Church history presents us with many examples of the reduction of Christian behaviour into obedience to a new law. It is not without significance that times of spiritual fervour have led to new directions in the pattern of Christian moral behaviour. The Evangelical Revival, for instance, was linked with the new insights of the Clapham sect.

Our subject, however, is not the dynamic of Christian morality, but the motive of Christian morality. Early Christian communities, both within the New Testament period and beyond, clearly had trouble with those who claimed the presence of the Spirit, and yet behaved in ways which Christians at large found distasteful and frequently immoral. The first letter of John has several hints of this problem in the community to which it was addressed. For this reason it was not enough to 'leave it to the Spirit'. The motivation and the content of Christian morality had to be expressed in language which could more easily be measured against the pattern of the life of Jesus.

The Pharisees

Superficially at least, it is possible to extract from the New Testament a list of ways of behaving which are reckoned as displeasing to God, even if the related task of compiling a list of ways of behaving which are pleasing to God is much more problematic. Obedience to the law may not be the pathway to eternal life, but the law does indicate the sort of life which pleases God. So it is quite reasonable to ask whether it is possible to compile a list of 'do's and don'ts' which might serve as a tentative framework for a Christian morality. Yet such lists, when attempted, have always broken down. Admittedly, the translation from the ethical system of Palestine two thousand years ago into one for an entirely different sort of society is by no means a simple task. But even assuming that such a task were possible, it would still produce a list, which in a major sense would be pulling in the opposite direction to the teaching of Jesus.

Part of the difference between Jesus and the Pharisees is to be found in the relative importance they attach to outward acts. By producing an extensive system of laws applicable to every circumstance of life it was possible for the Pharisee to achieve a complete obedience. Paul, in his days as a Pharisee, had done just that (Phil. 3:6). Jesus pictures a Pharisee thanking God (or should it be congratulating himself?) that he had observed the code of law down to the last, small command (Lk. 18:10ff.). Yet the Pharisee, according to Jesus, had not pleased God, whereas the sinful tax collector in the same story had done so. Jesus was not condemning the external morality of the Pharisee by such a story, but was making it clear that such an approach to pleasing God is a dead end. It is a dead end because it can lead a man to believe that he has attained perfection. It is a dead end because it is so open to abuse. The law code can be used as a framework for evading the spirit of the law, a sorry fact which has haunted legislators both ancient and modern. As Jesus points out, the Pharisaic method had managed to transform a commandment to honour parents into legislation which ignored them (Mk. 7:10ff.).

The Pharisees treated the Old Testament commands as a skeleton of law which needed to be filled out and particularized into the full corpus of laws and legislation which they observed. The observation of the sabbath, for example, needed to be spelt out in specific detail. What constituted 'working' for the purposes of this law? What length of journey was permitted on such a day? What was the exact duration of the sabbath? On the basis of the detail with which they invested the law, the Pharisees were able to condemn Jesus and his disciples for supposed contraventions, as when Jesus healed someone (*e.g.* Lk. 6:6ff.) or when the disciples plucked some ears of corn (Mt. 12:1). The Pharisees' method was to start with a scripture and travel outwards to a specific situation. God was pleased by the detailed external actions derived from particular biblical commands. Because of the danger of inadvertently breaking laws, they erected a 'fence' to ensure that no accidental infringements of the law occurred. Thus, when the biblical code allowed a maximum of forty stripes in punishment (Dt. 25:3), the Pharisees restricted it to thirty-nine stripes, just in case a mistake in counting was made. It mattered that the exact letter of the law was obeyed.

Jesus' teaching

The method of Jesus, on the other hand, started with the same scripture, but instead of immediately externalizing it into detailed legislation, he moved inwards to what that scripture revealed as to the nature of God and of his creation. He moved from the specific to the general. God was pleased no longer in obedience to detailed rules, but in acting in accordance with his revealed nature and the nature of his creation. To Jesus the sabbath is no longer a chain to restrict man's freedom, but a merciful provision of God for the benefit of man. He aptly summarized the two contrasting attitudes in 'The sabbath was made for man, not man for the sabbath' (Mk. 2:27).

It should not be thought, however, that Jesus' approach to the Old Testament led to a laxer approach than that of the Pharisees. Application of the same insights to other commands, such as the prohibitions on murder and adultery, showed that God willed not only the absence of the external act but also of the thought that fathered the act. Because Jesus moved the focus of attention from the external act to the underlying causes for the act, he moved the centre of morality from the overt action to the internal motive.[3]

The Epistles

This fundamental difference between Jesus and the Pharisees might seem to have been watered down in the household codes and sin lists found in the New Testament letters. The quotation at the beginning of this chapter shows how the presence or absence of various external acts is used as the sign of a true Christian. Because external acts are seen, they are the obvious, tangible signs of what a person is like. But the external acts are not seen as things in themselves; rather as factors pointing to an inward transformation. It is this transformation which lies at the heart of the apostle's concern. It is at this inward level that the letter-writers make their appeal. Thus Paul appeals to the Philippian Christians, 'Have this mind among yourselves, which you have in Christ Jesus' (Phil. 2:5). As the Christians at Philippi sought to establish a 'pecking order' in their community, Paul does not appeal to external qualifications but to internal motivation. A Pharisaic approach would presumably have set out a 'pecking order' based on some external criteria (charismatic or ecclesiastical gifts?) and then invoked sanctions against those who offended against the system, adding a certain amount of humanity to soften the harsher excesses of the 'law' so produced. It is sad to note that the Pharisaic method has prevailed over a larger part of the history of the church.

Paul's method, in contrast, was to shift the focus from external signs and acts to the internal motives of the Christians. Paul's appeal at the level of motive does not mean that he is not interested in the final act. His letters give ample evidence of his concern with the practical realities of life. His method, like the method of Jesus, is that by attending to the level of motive we do tackle the external acts as well. The reverse is not always true. The man who does not hate will not murder. If he does cause the death of another it will be an accident or because some higher demand is made (*e.g.* in a 'just' war). Clearly, Jesus reckons that the morality of an action is determined not only by its obvious end-product, but mainly by its inner motivation. Because Jesus sees the hidden motive as the true spring of action, he also teaches that it is not for fellow men to judge. God alone can see the hidden motive and, in the deep sense, he alone can judge. The lawcourts have to be largely concerned with external acts—men can see external acts, but can only infer inner motivation (although the difference between murder and manslaughter shows that, in the most serious cases at least, they do try to take inner motivation into account).

'Motivation' in contemporary usage

Concern for people's motives is not the prerogative of any one group. Men have always speculated on the reasons for others behaving in the way they do, *i.e.* they are interested not only in what people do, but also the motivation lying behind such actions. Such motivation is seldom a simple matter, but frequently a complex of conscious and unconscious elements. Psychological work over the past fifty years has produced an enormous volume of material on motivation. Unfortunately the word has been used in a narrower, technical sense than in normal conversation. Also, it is used within the deterministic framework of a science. Motivation is a word frequently used to describe the, often unconscious, forces behind actions performed. In such language a man's motive is not a consciously willed drive, but an inner, frequently unconscious or even irrational compulsion. Freud's use of the motivations of sex and aggression as the roots of human behaviour shows the way in which the word has been used.

The difference between the ways in which the word motivation is used is even more fundamental than this. In psychological use it describes something which lies at the root of an inevitable chain of cause and effect leading to an action. In normal usage it has to do with choices which are going to result in one action rather than another.

Motivation as a word thus has two distinct and yet closely related meanings in two different languages: one in the technical scientific language of psychology, the other in the personal language of human choice. The ways of seeking to reconcile these two languages, which describe the same situation but in different terms, have been explored in various studies during recent years.[4] From the point of view of this discussion 'motivation' is being used in its non-scientific sense. We are not seeking to find out how feelings of hate or lust or whatever arise in the human mind, but rather how the mind is to deal with such once they do arise.

Most men would cite the avoidance of pain and unpleasantness and the seeking of security and pleasure as motives which move them to behave in the way they do. But any illusion of a universal motivation disappears when we seek to give some content to pain or pleasure. The infinite gradation between the pleasure of being warm and the pain of being burned should warn us that dividing lines are very difficult to define. Sometimes what one man reckons as pain another will welcome as pleasure. One man will avoid crowds and seek the lonely hillside; another will find the loneliness painful and will seek the crowd. Indeed the same man may react differently on two different occasions.

Not only do men differ in their placing of the threshold of pain, but also in the relative importance given to differing types of pain. One man will find the pain of a guilty conscience more difficult to bear than the pain of hunger, and so will not steal. Another man in the same situation will value a clear conscience less than a full stomach. Because any public system of morality must be more consistent than human feelings, moral education in the past has placed considerable emphasis on one type of pain—the pain of a guilty conscience. The mechanism of conscience suits it admirably to this function, for unlike the other 'feelings' it can be educated prior to an event. For instance, the conscience can be fed with the information, 'it is wrong to steal', long before any temptation to steal occurs. In the temptation situation it will act as a 'moral flywheel' whose previously given moral momentum (in the form of moral education) will carry the person tempted past the dangerous situation.[5]

Motivation in the Bible

So far we have used the spectrum that goes from extreme pain to extreme pleasure as the reference point for talking about human motivation. The Bible, however, uses different axes around which to plot its moral ideas. The pain–pleasure axis takes man and his reactions as the criterion of moral choice. However refined this approach may become through the use of a conscience into which notions such as the commandments of God may be fed, in the end it is dependent upon men's feelings. As would be expected, the Bible is far more concerned about God and his reactions. For this reason we find the pain–pleasure axis replaced by the reward–punishment axis. This presupposes a reference point outside of man. That point could be sought in the world of nature, as in some systems of evolutionary ethics, or, as in the biblical ethic, the reference point is found in the will of God. Once this position has been reached it becomes possible to plot moral ideas on yet a third set of axes, this time with the axes labelled 'pleasing God' and 'displeasing God'.

The geometric analogy can be pressed further into seeing that it is possible to plot moral ideas on all three sets of axes, and thus the axes do have a relationship to each other. In theory at least it should be possible to transform from one system to another.

The biblical material is best considered in terms of the reward–punishment and the pleasing–displeasing God sets of axes.

Rewards and punishments

A most widely held view of human behaviour is that men behave as they do either to avoid punishment or to gain reward. The admonitions of teachers, magistrates and parents are frequently phrased in terms of 'Do this, or else such and such will happen'. The rewards offered or the punishments to be avoided differ considerably from society to society, but the basic idea of behaviour governed by a system of rewards and punishments is as wide as humanity. We would expect to find some scheme of reward and punishment in any comprehensive approach to behaviour. As we look at the New Testament we find many references to this theme, both in the teaching of Jesus and the apostles. Typical is Matthew 10:41–42: 'He who receives a prophet because he is a prophet shall receive a prophet's reward, and he who receives a righteous man because he is a righteous man shall receive a righteous man's reward. And whoever gives to one of these little ones even a cup of cold water because he is a disciple, truly, I say to you, he shall not lose his reward.' Similarly, Jesus also warns of punishment, for instance in Matthew 6:15: 'If you do not forgive men their trespasses, neither will your Father forgive your trespasses.'

It has been fashionable for a considerable time to denigrate as unworthy such appeals to future reward or punishment. We have been told that we should pursue virtue for its own sake, without a thought of reward. Although the surface meaning of such an attitude disregards any thought of reward, it is true to say that if a person felt there was no difference between doing right and wrong, if there was no sense of fulfilment in doing one, or of shame in doing the other, then most of us would consider that such a person gave no content to the word morality. Rewards and punishments in some form or another are essential to any practical system of morality.

This does not mean that any system of reward and punishment is ethically acceptable. Such a system could well be used as bribery —'pie in the sky when you die'. What matters is the relationship of this reward or punishment to the action prescribed which will secure that reward or merit that punishment. To most people there is something morally offensive in the idea that, for instance, one should tell the truth now in order to receive material rewards at a later date. The offence is contained in the sequence: tell the truth—material reward. Appeal to material reward seems totally unrelated to telling the truth. Bearing this criticism in mind, we can now further examine the Gospel material. The examples from Matthew's Gospel quoted above are instructive in two respects:

(1) Motivation in Matthew 10:41, 42 is found not in the hope of future reward, but in terms of the present situation: 'receive a prophet, because he is a prophet', *etc*. The reward is consequent to the act, not seemingly as an inevitable consequence, but as a gift from God.

(2) Reward or punishment is related to the act performed. The one who does not forgive is not forgiven; the one who receives a righteous man has a righteous man's reward. The relationship between the act performed and the reward promised is seen at its most obvious, yet at its most paradoxical, in the Beatitudes (Mt. 5:3–12). Here there is no straightforward, *logical* connection between action and reward, but rather the connection is to be found in the nature of God. Christ commends those actions and ways of life which are in accordance with the nature of God. Man acts in these ways as a sign of trust and obedience. Rewards are the eventual revelation of the nature of God which demonstrate that the earlier act of trust was not misplaced.

Almsgiving is commended, not to appear generous to others— if, indeed, our motive is to obtain other men's praise, that will be the sum of our reward (Mt. 6:2). It is commended not even for the benefit it will bring to the needy. Rather, almsgiving is to be an act of trust in God, whose nature is to be generous and lavish in his treatment of his creation. The motivation Jesus appeals to is one of trust in God's nature. The reward he promises is the out-working of this. Jesus teaches, not that God is a judge who rewards and punishes according to merit, but that he is a Father who gives generously. Despite the fact that many of the parables talk in terms of reward and punishment, the reward is always far more than justice would require. Thus the parable of the talents (Mt. 25:14–30), where the reward motif is very strong, sees the rewards more in terms of the generosity of the master than the deserts of the servants. Those who are prepared to give up all for the sake of the

Son of man are rewarded a hundredfold (Mt. 19:27–30). The emphasis of the parable of the labourers in the vineyard (Mt. 20:1–16) is again on the generosity of the owner who does not give in proportion to achievement, but according to his generous nature. The same can be noted in almost all the Gospel references. The idea of rewards as a result of meritorious service is swamped by the thought of a Father's generous provision over and above all deserving.

As frequently happens in the New Testament, an existing idea is taken and turned almost inside out as it is confronted by the grace of God. In an extensive article, Preisker sums up the New Testament evidence from the Gospels[6] as well as giving reasons for the retention of the word 'reward' as follows: 'Jesus speaks then of reward, but all thought of merit is unconditionally excluded. His reference to reward implies:

(1) that man stands under the eyes of the holy God;
(2) that he owes obedience to God as Lord and King;
(3) that man's salvation can be accomplished only by God himself;
(4) that only God's generosity grants a reward, and that it does so only to men with receptive hearts which are open to be blessed by the wonders of the kingdom of God;
(5) that reward is not a claim of just recompense, but the incomprehensible rewarding which derives from God's love which finds in the kingdom of God the beginning and completion of this overflowing generosity.'

In Paul, exhortations to moral behaviour are sometimes linked with thoughts of reward and punishment. In the wider context of total behaviour he himself runs the race to win the prize (1 Cor. 9:24–27). Such statements must be read carefully, noting particularly the prize offered and the dynamic which enables the race to be won. The reward is to 'know him [Christ]' (Phil. 3:10). He may be running for a prize, but he is 'trying to capture the prize for which Christ Jesus captured me' (Phil. 3:12, JB). The prize is 'in Christ Jesus' (Phil. 3:14). The power by which he contends for the prize is not his old life but 'Christ who lives in me' (Gal. 2:20). It is the Spirit who helps in our weakness (Rom. 8:26).

The two Pauline passages which deal at length with the subject of rewards are 1 Corinthians 3:9-15 and, later in the same letter, chapter 9:16-27. The first passage does not explicitly state the reward, but by implication it is the building erected on the foundation of Christ which survives 'the Day' (of judgment). In the context of the letter it is possible to see various structures which were being constructed in the Corinthian church. The different buildings had various slogans and watchwords associated with them, watchwords such as 'wisdom' (chapters 1 and 2) and 'freedom' (chapters 6, 8 and 9). Unfortunately watchwords and slogans not only contain truth, but frequently cloak error. It is true that 'all things are lawful for me' (1 Cor. 6:12); yet this is not the whole truth, so Paul has to remind his readers that 'not all things are helpful'. 'The Day' will burn up the mistaken deeds and doctrines performed under the slogan 'all things are lawful' and will leave only those which are of the gospel. A man's reward will be the joy of the realization that he had truly rooted and grounded his life in that gospel. Most of us recognize at least in others, the presence of 'blind spots' where they have not followed through in one area or another of their lives, the true understanding of the gospel. 'The Day' will reveal such blind spots for what they are.

Chapter 9 of the letter contains an interesting glance at Paul's own motivation. Although, as he argues from scripture, 'Those who proclaim the gospel should get their living by the gospel' (1 Cor. 9:14), yet he himself does not make use of this right. He proclaims the gospel free of charge in order to obtain a reward. The reward, however, is not some material benefit, but the joy and satisfaction which come to him by making the gospel 'free of charge' (1 Cor. 9:18), a reward, incidentally, that sounds very near to 'virtue as its own reward'.

In several passages both in Paul and elsewhere, reference is made to a future crown awarded by the Lord. In many of these references the crown is for all the redeemed who keep the faith to the end (2 Tim. 4:8; Jas. 1:12; 1 Pet. 5:4; Rev. 2:10, *etc.*). In other cases the crown refers to some trophy of the gospel, *e.g.* 1 Thessalonians

2:19 where the crown is the Thessalonian church and its faith. The crown is something for which a human agent bore some responsibility and which brings glory to God. As Jesus committed himself to the Father as an act of faith in the Father's goodness, a goodness which offered as its reward 'the joy which was still in the future' (Heb. 12:2, JB), so the Christian commits himself to God, not seeking to bring things to God (works), but accepting from God the promises (including those of rewards) which he makes. These rewards are not given in the sense of payments for services rendered, but as gifts for those who take God at his word and walk in the way he commands. 'Christians are told by the Spirit to look to faith for those rewards that righteousness hopes for' (Gal. 5:5, JB). The Galatians are warned not to look to the law to bring them justification (Gal. 5:4) and yet a few verses later they are told to obey the law as summarized in Leviticus 19:18: 'Love your neighbour as yourself' (Gal. 5:14). The reason given for obedience to the law is given as the preservation of the community. In such a context the law is seen not as a means of attaining righteousness but as laying down a pattern of life which is pleasing to God and to the advantage of men.

Rewards, then, in the New Testament, are not to be the aim of a course of action, but appear as part of its result. As Paul Ramsey puts it, 'Promise of reward may be the condition of action, the ground or the promise of strength, but reward is never the action's goal. Reward is always added to the nature of the act, not a direct result of it such as might become a part of the agent's own prudential calculation. If he were calculating the nature of his act would change, it would not be the kind of action for which reward is promised.'[7]

Pleasing God

The formulation of laws, 'You shall . . .', 'You shall not . . .', presupposes a reason for such commandments. The reason may be prudential, either referring to the present, 'Do not touch the fire, or else you will be burnt' or else to the future, 'Work well at school, and you will get a good job when you leave.' As we have already seen, some of the biblical commands are phrased in terms of rewards or punishments. One well-known instance is the fifth commandment, 'Honour your father and your mother, that your days may be long in the land which the Lord your God gives you' (Ex. 20:12). The majority of biblical commands in both Testaments do not carry such prudential considerations. The command is to be obeyed because it is of God. Sometimes there may be a thought that obedience is the proper demonstration of gratitude, as, for instance, is implied in the preamble to the Ten Commandments.

Although the equation is hardly ever made, it can be readily seen that what God commands equals the 'will of God' equals 'what is pleasing to God'. The 'will of God' is a term used fairly frequently in both the Gospels and the Epistles of the New Testament. Jesus teaches his disciples to pray, 'Thy will be done' (Mt. 6:10). The one who would enter the kingdom of God would be the one who carried out 'the will of my Father who is in heaven' (Mt. 7:21). God's will as used here and elsewhere is not an exclusively moral term, but it includes morality in its meaning. On some occasions it carries the sense of permissive will, as in the introduction to 1 Corinthians, 'called by the will of God to be an apostle' (1 Cor. 1:1). More normally the 'will of God' carries the thought of those actions, *etc.,* which are approved (or in some cases planned) by God. The 'will of God' is not an alternative way of saying 'actions prescribed by the law', indeed it carries with it an element of commitment to an unknown pattern of behaviour. Thus Jesus prays, 'Nevertheless, not as I will, but as thou wilt' (Mt. 26:39). To pray 'thy will be done' is not to commit oneself to a knowable ethical pattern, but to an attitude of trust in God as Father. Again we encounter Jesus' emphasis not on the outward act but on the inner attitude. Or, to recall the beginning of this chapter, a saint is one who ventures beyond the known into the unknown will of God because his eyes are not on the outward act but on the inward attitude of trust.

In the writings of Paul there seems to be a slight change of emphasis. The 'will of God' is more clearly related to a defined pattern of behaviour. In Romans 12:2 we find him prefixing his catalogue of specific instructions to his readers by reference to proving 'what is the will of God, what is good and acceptable and perfect'. Paul appeals to his readers to 'lead a life worthy of God, who calls you into his own kingdom and glory' (1 Thes. 2:12). They are to live holy lives because 'what God wants is for you all to be holy' (1 Thes. 4:3, JB); 'holy' as opposed to immoral in verse 7. Such a notion of pleasing God could easily remain a vague idea, but as we have already noted, Paul often uses the idea in a much more precise fashion to back up specific instructions; *e.g.* Colossians 3:20 tells children to be obedient to their parents because 'this pleases the Lord', a fact which is presumably known from the fifth commandment.

John makes the equation between obedience to the commandments and pleasing God simple and stark: 'This is what loving God is—keeping his commandments' (1 Jn. 5:3, JB). It would be perfectly possible to pile up other references from the rest of the New Testament which would say much the same thing, but once the point is accepted that God is pleased when his commandments are obeyed, further examination becomes repetitive. To lead a life that will bring credit to the beliefs held is a widespread plea from parents, schoolteachers, politicians and soldiers. There is one special case of 'pleasing God' which is the logical outcome of the discussion so far, and is also widely used in the Bible. Because God is consistent, what pleases him is what he himself would do in the same circumstance. Man created in the image of God is called upon to imitate God.

The imitation of Christ[8]

The appeal to 'do as I do' is a well-known teaching method in the field of human behaviour. Usually it is employed for teaching skills, but Paul is not afraid to use this method on more than one occasion; *e.g.* 2 Thessalonians 3:7: 'You yourselves know how you ought to imitate us.' The matter in question is the very practical one of idleness in a member of the Thessalonian church. Correction comes by the church copying the example of Paul who worked night and day so as not to burden anyone. It is a measure of failure on the part of the Christian ministry to have to say, 'Don't do as I do, do as I say.'

Yet the 'imitation' of Christ in the New Testament is not along these lines. In his actions Jesus did not present a pattern of human behaviour for all his disciples to follow. His teaching, the signs he performed, his sinlessness, his work on the cross were all necessarily unique. His clothing, his language, his manner of life and much else were incidentals that very few have even thought were to be the content of following him. Yet clearly he did expect his disciple to 'deny himself and take up his cross and follow me' (Mk. 8:34).

In John's Gospel we have the foot-washing incident (Jn. 13:1–15) where Jesus says to the disciples, 'If I then, your Lord and Teacher, have washed your feet, you also ought to wash one another's feet. For I have given you an example, that you also should do as I have done to you.' Despite the fact that the other command given at almost the same time, 'Do this in remembrance of me' (Lk. 22:20), has been observed carefully ever since, the foot-washing command has hardly been followed. There is no early record of obedience to this instruction as a literal command, except possibly in the ceremony of pedilavium or washing the feet of the newly-baptized. Only later generations turned an act of humility on the part of Christ into an occasion for ceremony for monarchs and high-ranking prelates. Such treatment by traditional Christianity of a straightforward command of Jesus clearly implies that it was understood in a non-literal sense. It was seen as an enjoinder to humility dressed in oriental clothes.[9] If, then, to 'imitate Christ', or to 'follow Christ', is not to be taken in a literal sense, how do the disciples understand it?

As Jessop points out there are several strands of Old Testament teaching which have to do with following God. The command in Leviticus to be holy as God is holy (Lv. 11:44; 19:2; 20:26) seems in its original context to have a largely cultic significance. Yet Peter's use of the command in the context of various moral exhortations shows that to him at least the disciples should be 'like God' in holy conduct. Being like God involved the whole range of conduct: towards the state, towards employers or employees, towards husbands, wives and children. Yet in what sense is it possible to be like God in a situation which God will never encounter? Before seeking the answer to this it is necessary to mention a word of warning on the whole subject of being 'like God' or 'like Christ'. Luther, aware of the dangers of the 'imitation of Christ' turning into a new form of legalism, wrote vigorously against the idea. This has left an indelible mark on German scholarship to this day.[10] Lutherans tend, therefore, to speak of Christ as an exemplar and not as an example. Legalism is always an error to which sincere Christians have been prone, so that Luther's warning needs to be heeded. The whole idea of imitation, however, is far too deeply imbedded in the New Testament to neglect it.

It is instructive to look at the way in which Paul uses the idea of the imitation of Christ in his moral teaching. Ephesians 5:21–33 deals with the relationship of husband and wife. As its basis Paul is probably using a 'code of Christian conduct' which underlies similar teaching in Colossians and 1 Peter. Paul adds to the bare commands a motivation in terms of the relationship of Christ and the church. In the part of the analogy which concerns us the husband is told to show his wife the same sort of love that Christ showed for the church when he died for her. Two points should be noted about this statement. First, that the point at which the 'imitation of Christ' is to be found is in his attitudes shown in the crucifixion. Secondly, the mere mention of the similarity between the husband/wife and the dying Christ/church relationship is thought to be sufficient to convince the readers as to the action they should take.

The same approach can be seen in 1 Peter 2:21 where Peter is dealing with the master/slave relationship, and in particular with the slaves' attitude to unjust punishment. He says, 'Christ also suffered for you, leaving you an example, that you should follow in his steps.' The example to be followed was willingly to accept unjust punishment, just as Christ did on the cross. Peter, like Paul, focuses on the death of Christ as the point at which imitation occurs. Similarly he doesn't argue his position; the mere presentation of the similarity between the master/slave situation and the accusers/

dying Christ situation is thought sufficient to cause those who read to think and act in the right way.

Other examples using this same approach are the exhortation to humility in Philippians 2:5 and the plea for generosity in 2 Corinthians 8:9. The point at which both humility and generosity are demonstrated is the cross. The drawing out of the similarity between a given situation and that of the dying Jesus is again thought to be sufficient incentive to act in the desired way. Normally speaking, references to being like Christ all refer to his death/resurrection (in a few cases to his ascension). It is surprising that with the exception of the foot-washing episode mentioned above (an example of humility for which a much stronger reference point became the crucifixion, as in Philippians 2) the exhortation to imitate Christ is not found in the events of his earthly life, whereas references to being like him in his death/resurrection (and sufferings) are frequent (*e.g.* Gal. 2:20; Eph. 2:1–6; Eph. 5:1f.; Col. 2:20; Phil. 3:10; Col. 3:3; 2 Tim. 2:11; 1 Pet. 4:13; Rom. 6:3f., *etc.*).

The issues raised by the idea of identification with Christ at the point of his death/resurrection have a much wider reference than moral behaviour, although (as Bruce Kaye points out in Part 1, chapter 4, pp. 75f.) it is never helpful to draw too sharp a distinction between the ethical and the theological in the pages of the New Testament. Moral and theological are two aspects of the same cluster of ideas. However, looking at the theological aspect, Paul makes use of the death/resurrection of Jesus as a paradigm of the Christian life. Baptism, the sacrament of Christian initiation, is depicted as a dying and rising from the dead: 'We know that our old self was crucified with him so that the sinful body might be destroyed, and we might no longer be enslaved to sin' (Rom. 6:6). This death is an experience which should result not only in a change of status before God, but also in a change of behaviour towards men (Rom. 6:12f.). The death to sin is not only a theological fact, but a moral step as well. The 'rising to life' is not only a phrase denoting the new dynamic of the Spirit, but also living a new sort of moral existence. The attitude of Jesus at the point of crucifixion, his humility before his accusers, his acceptance of injustice, his overflowing love and generosity towards those for whom he died, his faith and trust towards God his Father, are attitudes which the Christian is to reproduce in his own life. This is never put forward as a matter of a new law to be obeyed, but more in terms of etching out the pattern of Christ's death and resurrection which is already present in the life of the Christian.

Conclusion

We began our enquiry seeking to find out why the saint rather than the theologian held the key to Christian ethics, and why double-standard morality has been a continuing feature of Christian practice. With the idea of the imitation of Christ, especially in his death/resurrection, we come close to answering our enquiry. Whether we tackle the subject from the standpoint of Jesus' own words, or by the more general route of rewards and punishments, we end by finding behind Christian behaviour an attitude of trust in God: more specifically, a trust in the God who revealed his nature in the death and resurrection of Jesus. To trust him has both the negative (death) and positive (resurrection) aspects. The first aspect is more definable than the second, simply because it deals with the known attitudes God condemns rather than the infinite possibilities that are pleasing to God. This is the aspect of 'Thou shalt not . . .'. It is largely possible to contain this aspect within a code of rules. But as we have seen, such codes can easily be misunderstood:

1. because they are only part and never the whole of Christian morality
2. because the underlying motive of behaving in a certain way to please the God in whom we trust can so easily be changed into behaving in a certain way to earn the favour of a God we do *not* fully trust.

The resurrection aspect of trust is the more characteristically Christian. Having committed himself to the Father in the crucifixion, Jesus has to rely on God completely for what follows. The resurrection is not an act of the indestructible Jesus, but of the trustworthy God to whom Jesus had committed himself. If the dying aspect of a Christian's behaviour is a sign of his commitment to the will of God, the resurrection aspect is a sign of the commitment of God to the Christian. This is the realm of the gifts of the Spirit and is what gives Christian morality both its life and its unexpectedness. It is what makes God's saints, both known and unknown, such a challenge to our morality.

Too often, Christian moral teaching has centred on the first aspect. In consequence it has been parodied as a joyless (and if possible, minimizing) obedience to rules. The realization that Christian morality must contain more than this has led some of the more devout to try to go 'the second mile'. They may have been mistaken in some of their actions, but their reasons for trying are understandable. To re-use Gordon Stobart's football analogy quoted by Dr Packer in Part 2, chapter 3 (p. 186), once the groundwork of rules has been established and accepted the real game begins. Only then can the innovatory skill and artistry of the players have full rein. The dying aspect of Christian behaviour is largely concerned with defining the rules. But the real essence of football is not the rules, but the game the rules make possible. The real centre of Christian morality is not in the essential groundwork of rules, but in the Spirit-inspired 'game' which they make possible.

NOTES

1. In this chapter the word 'saint' is not used in a definable technical or theological sense, but rather to stand for a Christian of maturity, liveliness and deep trust in God.

2. See also Col. 1:21f.; Col. 3:5–10; 1 Cor. 6:9–11; 1 Pet. 4:3, *etc.*

3. It is important not to overstate the case. Motives do matter to the Pharisees; overt acts do matter to Jesus. See T. W. Manson, *Ethics and the Gospel* (SCM Press, 1960), chapter 2.

4. See, for instance, the mind–body problem in I. C. Barbour, *Issues of Science and Religion* (SCM Press, 1966), pp. 351f. See also the previous chapter, p. 173.

5. Such a notion of the mechanism of conscience is morally neutral, and it would seem to suggest that a conscience can be programmed completely at the will of the programmer. Although conscience will then be heard as the 'voice of God' it will in fact be the voice of tradition, education, *etc.* Yet, as Dr Packer points out in the previous chapter, this is by no means the whole story, for the conscience also pronounces on the programmer, and any hint of manipulation or double standards will result in a radical change in the programme followed by the conscience. Trust is prior to morality in this matter. A person believes his conscience mirrors truth.

6. In G. Kittel (ed.), *Theological Dictionary of the New Testament*, IV (Eerdmans, Grand Rapids, 1967), pp. 695ff.

7. Paul Ramsey, *Basic Christian Ethics* (SCM Press, 1950), p. 133.

8. For a study in depth see Jessop, *The Imitation of God in Christ* (SCM Press). See also Dr Packer's paragraph on this theme in the previous chapter.

9. It is possible to claim that the church has been misguided in its understanding of the foot-washing command, but the lack of later New Testament reference, the almost universal understanding of the later church, across all denominational boundaries, as well as the practical difficulties facing any sizeable group of Christians seeking to follow the command literally, all go to suggest that a non-literal understanding of the command of Jesus is the right one.

10. See, for instance, H. Thielicke, *Theological Ethics,* I (A. and C. Black, 1968), p. 185.

5

Social ethics

David Bronnert

'I will preach about *Playboy* because that is a moral issue, but not about starvation for that is a political issue.'[1]

Few Christians would enunciate the division between social and personal ethics in so stark a manner, yet such an extreme position is not so dissimilar to the working theology of many. Personal ethics—sexual morality, financial integrity, truthfulness, family relationships, compassion for those in need, and evangelistic zeal—are recognized as a proper concern for the minister and for the Christian; they may be preached about and publicly prayed for without fear of criticism. The Third World, justice in society, educational ideals, racism, the population explosion are a different matter—these belong to the secular and political realm; whether there is a Christian view is debatable, and controversy is best avoided.

The result of such a divorce is that tacit support is given to whatever is the prevailing view; the unspoken assumptions and the expressed opinions are those of the social and national group to which the Christian belongs, without these views being affected by his commitment to Christ.[2] Thus there are massive problems to which Christians are contributing even while they practise a high standard of personal ethics. In South Africa it is not at all uncommon for white Christians to be friendly and courteous to black people on a personal basis, while supporting in one way or another a system that gives a massive insult to the human dignity of the same people. Again, many Christians contribute generously to relief agencies like OXFAM, while accepting the system of trade that enables them to have an increasing affluence and that makes the poor poorer every year; a hundred pounds gained through the

216

Social ethics

system may be tithed generously but the recipient still is in possession of ninety!

Scripture lends no support to this separation of life into compartments. In the beginning, God created human beings in society, not as isolated individuals: 'God created them . . . God blessed them . . . God said to them' (Gn. 1:27–28). The individual does not exist in isolation, but is bound up in a network of social relationships. God's concern with the whole fabric of human life is often expressed in the Bible in both judgment and mercy. In the flood (Gn. 6:11–12a), a community was judged because of its internal strife, a distortion of God's will for human society. The prophets are full of condemnations of social evil both within and outside Israel: Amos strictures Damascus, Gaza, Tyre, Edom, Ammon and Moab for sins against humanity, justice and brotherhood, before he turns his attention to Judah and Israel (Am. 1 and 2).

In Amos there is none of the, now-common, polarization into those concerned about social justice versus those concerned about sexual misbehaviour. He is passionate in his anger about those who 'sell the righteous for silver and the needy for a pair of shoes. . . . You cows of Bashan, . . . who oppress the poor, who crush the needy. . . . Who lie upon beds of ivory, and stretch themselves upon their couches, and eat lambs from the flock, and calves from the midst of the stall; who sing idle songs to the sound of the harp, and like David invent for themselves instruments of music; who drink wine in bowls, and anoint themselves with the finest oils, but are not grieved over the ruin of Joseph!' (Am. 2:6; 4:1; 6:4–6). He is just as passionate in this as in his distress over 'religious' and 'sexual' sins: 'They have rejected the law of the Lord, and have not kept his statutes. . . . A man and his father go in to the same maiden, so that my holy name is profaned. . . . You made the Nazirites drink wine, and commanded the prophets, saying, "You shall not prophesy" ' (Am. 2:4, 7, 12). Amos does not see 'social' and 'private' as separate issues; all evils are viewed as offences, and against God. He vehemently rejects any attempt to make religious observance a substitute for the right actions in society: 'I hate, I despise your feasts. . . . Take away from me the noise of your songs. . . . But let justice roll down like waters, and righteousness like an everflowing stream' (Am. 5:21, 23, 24).

Equally, when God acts in mercy he shows his concern with the whole of life and not simply for a part labelled 'spiritual'. In the exodus, God showed his concern for an oppressed people who were involved in a physical, social bondage that included racism, genocide, Uncle Tomism and hypocritical liberalism. This is what is referred to when it is recorded: 'The people of Israel groaned under their bondage, and cried out for help, and their cry under bondage came up to God' (Ex. 2:23).

Changing individuals rather than society?

It is often argued that the Christian way to change society is to change individuals rather than to seek to apply Christian principles to society, '. . . After all, if the world were converted its problems would be solved.' Undoubtedly, any movement for reform that does not pay attention to changing men's minds, and the attitudes and behaviour of individuals, is bound to run into the sand; but the argument is nevertheless weak. It forgets to ask the question, 'What are these changed individuals to do?' If they follow their mentors and ignore social action and engage in evangelism, the world is likely to get worse not better. To postpone action until the world is converted is to postpone it for ever, since no-one seriously supposes that this will be achieved before Christ's return. The quite evident and intolerable disorder and injustice in the world will not be affected for the better by people becoming Christian, unless the implications of the gospel are understood and applied in the realm of economics, education, work, medicine, housing and social relationships. The whole of South Africa becoming Christian (a good proportion claims to be already) would not affect the fundamental injustice of £12 per annum spent on the education of a black child while £120 is spent on a white, unless a radical change in the society were to follow. Such a change would involve not only the loss of control by the white group, but lower educational standards for their children, inferior opportunities at work, poorer housing and fewer leisure facilities.

An extension of the same argument is the common observation

that 'Christians may support any of the major political parties in Britain'; the implication being that while the individual's course of action is plain in his personal relationships, any number of alternative policies are compatible, at the social and political level, with a Christian profession. It must, of course, be conceded that the major parties present alternative 'package-deals', and as such will contain items a Christian will legitimately like and dislike. As the issues at stake and the gifts and character of the men concerned have to be weighed, it is to be expected that even well-informed Christians will vote for different parties; but that is not to say that it is simply a matter of personal judgment which policy or ideal is followed. Douglas Crawford argues that for the Christian, integration and apartheid are equally legitimate alternatives provided they are done in a spirit of love.[3] Gervase Duffield suggests that an increase or a decrease in money for world development could be equally attractive to the Christian conscience.[4] If this were true, it would constitute a devastating blow to the credibility of Christianity: like a horoscope capable of such variety of interpretations as to be irrelevant to many of the crucial moral and ethical questions that are facing mankind.

A low priority ?

A concern for society is criticized by some Christians as a pre-occupation with this world rather than eternity: since the apostles and Jesus himself did not engage in a political crusade against the evils of their day, it cannot be incumbent on Christians to do so now. Such an argument neglects the different context in which the Christian life has to be lived; the early Christians were not powerful or influential members of society; rather they were at the receiving end of 'the system'. The situation of Christians in Russia and America is very different: in one an 'out' group facing an authoritarian and repressive regime; in the other, possessing democratic rights in considerable numbers and with real influence in the seat of government. In any case the New Testament has many social implications:

'(Jesus) said also to the man who had invited him, "When you give a dinner or a banquet, do not invite your friends or your brothers or your kinsmen or rich neighbours, lest they also invite you in return, and you be repaid. But when you give a feast, invite the poor, the maimed, the lame, the blind and you will be blessed, because they cannot repay you" ' (Lk. 14:12–14).

'Come now, you rich, weep and howl for the miseries that are coming upon you. Your riches have rotted and your garments are moth-eaten. Your gold and silver have rusted, and their rust will be evidence against you and will eat your flesh like fire. You have laid up treasure for the last days. Behold, the wages of the labourers who mowed your fields, which you kept back by fraud, cry out; and the cries of the harvesters have reached the ears of the Lord of hosts. You have lived on the earth in luxury and in pleasure; you have fattened your hearts in a day of slaughter' (Jas. 5:1–5).

There is a demand not only for an inner change, but for positive action towards those who are deprived: a change in material and economic terms as well. The passion of the eighth-century prophets had clearly not evaporated in the apostolic era.

When the context of the church changed in the time of Constantine Christians were involved in the ordering of society. It is common to deplore the transition involved, yet it was an inevitable consequence of the spread of Christianity and the impact of its teaching. Unless the Christians retreated into an anchoretic existence, or accepted the pagan *status quo,* they had to apply the New Testament to their society, its laws and its customs. The deplorable consequences of the conversion of Constantine came from the failure to do this thoroughly and consistently, not from the attempt to do it at all. If Christians are to be faithful to Christ in the modern world with its massive evils that warp and destroy so many human beings they cannot say 'our plan is not to reform society, but to witness to Jesus Christ'.[5]

In the New Testament, thought of eternity does not lead to indifference to what happens in the present world; rather Jesus teaches that the result of thinking about eternity, his second coming and the day of judgment, is to be action in time (Mt. 25:31-46). Behaviour in society has an eternal significance, not simply a temporal one; all the more reason then for working for justice and humanity if this is to find its fulfilment and reward in the 'new heavens and the new earth'. What is new is to be ushered in by God rather than created by men (Rev. 21:1-2), but this does not mean that the believer should be unconcerned with society or justice until that day (it could equally be argued that personal morality can similarly be left until that time); rather the Christian is called to live in anticipation of that event.

The basic principles

Scripture does not present a detailed Christian social order, but it does give clear guidance in the form of basic truths about God and man: what God requires of man in the realm of justice, humanity and brotherhood—and what God detests. The approach can be expressed in St Paul's words, 'Let each of you look not only to his own interests, but also to the interests of others' (Phil. 2:4). That implies the recognition that others have a value and worth equal to one's own; other families, other communities, other nations have a value and worth equal to one's own family, community and nation. They too are 'made in the image of God' and share in all the glory and all the shame of being human. So the Christian cannot support his sectional interest because it is his. He ought not to defend an élitist system of education because his children will benefit from it, nor oppose increases in his taxation if this makes for a more just society, nor excuse his race or his nation's self-interested actions.

The foundation principle is the fact that 'man is created in the image of God'. Because this is true God has given him certain 'rights' by virtue of his creation. These belong to man as the gift of God, and no man is entitled to relieve another of these rights without sufficient cause; nor should an individual feign to bestow such rights on another, though he may need to restore what already belongs to him. Before exploring any further 'the image of God', it is necessary to anticipate two common objections to seeing justice as the foundation principle. Surely love rather than justice is the Christian principle, and does not the Bible emphasize a man's duties rather than his rights? Love may go beyond justice, but it can never justify giving less to a man than justice. Love goes beyond justice when, out of regard for the welfare of others, a man sets on one side what is due to him. He may refuse to accept what he is entitled to either in recompense for a wrong done to him, or in sharing in some aspect of human fulfilment. Love involves a caring consideration for the best interests of others. What does the other need? What is due to him? Love can never be a reason for depriving another of his rights; rather it demands justice for him as the minimal requirement. Love finds expression in a concern for justice, not a denial of it. Duties and rights are interrelated. Undoubtedly the New Testament emphasizes the obligation to be concerned with the rights of others rather than the demand for one's own rights, though the latter is not entirely absent (Acts 16:37; 2 Cor. 11:20f.). If a Christian is to know his duty, he has to consider what are the rights of others; and a community has to evaluate rights and obligations for the same reason.

What rights do men possess? All men are made in the image of God and accordingly all have the right to belong to the one human family. They have a right to the society of others in the complex web of personal, family, work and social relationships that make up a truly human existence. Men may forfeit, through their own actions, some of the expressions of this right to belong, but even then they still belong and still have a worth which others must not disregard. Segregation, whether done by custom or by law, is a fundamental contradiction of this basic right. Racial segregation is a glaring example of such a contradiction: men and women are excluded from the society of others not on the ground of their behaviour but on the basis of appearance. In practice the full expression of their humanity is disallowed. Often the treatment of the aged in Western societies is another contradiction of the full human dignity of all: they may be despised or disregarded because they are no longer producers, and cut off in practice from the rest of humanity, as a species apart. The Christian should seek a world in which the human race is seen as essentially one, and every individual has a value in his own right. He will be opposed to every evil that divides and separates, that makes for an impersonal, dehumanized society, and that robs people of their worth.

All men have a right to share in the earth and its riches, because God has given the earth to them as a whole; they have a right to possess it. All that makes for human fulfilment in education, culture, leisure and enjoyment belongs to man 'made in the image of God'. Though capacities and interests vary, no-one has inherently a greater or lesser right to share in the resources made available to mankind. The imbalance between the rich and poor nations of the world is a flagrant distortion of God's will, as is the discrimination within nations that gives, through accidents of birth or appearance, unequal opportunity and privilege. The Christian will want to work for a world with a more equitable distribution of the given material resources; he will be against privilege, and concerned for the deprived, even when that is to the disadvantage of his immediate family and group.

The fact that all are made in the image of God does not mean that each individual is identical; far from it. An essential element in being in the image of God is personality—the right to be oneself! The fact that a man's national, cultural, economic and family group is known, does not predetermine every detail of his behaviour; he is himself and no other. The Christian will be wary of pre-judging individuals; labelling them, stereotyping them, depriving them of their reputation without examining their character and actions. He will work for a human society where individuality is not crushed, where character is valued rather than superficial appearances, and where people seek to understand and to accept each other rather than to condemn and to reject.

All other actions and attitudes spring from this foundation. The ideal of the Marxist, 'to each according to his need, from each according to his ability', ought to be fully embraced as a biblical ideal; though the neglect of human individuality and worth that has accompanied it, is the very reverse. Western society has tended to lay its emphasis on human liberty; again a biblical truth of major importance, yet one that can easily degenerate into freedom for some to exploit others. A concern for human freedom in isolation easily breeds the spirit of competition rather than co-operation for the common good; the praiseworthy desire to excel is corrupted into a desire to do better than others and to have more than others.

The dimensions of evil

The attainment of ideals is always difficult and never complete in human society, because man does not now possess his primordial innocence. What allowance ought to be made by Christians for that unpleasant but inescapable factor in human affairs? It is essential that the dimensions of evil are not underestimated, for the Fall has affected every part of life. In Genesis 3 and 4, not only man's relationship with God is affected, but also his relationship with the created world, with his wife, with his brother (Cain and Abel); human institutions and customs are included (Cain built a city, Lamech married two wives). Bonhoeffer puts it well: 'It is not realised in all seriousness that the world is fallen and that now sin prevails and that creation and sin are so bound up with each other that each human order is an order of the world and not an order of creation.'[6] Sin and evil are woven into the fabric of society; fallen humanity is exhibited not only in the criminal, but in the police, the law-abiding public, the institutions of the state, the language and the practices and intentions of the law. Claims to perfection must be viewed with more than a degree of scepticism, whether those claims are made by an individual, a group, an institution or a system.

All this does not mean that there are no differences between men or between societies; there are better and worse, some societies are more just and compassionate than others, but human life operates in the realm of comparatives not absolutes. For while there is an idealistic side even in the worst of men and societies, self-interest is, to a great extent, at the root of individual and group behaviour. 'No-one is born prejudiced against others, but everyone is born prejudiced in favour of himself' (D. Stafford Clark). Reinhold Niebuhr has no illusions about the individual: 'Even the most rational men are never quite rational when their own interests are at stake'; but as for the group, 'The larger the group the more certainly will it express itself selfishly in the total human community.'[7] In the behaviour of both individual and group, the New Testament sees not only 'the flesh', but demonic forces at work, in the mind of the individual (2 Cor. 4:4), and in the values, customs and life-style of the group (1 Jn. 2:16).

The difficulty confronting many, if not most, people is that of recognizing that the situation which benefits them and their immediate circle, may be so unfair to others that for a just society a radical alteration is required. John Murray provides an illuminating example: 'It is simply a fact that God has not ordained equality of distribution of gift or possession. And because this is so, it is impossible to put equality into effect. Some are more capable of increasing their possessions: they are more provident, diligent, industrious, progressive.'[8]

No-one would quarrel with the fact of diversity of gift, but a close correlation of virtue and prosperity in the present world (ordained by God!) is ludicrous, both in America, where Murray was writing, and in the world at large. The fact that it takes six months for a labourer in Africa to earn what his counterpart in Britain earns in a week has no conceivable connection with their personal virtues. Within American (and British) society, there are those who are born losers, and the pattern of housing, education and employment, added to the deprivation experienced by their parents, conspires to keep them underprivileged. To blame the victims of society for their misfortunes and to attribute virtue to the successful and the wealthy is a complete inversion of the teaching of Christ. Walter Rauschenbusch's words are much to the point:

'As long as a man sees in our present society only a few inevitable abuses and recognizes no sin and evil deep-seated in the very constitution of the present order, he is still in a state of moral blindness and without conviction of sin. Those who believe in a better social order are often told that they do not know the sinfulness of the human heart. They could justly retort the charge on the men of the evangelical school. When the latter deal with public wrongs, they often exhibit a curious unfamiliarity with the forms which sin assumes there, and sometimes reverently bow before one of the devil's spiderwebs, praising it as one of the mighty works of God.'[9]

The relationship of realities to ideals

The implications of the extent of evil are very many; not only does the ideal not now exist, but in this world the ideal society is unattainable. Furthermore, these forces are at work within the Christian and the Christian community, even though the Holy Spirit is at work to lead and to direct in a different direction and toward different goals. Neither revolution nor revival will usher in an ideal state of affairs; though both in different ways may contribute to a better social order. Increased decay is also another possibility.

Although this is the case, Scripture nowhere gives encouragement to men to abandon the goals and the ideals, and to give way to inertia or despair. While there is in the Bible an attempt to provide limitations on the consequences of human perversity and folly, because it exists, there is no abandonment of God's requirements. God's law is intended for all men, for, whether they acknowledge it or not, they are created by him and are answerable to him. Does this mean then that the Christian should be aiming to get the law of the land to conform to the law of God? He will certainly wish to see the laws, customs and attitudes of his country and the international community reflecting the will of God; but that is not necessarily the same thing as conforming to the law of God. The expression 'the law of God' has sometimes an implication of coercion, whereas the will of God includes the freedom to defy the law of God; not an unlimited freedom, as others then would soon be robbed of freedom to live and act, but a real freedom none the less; for God 'makes his sun rise on the evil and on the good, and sends rain on the just and on the unjust' (Mt. 5:45). The law of the land has a significant role in restraining the inhumanities of men, in minimizing the evil consequences of human waywardness, and in redressing injustice; but it is not the sole or the chief instrument for achieving God's will on earth.

In the drafting of laws, the Christian will want, or ought to want, the ideal provided by God to be kept fully in view while recognizing the limitations occasioned by human sin. It is, however, all too possible for the proper function of the law in minimizing evil and redressing injustice to become distorted into a reinforcement of injustice; a siding with the sinner rather than the sinned-against. In Scripture, the ideal of a life-long union of one man and one woman in marriage is maintained, while in the Old Testament divorce was regulated to limit the evil done. This attempt to give a measure of protection to the divorced woman, became in the hands of men a new 'ideal' bestowing divine approval on the oppressive conduct of the strong in their treatment of the weak. So it must always be asked: 'Is the expressed intention of the law and its actual operation such as to reduce the evil done to the weak? Or is it in practice simply reinforcing the wrongdoer's actions?' Thus a law against racial discrimination, seeking to protect the disadvantaged, is acceptable even though this infringes the human freedom to choose. On the other hand, to write racial discrimination into the law (as for instance in immigration law), whatever the stated intentions, is not acceptable as a concession to human sinfulness; for this adds the weight of the law to the side of the prejudiced, and deprives the sinned-against of their rights.

It is not uncommon for a practice that has certain beneficial effects, to be exalted, for that very reason, into a new and basic principle. No one could deny that competition, for instance, has advantages over monopoly; the latter almost inevitably leads to the misuse of power while the former has encouraged initiative and hard work. But that is very far from making competition a divine order of creation, providentially harnessing individual self-interest to the common good. It may be a lesser evil, but it brings many unfortunate consequences in its train, and it is not the Christian ideal of co-operation and service. Similarly, hierarchical organization in human affairs is much better than anarchy, but the Christian ideal remains 'You are all brothers of one another and have only one Teacher' (Mt. 23:8, GNB) and that must be allowed constantly to challenge social stratification whether in church or society.

The extent of obligation

There are many formidable obstacles in the pursuit of a more just world. The complexities of human society include the need to interact with others in discussion and work, the many conflicting interests involved and, perhaps most significant, the mechanics of a technological world. The people who have the power and influence to change situations are also the group most likely to be benefiting from the existing order. The temptation is always present to reduce God's requirements to the level of what is easily attainable, and then to feel content with small virtues. This was the burden of Jesus' condemnation of the Pharisees, for they tithed 'mint and dill and cummin, and have neglected the weightier matters of the law' (Mt. 23:23).

The individual has more direct control over his private life than over his local community, his country and the international community, so the retreat into personal affairs is understandable. It ought, however, to be obvious that the larger the scale the greater the impact of any action or achievement; and inevitably the individual is part of the larger community, deriving benefits from it and sharing in its evils. The Christian Aid slogan, 'Give a man a fish and you feed him for a day; teach a man to fish and you feed him for life', points to the need to go to the roots of the problem rather than simply to treat symptoms. It is not enough for the individual to give money towards a crisis in a developing country, if his government controls the terms of trade to the disadvantage of that same country. All this involves working with others who may not be Christians, but who, because they are men, have a concern for the welfare of others. This is not to suggest that the plight of someone in trouble can be dismissed in the pursuit of lofty goals. Some Marxists may say that they will not do 'ambulance' work for that will prop up the present system, but the Christian cannot look at individual distress in that way. The good may be finite, but it represents the ideal-in-the-making, an earnest of good intentions in the larger and more significant realm, for 'as often as we have the chance, we should do good to everyone' (Gal. 6:10, GNB). After all, a good doctor will provide ointment to soothe the symptoms, while giving antibiotics to deal with the cause.

The challenge for the Christian is to put into concrete terms the revolutionary style of life lived by Christ; to translate into economics, education, politics, international relations the claim that in Christ he 'is a new creation' who looks at no-one, and no situation, from a simply human point of view of self-interest and self-concern. There needs to be a recognition that wittingly and unwittingly he has contributed to the ills of humanity, and that situations that are of benefit to him and his immediate circle are part of that. A love for others will result in the Christian being concerned for the total good of others, material, social and spiritual. A concern for the social and material should not be a substitute for a concern for man in his relation to God, nor should it be viewed as a convenient bridge to the spiritual. Rather, because he knows God, he reflects the character of God: 'I am the Lord who practise steadfast love, justice, and righteouness in the earth; for in these things I delight' (Je. 9:24).

NOTES

1. See for instance *The Other Side,* March/April, 1972, p. 4.
2. But *cf.* Part 2, chapter 4, p. 193.
3. Douglas Crawford, *High Tension* (Lakeland, 1969), p. 68.
4. Gervase Duffield, in *The Churchman,* Spring 1971, p. 5.
5. John Williams, *Living Churches* (Paternoster, 1972), p. 34.
6. Dietrich Bonhoeffer, *No Rusty Swords* (Fontana, 1970), p. 162.
7. *Moral Man and Immoral Society* (SCM Press, 1963), pp. 44 and 48.
8. J. Murray, *Principles of Conduct* (Inter-Varsity Press, 1957), p. 92.
9. W. Rauschenbusch, *Christianity and the Social Crisis* (Macmillan, New York, 1907), p. 349.

6

Public law and legislation

Norman Anderson

Introduction

Hitherto in this book we have been concerned primarily with questions of morality and the law of God in the biblical sense. In ancient Israel there was, indeed, comparatively little difference between the two. As in Islam, both morality and law had their basis in divine revelation, although there was ample scope for this to be systematized and extended by analogy to cover new problems and ever-changing circumstances. Theologically speaking, therefore, the dictates of the law and the demands of morality were virtually synonymous, for the divine law was regarded as covering every aspect of human life. All the same, there must have been a certain difference between morality and law in the theological sense (*i.e.* the precepts or teaching of the way of life which was prescribed by God for his creatures), on the one hand, and law as a lawyer interprets that term, on the other.

To begin with, there must always have been (again, as in Islam) a distinction between those precepts which were justiciable and enforceable in human courts and those which must necessarily be left to the bar and sanctions of eternity; and this corresponds closely to the line of demarcation which a lawyer habitually draws between law and morality. Whereas morality can and should make maximum demands, moreover, the law (in so far as human tribunals are concerned) must normally content itself with enforcing what is comparatively minimal. No court can force a man to love either God or his neighbour, for example; all it can do is seek to prevent or punish specific acts of disobedience to God's law or infringements of the rights of other people. Similarly, courts largely concern themselves with acts that have been done and words that have been spoken; for no human judge is really competent to assess a man's inward thoughts and intents—although he may, indeed, have to do his best to infer whether an act was intentional or accidental. There are, moreover, an almost infinite number of possible gradations in guilt, based on personality, temperament, upbringing, circumstances, knowledge and provocation. Human justice must inevitably, therefore, be somewhat rough and ready; and this is, no doubt, in part the reason why many of the prescribed penalties of the sacred law were, in all probability, comparatively seldom imposed in practice.

The law of the land

But what attitude should the Christian take today to the civil and criminal law of the state in which he happens to live and the legislation which proliferates from day to day in modern life? Should the moral injunctions of the New Testament be enforced, ideally speaking, by the secular law? In general this would be quite impracticable, for there is very little 'law', in the legal sense, in the New Testament (except, as some would consider, in such matters as marriage and divorce), and its exceedingly exacting moral requirements could scarcely be the subject of litigation, or be enforced either by civil remedies or criminal sanctions. What then of the law of the Old Testament, a great deal of which does in fact take the form of legislation or case law which could in theory be enforced today? Is this what a Christian should advocate in a democracy, or impose under any such form of government as would enable him to do so? After all, Jesus said he had come not to destroy the law and the prophets, but to fulfil them.

It is helpful in such a context, I think, to follow Article 7 of the Thirty-Nine Articles of the Church of England in classifying the Mosaic law under the triple headings of moral law, ceremonial law and civil law—however alien such a classification would have been to the minds of those who lived under that law in Old Testament times. The moral law (which may in part, perhaps, be identified with what Jesus termed the 'weightier matters of the law') was fulfilled by him in his perfect life of unswerving obedience to its requirements, in his atoning death of vicarious acceptance of the sanctions incurred by those who had broken and even defied its precepts, and in his reinterpretation and reimposition of those same principles on his redeemed people. The ceremonial law, on the other hand, was in essence largely an adumbration of what we might term the way of grace, teaching that sinful man could never saunter, as it were, into the presence of a holy God, but that there was none the less a ready welcome for the repentant sinner through the blood of sacrifice and the water of cleansing. But this way of grace was enunciated, in the Mosaic system, in a largely legal framework; and St Paul makes it clear that the Jewish people as a whole, instead of being driven by the moral law to throw themselves on the mercy of God by a believing recourse to the ceremonial law, all too often constructed out of the moral and ceremonial law together a way by which they hoped to 'establish their own righteousness' and thus earn salvation. This ceremonial law was, moreover, fulfilled by our Lord in a somewhat different sense from the way in which he fulfilled the moral law; for the sacrificial system, for example, was in essence only a signpost pointing on to the supreme sacrifice he was to make; the animals so sacrificed were mere types or symbols of the 'Lamb of God' who was to come; and the ever-repeated sin offerings found their full and final fulfilment when he 'bore our sins in his own body on the tree'. Now that he has died for our sins, been raised again for our justification, and entered into the presence of God for us, there is no place for any repetition whatever; and the priestly orders, courts and curtains of the tabernacle and temple have lost all significance, save only for the light they still throw on the redemption that he has wrought.

But what of the civil and criminal law of the Old Testament; of crime and its punishment; of civil wrongs and their remedies; of debt and its payment or release; of marriage and divorce; and of civil status, slavery and manumission? It is this part of the Mosaic law which largely represents what a lawyer regards as law today—and which also, it may be said, approximates most closely to other ancient codes, whether Semitic or Sumerian. How, if at all, can it be justly said that Jesus fulfilled this section of the Mosaic law?

This part of the law, it must be remembered, was promulgated or permitted in order to keep the peace, and to regulate human relationships, in first a nomadic and then a pastoral community—which was, indeed, God's 'chosen people', but had most of the faults and failings of other nations in a similar stage of civilization and development. It was to this nation, moreover, that Jesus came as their Messiah; but they would not accept him as such. So he told them, in no uncertain terms, that the 'kingdom of God' would be taken from them and 'given to a nation that yields the proper fruit' (Mt. 21:43, NEB); and the apostle Peter made it abundantly clear that this had indeed happened when he wrote to Christians 'scattered throughout the provinces of Pontus, Galatia, Cappadocia, Asia, and Bithynia' as a 'chosen race' and even a 'holy nation' (1 Pet. 1:1 and 2:9, GNB).

Today, therefore, the church is not a nation-state, governed by the civil and criminal precepts and regulations of the Mosaic law—some aspects of which fell far short of the divine ideal for humanity, and were promulgated only because of the hardness of men's hearts (Mt. 19:8). Instead, the church is the community of the redeemed from all nations, on whom the moral law of God is incumbent in all its fullness, but who are governed in matters criminal and civil by the legislative enactments and customary law of the countries to which they owe human allegiance. So the 'civil' precepts of the Mosaic law, too, have—since Christ's advent—fulfilled the function for which they were designed.

What then should be the attitude of the Christian today to the law of the nation to which he belongs? About this the New Testament teaches unequivocally that he is to be subject 'to every human institution for the sake of the Lord, whether to the sovereign as supreme, or to the governor as his deputy for the punishment of criminals and the commendation of those who do right' (1 Pet. 2:13, 14, NEB). So resistance to the secular government represents, in general, resistance to what has been ordained by God for the good of his people, who will, therefore, 'have themselves to thank for the punishment they will receive' (Rom. 13:2, NEB); and the Christian is under a moral as well as a legal obligation to pay his taxes and fulfil all his civic duties.

But this moral obligation is not, of course, absolute, for where there is a manifest clash between obedience to God and obedience to the secular government, then obedience to God must necessarily come first (Acts 4:19). In extreme cases, moreover, a government may so fail to fulfil its God-given functions of promoting virtue, discouraging vice and maintaining law, order and the public good that it may forfeit the right to men's obedience, and may have to be overturned in favour of a new regime—for the Old Testament records a series of instances when God intervened in judgment on nations and their rulers, and even commanded men to act as his instruments in this respect. But these are balanced by many injunctions in the New Testament to suffer personal injustice and abuse rather than resort to violent resistance; and the conditions which would have to be fulfilled in any doctrine of a 'Just Revolution' are even more stringent than those which must govern the concept of a 'Just War'.

Christian legislation?

There are, then, some general guidelines for the attitude which the Christian should adopt to the secular law if he lives under any sort of autocracy. But what should be his attitude to the secular law should he be in a position to impose it, or at least to influence its nature and application? Should the law of a modern state, ideally at least, approximate to the civil and criminal law of ancient Israel, and should the moral teaching of the New Testament be embodied, so far as this is in fact practicable, in legal precepts designed to govern the lives of Christians and non-Christians alike? Alternatively, what criteria should a Christian adopt as to the form that the civil and criminal law of a modern state ought to take?

These questions, in their turn, entail a number of subsidiary questions of great importance. Is God's revealed will, in matters moral and legal, incumbent on man as man or only on the Christian as one who has accepted God's sovereignty? Should the precepts in which this will finds its expression be enforced, so far as this is possible, on believer and unbeliever alike? How far, indeed, is it ever appropriate to call the criminal law in aid to enforce moral precepts? And are God's standards of moral behaviour, and indeed

of penal sanctions, absolute and unchangeable, or do they vary—to
to some degree at least—from age to age and civilization to
civilization?

Maker's instructions

First, then, is God's revealed will, in matters moral and legal,
incumbent on man as man or only on those who have accepted
God's sovereignty and who believe in his revelation? Here the
answer must surely be that God has revealed and enjoined what is
beneficial for man as man, rather than for any particular section
of mankind. His moral precepts and laws must, therefore, be
regarded as our Maker's instructions for the human creatures he has
brought into being, and only in so far as they obey these instructions
will they be able to fulfil his beneficent purposes and enjoy the full,
happy and satisfying lives which he intended them to live. But the
Bible is emphatic that man is no longer in his original state of
innocence and that sin has infected his heart, mind, will and even
conscience, so he can never in this world rise to the heights of full
and perfect humanity. This life has only been lived once in the
whole course of human history: by Jesus Christ our Lord. But to
fall short of that standard is still sin, in the case of believer and
unbeliever alike. And this is, indeed, a universal malady, for 'all
have sinned, and fall short of the glory of God' (Rom. 3:23).

All the same, sin only becomes positive transgression when the
divine prohibition of the thought, word or action concerned (or,
indeed, the divine command to do this or that) is known and either
neglected or defied. The Jew who knew the law revealed on
Sinai had, no doubt, a much fuller realization of the divine law and
will than did the Gentile, on whose heart the basic requirements of
that law were written in much less explicit terms; but written, in
some measure, they were.[1] So, too, today; for Jesus taught that the
servant who does not know his Lord's will will be 'beaten with few
stripes' compared with the punishment incurred by one who knows
his Lord's will but ignores or defies it. Again, the Christian is heir
to a supernatural grace which enables him to conform to the
standard God has revealed much more closely than is possible
for one who has not come into living fellowship with God in

Christ by his Spirit. So, again, there is a real sense in which his responsibility will be the greater.

Freedom of thought

Secondly, then, should the precepts in which the divine will finds its expression be enforced, so far as this is possible, on believer and unbeliever alike? In the very mixed society of today, in which men and women of different religions and no religion are members of the same nation and represent different elements in almost every community, can it validly be argued that Christian moral standards should underlie all secular legislation? Can the Christian, it is asked, impose *his* ideas of morality on those who do not share the faith and foundations on which that morality rests? In a democracy, of course, the answer to this question—on the surface at least—is comparatively simple, for the Christian cannot, in the very nature of things, impose his ideas on a resistant majority. All he can do is to try to convince his fellow citizens either of the validity of his faith (and therefore the duty of obedience to the precepts and way of life which it enjoins), or else of the intrinsic benefit of adopting some of those precepts and moral standards whether the basis on which they are enjoined is, or is not, itself accepted. And even if Christians happen to be in a majority, or to be in a position in which they can in fact impose legislation—and would necessarily wish that the law of the land should approximate, as closely as possible, to the law of God—it would still, I think, be incumbent upon them to give others that freedom of thought (and, within appropriate limits, of action) which they would themselves demand from a non-Christian government.

Enforced morality?

Thirdly, how far is it ever appropriate to call the criminal law in aid to enforce moral precepts? This is, today, an exceedingly controversial subject which has occasioned a major debate between Lord Devlin and Professor H. L. A. Hart—to say nothing of many other participants. The current discussion had its origin in Lord Devlin's Maccabaean Lecture in 1958 on 'The Enforcement of Morals', in which he challenged the basic assumptions (although not, indeed, the practical recommendations) of the Report of the Committee on Homosexual Offences and Prostitution:[2] namely, that the function of the criminal law 'is to preserve public order and decency, to protect the citizen from what is offensive or injurious, and to provide sufficient safeguards against exploitation and corruption of others, particularly those who are specially vulnerable because they are young, weak in body or mind, inexperienced, or in a state of special physical, official or economic dependence'; but that it is *not* the function of the criminal law 'to intervene in the private lives of citizens, or to seek to enforce any particular pattern of behaviour, further than is necessary to carry out the purposes we have outlined'.[3] Against this thesis Lord Devlin argued that a society is held together not only by its political structure but also by a shared morality; and that just as every community has the right to protect its political integrity by the law of treason, so it must also have the right, in suitable circumstances, to safeguard its ideological integrity by means of criminal sanctions.

This viewpoint was immediately challenged by Hart, who championed, in general terms, the thesis of John Stuart Mill (on which, indeed, the basic assumptions of the Wolfenden Report had themselves been founded) that 'the sole end for which mankind are warranted, individually or collectively, in interfering with the liberty of action of any of their number, is self-protection'. So 'the only purpose for which power can be rightly exercised over any member of a civilized community, against his will, is to prevent harm to others. His own good, either physical or moral, is not a sufficient warrant. He cannot rightfully be compelled to do or forbear because it will be better for him to do so, because it will make him happier, because, in the opinion of others, to do so would be wise, or even right.'[4] It was not that the community, in Mill's view, had no concern with the behaviour of its individual members. It certainly had; and it had the duty to try to influence that behaviour by advice and by moral persuasion of all sorts. But the sphere of the criminal law should be rigidly confined to the prevention of harm to others or to the body politic, and the protection, even against themselves, of those who were not adult, sane members of a civilized community.

Paternalism

Hart, however, does not in fact go all the way with this. Instead, he believes that the criminal law, while it should never be used to enforce moral standards as such, can rightly be called in aid, on occasion, to exercise what he terms a 'paternalistic' function —as, for example, to protect even a sane, adult member of a civilized community from ready access to hard drugs. The Christian would certainly agree. But once this principle of paternalism is admitted, it is clearly a matter of debate where the line should be drawn. Hart himself would allow criminal sanctions against peddling hard drugs, as we have seen, because of the manifest harm they cause and the ease with which even a civilized adult becomes addicted to them; against cruelty to animals, even in secret, because of the physical pain this can be shown to entail; and against a bigamous marriage, even where both parties are fully cognizant of all the circumstances, because of the offence this causes to the sensibilities of many members of the community. But he would explicitly disallow such laws as those which penalize various forms of homosexual behaviour between males, bestiality, incest, living on the earnings of prostitution, or keeping a brothel, *etc.*[5]

His opposition to 'paternalism' in this sphere rests, I think, on two different factors: first, that he has a doctrinaire objection to any enforcement of 'morality', as such, by means of criminal sanctions; and secondly, that he has succeeded in convincing himself that there is little, if any, evidence that such things 'do any harm'. But the Christian would certainly ask why the principle of protecting a man by means of criminal sanctions against such physical harm as he might otherwise inflict on himself, or allow someone else to inflict on him (both of which would have been anathema to Mill), should not be extended to the infliction of moral harm? Does the difference consist only in the fact that physical injury is easier to demonstrate, prove and quantify? This may be conceded. Or is the basic assumption that the damage which drugs may cause to physical health cannot be gainsaid, whereas what is commonly regarded as moral evil amounts to no more than a deviation—which allegedly 'causes harm to no-one'—from accepted norms which are themselves relative and questionable? This would represent a radical departure from the basic assumptions of the Wolfenden Report, which called, as we have seen, for 'sufficient safeguards against exploitation and corruption of others, particularly those who are especially vulnerable'. The idea behind these words certainly goes beyond an 'exploitation' which consists in nothing more than an inducement to agree to a proposal which, had the individual been older, stronger or less dependent, he might well have refused; for the word 'exploitation' is immediately followed by 'corruption'. This clearly implies that there *is* such a thing as moral corruption and that certain acts or behaviour are liable to cause it—a proposition about which the Bible leaves the Christian in no doubt whatever. Is it, then, suggested that behaviour which tends to corrupt the young, weak, dependent or uncivilized has no such effect on the mature, strong, independent and civilized? Or is the argument, on the contrary, that certain behaviour is liable to corrupt people of any age or condition, but that those who are not especially vulnerable to exploitation must be allowed to submit themselves to such corruption—or at least the possibility of such corruption—if they so wish?[6]

If, then, the criminal law may legitimately adopt a somewhat 'paternalistic' role, as even Hart accepts, it would seem to follow that there should be no objection, in basic principle, to its being used to protect individuals from any sort of injury, or to preserve the basic institutions of society (such as marriage and the family) from any attack on their integrity. But this does not mean that criminal sanctions ought in fact to be imposed in every such case; for there are a number of criteria which should always be taken into consideration before legislation is invoked.

Other criteria

First, the question must be asked whether such a law would command sufficient public support to make it viable. It is possible, of course, even in a democracy, for legislation to be passed by the legislature which would not be approved by the majority of citizens in a referendum (a fairly recent example of which can, almost certainly, be found in the abolition of the death penalty for all kinds of murder), although such legislation could not survive very long against widespread and determined opposition. But this is not to suggest that the law should never lead, rather than follow, public opinion; for legislation designed to prevent, or at least penalize, racial segregation and discrimination may well, if consistently enforced, 'help to bring about a change in attitude, in behaviour and eventually in moral convictions'.[7] The point at issue is that it is generally speaking inadvisable for the law to run fundamentally contrary to public opinion.

Secondly, would such legislation be enforceable, with any semblance of equity, by the police? For, if not, then it would inevitably bring the law itself, and its enforcement agencies, into disrespect.

Thirdly, would such a law be likely to involve, or open the door to, evils so great as to outweigh the benefits it is designed to effect? Would it, for example, entail such an invasion of privacy, such a danger of widespread blackmail, such a political or ideological dictatorship,[8] or such a restriction of individual liberty and the rightful exercise of moral choice, that it must be judged to be inexpedient in the interests of society as a whole?

It is on principles such as these that proposed legislation must be assessed, or existing legislation reassessed, both by Christians and non-Christians. Nor are these principles confined to the criminal law, for they extend to the civil law as well. An obvious example of this may be found in the law of divorce. It is, of course, possible to forbid divorce in all circumstances, as is the case in Malta today. To many Christians this would represent an enforcement by the State of biblical teaching, since Jesus himself taught unequivocally that God, our loving Creator, intended that we, his creatures, should find our sexual, psychological and spiritual fulfilment in the life-long fidelity of monogamous marriage. If, then, this represents God's 'moral law', is it not, always and everywhere, incumbent on the Christian at least? This certainly represents the firm conviction of many. Others, however, would not only point to tragic cases of marriage breakdown, even among Christians (followed, on occasion, by a second marriage which seems to be manifestly blessed of God), but would insist that the New Testament may itself be held to permit divorce and remarriage in certain circumstances.[9] Nor is it altogether clear what precisely is involved in the phrase 'what God has joined together',[10] or even in the subsequent injunction 'let not man put asunder'.

Law in a pluralistic society

But a further, and essentially different, question is whether the rigorous provisions of the moral law can or should be imposed on non-Christians in a pluralistic democracy by civil legislation, or to what extent they should be so imposed even if Christians were in a position to do so. Here it is relevant to note that the Mosaic law itself made certain concessions, and that Jesus did not in any way suggest that these were not made by divine permission. If, moreover, it is asked why such concessions were permitted, the New Testament answer is because of the 'hardness' of men's hearts, which presumably means that fallen men and women cannot (and do not) live up to what God has designed for them. But this is not to suggest that God has one standard for the marriage of Christians and another for that of non-Christians, for it seems clear that the creation ordinance of marriage was intended for man as man; and Christians, like everyone else, are fallen creatures, although they are heirs to a supernatural grace which can enable them to approximate much more closely to the divine ideal than would be possible for them if left to their own unaided efforts.

What, then, should the Christian urge upon his fellow men in a pluralistic society? He should, as I see it, unhesitatingly proclaim that life-long fidelity in monogamous marriage is God's creation ordinance for man as man, and that anything less falls short of the divine ideal. But he should not seek rigidly to impose this by law on his fellow citizens, even if he were in a position to do so; nor should he, in a democracy, campaign for such a law. Instead, he should advocate legislation that is designed to uphold the status and permanence of the marriage bond as much as is compatible with providing relief where this appears to be really necessary; for it seems distinctly doubtful whether the institution of marriage is not brought into even greater disrepute by broken homes, illicit unions and illegitimate children than by legal provisions which allow men and women to give a decent burial, in appropriate circumstances, to a marriage which is already dead, and then to contract another legal union. Even so, there may always be a further distinction between what the Christian believes to be desirable in this context, provided public opinion will support it, and what he will settle for as the maximum that can reasonably be expected.

Examples of cases in which there is a moral problem in regard to criminal law can be readily found in the contemporary debates about abortion, euthanasia, sex relations and pornography. The basic principle behind the first two is that of the sanctity of human life, and behind the second two the moral welfare of society. In each case, moreover, there is for the Christian both a theological and sociological problem. In regard to abortion and euthanasia, for example, the biblical principle of the sanctity of life would seem to rule out either 'abortion on demand', in the sense that a woman may insist on the removal of an unwanted foetus in exactly the same way in which she may require the extraction of a troublesome tooth, or any deliberate act which is intended to bring a human life to a premature end. But the problem remains as to how this basic principle is to be applied in the specific context of whether (and when) an embryo is to be regarded as having attained the status of a human being, and whether a man or woman is still to be so regarded if kept 'alive', in a purely biological sense, only by artificial means after the central nervous system has suffered an irreversible breakdown. This last point, together with the whole question of what, precisely, constitutes death, has assumed a new and urgent importance in the context of the transplantation of organs from a 'dead' donor to a living recipient.[11] Further problems concern the circumstances in which there is a conflict of interests between the life of the foetus, as at least an inchoate human being, and the life or basic health (whether physical or mental) of the mother, as a developed human personality, on the one hand, and the circumstances in which an elderly person should be allowed to die in peace, rather than have his life prolonged by means of some hazardous operation or painful treatment (or, indeed, resuscitated in a terminal illness), on the other. In all these cases, moreover, the ethical principle of the lesser of two evils may well be applicable.

Yet again, the Christian may have to distinguish between what he considers to be right or wrong *per se,* and therefore what is incumbent upon him in his own life or in what he recommends to others if they ask his advice, and what he believes the criminal law should impose on all, in so far as he is in a position to influence this. He could certainly reinforce his theological convictions in such circumstances by the sociological considerations that either 'abortion on demand' or 'euthanasia on demand' would not only tend to cheapen the community's regard for human life, but would also give rise to a host of problems such as whether the individual concerned would not have changed his mind if the action demanded had not been taken when it was; whether legislation authorizing such action would not, of itself, bring psychological pressure to bear on a sensitive person; and whether the relationship between doctor and patient, or between different members of a family, might not be seriously impaired.

Questions of sex relations pose a very different problem. Adultery and fornication are unquestionably sinful, on any biblical view, and have sometimes been punished as crimes by the civil law. But this is rare today because, *inter alia,* public opinion would not support it, because it might entail an unacceptable invasion of privacy and open the door to widespread blackmail, and because the law could not be equitably enforced. Similarly, the Bible leaves us in no doubt that indulgence in lesbian practices is both sinful and contrary to nature; but such practices are not normally punished as crimes. It was for these reasons that criminal sanctions for homosexual acts, committed in private between two adult and consenting males, were recently abolished in this country. To say that such acts have now been 'legalized' is, however, both untrue and misleading, for adultery, fornication and homosexual practices are still regarded in law as immoral, and therefore devoid of legality;[12] but they are not proscribed by the criminal law, except, of course, in the case of one who is young. Prostitution, again, is not *per se* subject to criminal sanctions; but it is a crime to solicit, to live on the proceeds of prostitution or to keep a brothel. This means that a wide variety of sexual sins is not subject to criminal sanctions in our society; but such sanctions are still available, in theory at least, to preserve public decency, to protect those who are especially vulnerable, and to penalize those who seek to exploit for financial gain the moral weaknesses of third parties. And many Christians, and others, would agree that it is right to call the criminal law in aid in such cases, both to protect those who need protection and on the principle enunciated by William Temple when he said: 'To say that you cannot make folk good by Act of Parliament is to utter a dangerous half-truth. You cannot by Act of Parliament make men morally good; but you can by Act of Parliament supply conditions which facilitate the growth of moral goodness and remove conditions which obstruct it.'

Somewhat similar principles apply to pornography and obscenity. To impose a rigid censorship on books, magazines and newspapers, in the sense that they would have be 'passed' by some person or body before publication, would throw the door wide open to political or ideological dictatorship. But the law should prohibit any public display or unsolicited distribution of grossly indecent material, since it is the proper function of the law, as we have seen, to protect those who need protection (*e.g.* the young, and all those who do not want to have such material foisted upon them). And, on precisely the same principle, those who seek, for financial gain, to exploit others, whether as actors or models for pornographic plays, films or photographs designed for public display, should be liable to criminal sanctions.[13]

In conclusion

Two further questions remain. First, the problem of what may be termed moral principles of abiding validity as against principles which are only relative, and which vary from age to age and civilization to civilization.[14] This problem has been discussed at some length elsewhere in this volume, together with the whole question of 'situation ethics'. It is sufficient to observe in this context, therefore, that positive law can always be modified or changed, but that unless it is so changed it remains the law—although circumstances frequently determine the view which the criminal law will take of certain actions, and will also be taken into account by the courts in mitigation of an offence.

But this leads to the final problem: that of a law which is itself flagrantly unjust. The attitude that should be taken by the Christian in such circumstances will, of course, depend on what, precisely, the law enjoins; but in the final analysis he is under obligation, in all such cases, to 'obey God rather than men'. But what view should he take of such a law *per se*: that it is valid law, if it has been promulgated in the right way, even if it is morally wrong and ought to be disregarded; or that it should not really be regarded as 'law' at all, in the proper sense of that term? This poses the age-old problem of positive law *vis-à-vis* 'natural law'; and it is a phenomenon of life that lawyers who live under a government which normally respects the rule of law, and is comparatively just, are apt to concentrate exclusively on positive law and to treat the concept of natural law with something akin to tolerant amusement, but as soon as they find themselves subject to a despotic dictatorship they begin to appeal to an abstract standard of justice against which all positive enactments must be assessed. It was so in Germany before, during and after the Hitler regime. Before Hitler, German lawyers were, in general, uncompromising 'positivists'; but many changed their minds and began to champion the doctrine of natural law under Nazi oppression. After the war, moreover, not only academic jurists but even the courts themselves refused, on occasion, to recognize some of the Nazi enactments as having the force of law at all. This question is, of course, in part a matter of pure semantics and in part a factor of practical importance. Is an unjust law to be regarded as law, but bad law and law which ought to be changed, or is it to be denied the dignity of being classified as law at all? If the first, then is it to be obeyed and enforced (or at least recognized) until it is changed, or is it to be disobeyed and even ignored in practice? This is the vital point; for if, in fact, it is to be ignored, then the way in which it is classified is largely a question of academic interest.

This difficult problem of apparent discrepancies between the law of the State, on the one hand, and natural justice, on the other, can only be resolved by treating each case on its merits. The Christian will probably conclude that it is his duty to obey the law of the State unless he is convinced, beyond any reasonable doubt, that it is unjust; for chaos and anarchy are major evils. Even when he is so convinced, moreover, he will almost certainly decide that there are some cases in which he must obey even an unjust law unless or until he can get it changed by constitutional means; other cases in which he cannot in conscience obey it at all, whatever the consequences may be; and yet others in which the circumstances are so extreme that passive disobedience may rightly give place to open and even forcible resistance.[15]

NOTES

1. *Cf.* Part 1, chapter 6, pp. 116ff.; Part 2, chapter 1.

2. 1957 Command Paper 247 (commonly known as *The Wolfenden Report*).

3. *Ibid.*, paras. 13f.

4. See J. S. Mill, *On Liberty* (Longmans, 1859); reprinted in *Utilitarianism, Liberty and Representative Government* (*Everyman's Library* No. 482, J. M. Dent, 1910), pp. 72f.

5. H. L. A. Hart, *Law, Liberty and Morality* (Oxford University Press, 1963), pp. 25f.

6. *Cf.*, for a fuller discussion of these points, J. N. D. Anderson, *Morality, Law and Grace* (Inter-Varsity Press, 1972), p. 71.

7. Morris Ginsberg, *On Justice in Society* (Penguin, 1965), p. 235.

8. Even Christians, moreover, can be sadly mistaken in their interpretation of the divine will, and grossly intolerant in imposing this interpretation on others, as history has often demonstrated.

9. *E.g.* the 'Matthean exception', where the other party has committed adultery, and the 'Pauline privilege', where a non-Christian spouse refuses to go on living with a partner who has become a Christian (and this principle has been extended, in most of the 'Reformed churches', to any case of genuine desertion).

10. Witness recent extensions in the grounds on which Roman Catholic courts will give decrees of nullity.

11. These (and related) questions are much more fully discussed in my lectures on *Issues of Life and Death* (Hodder and Stoughton, 1976), chapters 3 and 4.

12. As can be seen from the fact that a contract or agreement for such purposes will not be accorded any legal recognition or enforcement, and that solicitation for such purposes is a criminal offence, *etc.*

13. *Cf. Pornography: The Longford Report* (Hodder and Stoughton, 1972), especially pp. 207ff., and 366ff.

14. *E.g.* the abiding principle of decency and modesty, as against changing views of how, precisely, decency and modesty are to be defined.

15. I have discussed this complex question in some detail in chapter 4 of *Morality, Law and Grace* (Inter-Varsity Press, 1972).

Index of main Bible passages

Index of authors

Aquinas, T. 175f.
Barth, K. 118f., 153, 154–156
Bonhoeffer, D. 153, 154–156, 224
Brandon, S. G. F. 101f.
Brunner, E. 153, 154–156
Bultmann, R. 153, 156f., 166 n.16
Calvin, J. 104–107
Crawford, D. 219
Lord Devlin 236–240
Dodd, G. H. 95 n.6, 96 n.12, 118
Duffield, G. E. 219
Epictetus 80ff., 99
Fletcher, J. 151ff., 157–162, 164, 165
n.3, 166 n.6
Freud, S. 178, 200
Gustafson, J. 162
Hart, H. L. A. 236–240
Jessop 210
Kasemann, E. 117
Kidner, F. D. 170f., 191 n.2
Ladd, G. E. 150 n.6
Lewis, C. S. 190, 192 n.8

Luther, M. 93, 211
Mill, J. S. 236f.
Murray, J. 121 n.1, 162f., 225
Niebuhr, R. 224f.
Nowell-Smith, P. 132
Nygren, A. 119
Oden, T. 157
Pierce, C. A. 176f.
Preisker, H. 205
von Rad, G. 22 n.1, 170
Ramsey, P. 152
Rauschenbusch, W. 225f.
Robinson, J. A. T. 151ff., 157–162
Sanders, E. P. 18f.
Schnackenburg, R. 91, 97 n.35
Schweitzer, A. 76
Seneca 98, 104
Sherwin-White, A. N. 103
Sibbes, R. 192 n.8
Stafford Clark, D. 224
Temple, W. 244
Yaron, R. 36

Index of subjects

abortion 34, 242f.
Acts, book of 67–69
Adam–Christ motif 117, 120
adultery 34ff., 142, 243f.
anarchy 133f.
authority 46–50, 102, 105ff., 219, 233f., 245

behaviourism 172–175
berît 7
blessings 12f., 14f., 28

capital punishment 42f., 239
case law 11, 25
censorship 244
Christlikeness 144–149, 209–213
commandments 11, 64f., 66, 70, 79, 134f., 148, 164, 198
communalism 111
conscience 116, 175–178
corporate guilt 39, 40
courts (OT) 45f.
covenant 3–22, 114f., 145
— Davidic 13f.
— in Jesus' teaching 17, 19–21
— in the NT 17–22
— in Paul 17, 21
— Sinaitic 7–13
'covenantal nomism' 18–20
creation ethics 129–149
curses 12f., 14f., 28
'cutting off' 43

Dead Sea Scrolls 19
Decalogue 11, 24, 27–38, 64f., 140ff., 152, 180
divorce 36f., 61f., 132, 136, 227, 240

eschatology 84–86, 88, 108, 220f.
Essenes 18f.
ethics in the Epistles 72, 75f., 88–90, 93–95

euthanasia 242f.

Fall 136f., 224–227
fasting 61
food laws 30
freedom 79ff., 171f., 223, 226, 236
fulfilment of the law 55ff., 69f., 76f., 79ff., 83f., 120, 148

Gentiles 68, 115ff.
gospel 74ff., 79, 84
Gospels 53–67
government 45–50, 62f., 98ff., 105ff., 228, 234
grace 3–7, 14, 16–18, 53, 86

Herod 100f.
honesty 134, 135
household codes 110f.
human nature 132–136, 144, 163, 168–175, 181f.

image of God 145–149, 169–171, 221f.
intuition 143

Jesus Christ and the law 53–67, 69–71, 73, 146f., 198f.
'just' war 134, 200, 234
justice 217f., 221–224, 231, 245

kingdom ethics 149 n.6
kingdom of God 20, 21, 54f., 59

law
— ceremonial 30, 58f., 63, 232
— civil 28, 41, 102f., 231–233
— criminal 28f., 41, 231, 234, 237–240, 242
— cuneiform 25–27, 33, 39
— enforcement 44–46, 236f., 240
— in the Epistles 73f., 76–80, 207

251